A VOTER'S GUIDE TO THE US ECONOMY

- 2012 -

An Almanac of Politically Relevant Economic Information

Robert L. LeBoeuf

Cover artwork by Judith Woodbury

ISBN-13: 978-1475064384

ISBN-10: 1475064381

CONTENTS

FIGURES

TABLES

PREFACE

This book grew out of a series of regular, ongoing dinners with friends, at which the host would choose a topic and we would go around the table expressing our views. A free-for-all discussion would ensue. I love those discussions, but it has occurred to me that virtually all the conversations suffered from a lack of clear concept definitions and objective data. After many of these dinners, my wife Christi and I found ourselves searching for facts to support or refute positions asserted at the dinner.

Many of our dinner topics were inherently economic. Often the economics lay beneath a veneer of politics, and the conversations became a muddle of how the world should be, versus how it is. I've concluded that economics isn't just for economists, as much as economists would have you think otherwise. Voters make important decisions that are basically economic without benefit of understanding either the underlying concepts or the data.

This book has two purposes: to help voters understand the dialogue about economic issues; and, to help them decide, on the basis of clear, correct information, which candidates best represent their economic interests. It is not a textbook to be studied and learned. Rather, it is a quick reference resource with some background information to be consulted and occasionally pondered.

An often-used quote that originally may have come from Bernard Baruch in 1946, states that people are entitled to their own opinions, but not their own facts. I have attempted in this book to be completely neutral in my presentation of both definitions and facts. As the reader will find, government statistics can be misleading. Definitions can be changed and data can be selected to support particular outcomes. My promise to the reader is that I have chosen the most authoritative sources for the data presented, and I have presented the concepts surrounding the data as fully and dispassionately as I could.

Having said that, I must ask the reader always to be mindful of Josiah Stamp's commentary on statistics:

> "The government are very keen on amassing statistics. They collect them, add them, raise them to the nth power, take the cube root and prepare wonderful diagrams. But you must never forget that every one of these figures comes in the first instance from the village watchman, who just puts down what he damn pleases."
>
> *Josiah Stamp*

ACKNOWLEDGMENTS

The inspiration for this book came from a dinner group of neighbors including Elizabeth Young and Bob Lovell, Gail and Bob Leibowitz, and Janet and Chester Kauffman. The dinners are wonderful, and the conversations make me look for answers and try to confirm things I think I already know.

I am doubly indebted to Liz Young, because she not only helped inspire this book, but she took the time to review it for me.

Benjamin Mandel of the Bureau of Economic Analysis helped me via e-mail with answers to questions on the National Income and Product Accounts. I'd like to acknowledge someone at the Bureau of the Public Debt in similar fashion, for similar reasons, but I don't think OPDA@bpd.treas.gov is a real person. In any case, whoever you are, thank you.

My wife Christi not only helped inspire this book, she helped create it. She encouraged me and challenged me, asked for clarification, and reviewed the ongoing work several times. Without her support, there would be no book.

Any errors are mine alone, and not the fault of those who generously contributed their time to this effort.

Finally, I extend a loving thank you to my parents Louis and Rita LeBoeuf, who supported me in so many ways over the years. Thanks, Mom and Dad.

PART 1.   SOME BASICS

1. INTRODUCTION

Economics addresses the allocation of limited resources among competing uses. Good economic decisions must be based not only on the preferences of the entity making the decision, but on the economic facts underlying the decision.

Economic issues once again will be at the heart of the 2012 US presidential election. Most voters have little economic training, but everyone makes economic decisions every day, be it which job to take, or what product to buy. If the voter has the correct information, he or she has a better chance of making informed decisions that affect the country's economic standing and future.

Politicians, however, sometimes deliberately try to mislead. They want events interpreted in their favor, so they select facts that support them and ignore ones that don't. They've been known to bend the facts, and I've heard that some of them even have lied on rare occasions! It's your job as a voter to understand what politicians are saying, and equally important not saying, and determine the truth.

This book presents economic information that bears on every voter's decisions in the 2012 presidential election. Part 1 deals with some basics. It is a necessary and I hope helpful tutorial on five concepts: measuring rates of change, "per capita", data adjustments, data sources, and, for reference purposes only, a graphic that concisely shows who has been in charge of the White House and Congress, and to a large degree of our economy, from 1989 through 2011.

Part 2 talks about the economy, including economic production, unemployment and employment, income and wealth distribution, and taxes.

Part 3 describes federal spending, including the budget, federal receipts and expenditures, debt, health care, Social Security, military spending, federal regulation, and the true cost of federal governance.

Part 4 addresses international topics: immigration, international trade, foreign aid, and the United Nations.

The data presented in the following chapters are facts, whether you are a Democrat, an Independent, a Libertarian, or a Republican.

Presentational Note

You will see most of the data series begin in 1989. It's an arbitrary choice, but I wanted at least 20 years, and 1989 is a beginning point for some of the data series. The ending year depends entirely on data availability.

---

2. RATES OF CHANGE

How economic data change over time often has greater significance than their absolute levels. It is important, therefore, to know how changes are defined and calculated. This section will be short and simple, but it really is key to understanding much of what follows.

Basically, there are three ways to characterize how much a particular measure changes over time. One way is to use **absolute change**. For example, if the economy grew from 150 to 250 in 10 years, the absolute change would be 100. (Let's not worry about units of measure for now.)

Another way to characterize the change is to use **percentage change**. That's easy. Divide the absolute change (100) by the starting value (150) and you get a change of 67 percent.

But what if you want to know the average annual rate of change over the 10 years? You have two choices: simple and compound. The **simple annual growth rate** is calculated by dividing the total percentage change for the period by the number of years in the period. In our example, 67 percent total growth divided by 10 years equals a 6.7 percent simple annual growth rate.

A more complex, but more frequently used measure of annual change is the **compound annual growth rate (CAGR)**. You still use the percentage change for the period, and the number of years in the period, but now you must use a more complicated formula:

$$\text{CAGR} = (\text{percent change})^{(1/\text{no. of years})}$$

Or if you prefer to use Excel and a slightly different formula:

$$\text{CAGR} = \text{POWER}((\text{End Value/Start Value}),(1/\text{No. of Years}))-1$$

If the math leaves you a bit bewildered, look at table 2-1. It shows that a simple growth rate adds the same percentage of the base-year value in each succeeding year, and a compound growth rate uses the increasing annual number as the base for applying the growth rate each year. The formulae above come at the problem from the opposite direction. Given a certain percentage change over a specified number of years, the formulae yield the compound annual growth rate.

Table 2-1: Simple and Compound Growth Rates

Year	Simple Rate (5%)		Compound Rate (5%)	
1	Starting Value	$100.00	Starting Value	$100.00
2	$100 + $5	$105.00	$100.00 x 1.05	$105.00
3	$110 + $5	$110.00	$105.00 x 1.05	$110.25
4	$115 + $5	$115.00	$110.25 x 1.05	$115.76
5	$120 + $5	$120.00	$115.76 x 1.05	$121.55
6	$125 + $5	$125.00	$121.55 x 1.05	$127.63
7	$120 + $5	$130.00	$127.63 x 1.05	$134.01
8	$135 + $5	$135.00	$134.01 x 1.05	$140.71
9	$140 + $5	$140.00	$140.71 x 1.05	$147.75
10	$145 + $5	$145.00	$147.75 x 1.05	$155.13

Note that for purposes of calculating the compound annual growth rate, the number of years used in the formulae is the last year of the period minus the first year. For example, the period 2000 through 2010 is a ten-year period, because the rate is applied ten times. The first year is the base, so it is not counted in the compounding formula.

Either way, the result in our example of a change of 100 over 10 years is a compound annual growth rate (CAGR) of 5.2 percent.

Whenever you hear a rate mentioned, you need to know what kind of rate it is. It matters, because choosing the type of rate is the occasion for mischief. The simple rate always will be higher than the compound rate for the same period, but the compound rate probably will be more realistic.

Choosing the type of rate is mild mischief, however, compared to the mischief that can be created by judiciously picking the period of observation. Few data series change at a uniform rate over time. By carefully selecting when the period starts and how long it is, one can manipulate the perceived average rate, sometimes dramatically.

My message to you here is to be skeptical. Understand what kind of rate is under discussion, and determine if the period covered makes sense on its face, or was chosen to influence the result.

3. PER CAPITA

Many of the economic concepts in subsequent chapters will be expressed in per capita terms. The phrase **per capita** means for each person. If you have 100 people spending a total of $1,000, per capita spending for the group is $10 ($1,000 divided by 100 people equals $10 per person). To determine the average value of anything per US citizen, we must know the US population.

Figure 3-1 shows the US population over the period 1989-2011. Its compound annual growth rate is 1 percent, and the growth is very even, except for 1999-2000, when a bit of a jump occurred. This jump may be more statistical than demographic, since it occurred at the time of the 2000 census. At the end of 2011, the Census Bureau estimated US population to be 313,019,575, including the resident population plus armed forces overseas.

Figure 3-1: Population, 1989-2011

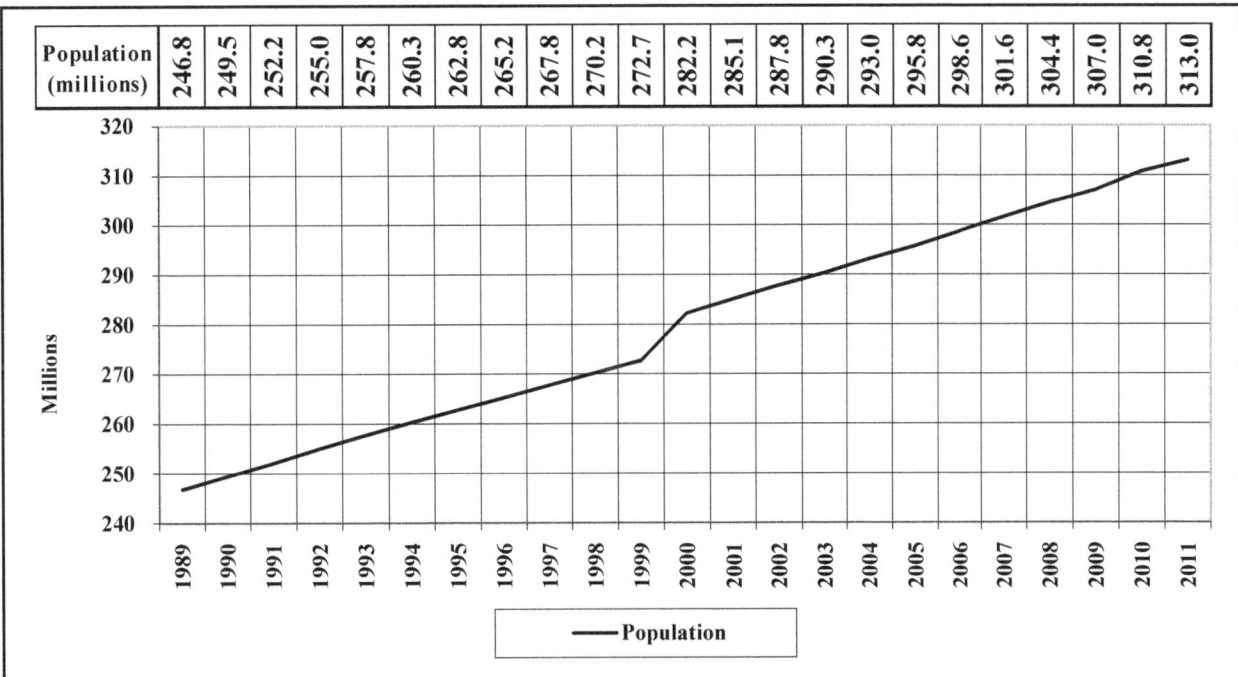

Source: http://www.census.gov/popest/data/national/totals/2011/index.html

---

Presentational Note

In figure 3-1, and in most of the figures that follow, the data are time series. That is to say, the values are presented over units of time, usually years. The years appear at the bottom of the graph (along the x-axis), and all the information above the years correlates to the years. The values represented by the graph appear above the graph and align with the appropriate years along the bottom of the graph.

The convention used throughout the book for multi-series figures will be for the data series names at the top of the figure and the data series names in the legend to appear in the same order when read bottom to top and left to right, respectively.

---

4. DATA ADJUSTMENTS

Economic data are subject to influences that can present a misleading impression of the situation being measured or estimated. Economists and statisticians strive to use techniques that offset some of the influences that they deem to be potentially misleading. They continually attempt to balance statistical purity with conceptual veracity.

Two types of data adjustments are widely used and you should understand them: adjusting for price inflation and adjusting for seasonal influences.

4.1 ADJUSTING FOR PRICE INFLATION

In subsequent chapters, we will discuss income, economic output, and other economic data that frequently are adjusted for price inflation. Economic output can be measured by quantity, or by value. Measuring by quantity is possible in concept, but impossibly difficult in practice. Imagine counting all the shoes, cars, vegetables, and myriad other products and services and trying to conceive of a simple, concise metric to reflect this production. A much better way is to add the value of all the goods and services produced to come up with a single dollar value to represent total production. Much better, but with a big problem. Prices change over time. These changes may reflect the quality of the goods produced, the relative availability of the goods, or the value of the dollar.

The situation with wages is similar. In order to establish the purchasing power of wages, one must know how price inflation is affecting the value of goods purchased with the wages. In the next section, we will look at inflation indices and see how to rebase them.

4.1.1 What is an Index

An index is a series of numbers that show how another series of numbers changes. Using an index facilitates comparing changes among disparate data over time and applying adjustments to data. See table 4-1 for a simple example of how an index is calculated. The example data series runs from 2000 through 2005 (column 1) and the index is calculated from the data series values (column 2) by dividing each data series value by the data series value of the selected base year. In table 4-1, the base year is chosen to be 2000 and each year's value (including the base year) is

Table 4-1: Calculating and Re-Basing Indices

Year (1)	Data Series (2)	Calculation (3)	Index (2000=100) (4)	Calculation (5)	Index (2003=100) (6)
2000	225	(225/225)x100	100	(225/253)x100	89
2001	231	(231/225)x100	103	(231/253)x100	91
2002	242	(242/225)x100	108	(242/253)x100	96
2003	253	(253/225)x100	112	(253/253)x100	100
2004	300	(300/225)x100	133	(300/253)x100	119
2005	375	(375/225)x100	167	(375/253)x100	148

divided by the base year value (225) and multiplied by 100 (column 3) to create the index (column 4). The table also shows how one can very easily change the base year of an index, or re-base it. Simply select a different base year and divide the data series values by the base-year value. In the example, the series is re-based from 2000=100 to 2003 =100 (columns 5 and 6).

One can rebase using either the original data series or an index of that series. The result will be the same.

4.1.2   Inflation Indices

There are two primary measures of inflation. One is the Consumer Price Index (CPI), which is produced by the Bureau of Labor Statistics (BLS); the other is the Personal Consumption Expenditures (PCE) price index, prepared by the Bureau of Economic Analysis (BEA). Since the PCE price index frequently is referred to as the BEA chain-style index, we will refer to it as the BEA index. These two indexes are constructed differently and tend to behave differently over time. For example, in the fourth quarter of 2010, the CPI rose at a 2.6 percent annualized rate, while the BEA index rose at a 1.7 percent annualized rate, a difference of 0.9 percentage points.

For a concise but somewhat technical explanation of these indices, see *Focus on Prices and Spending, Consumer Price Index: First Quarter 2011*, US Bureau of Labor Statistics, May 2011, Volume 2, Number 3.

4.1.2.1   BLS Consumer Price Index (CPI)

The CPI actually is a family of indices that measure the average monthly change in the prices paid by a sampling of consumers for a fixed market basket of goods and services. It is calculated by specifying a single base period set of prices and then valuing the output of all periods using those prices.

The CPI covers "out-of-pocket" expenditures, including user fees (such as water and sewer service) and sales and excise taxes paid by the consumer, but excluding income taxes and investment items (such as stocks, bonds, and life insurance). The CPI is estimated from a set of samples of urban areas, of consumers within those areas, of retailers and other outlets, and of specific, unique items purchased.

The broadest and most comprehensive CPI is called the All Items Consumer Price Index for All Urban Consumers (CPI-U) for the US City Average, with 1982-84 as the base period for the index. It is the "official" CPI reported in the media.

4.1.2.2   BEA Chain-Type Index (BEA)

In 1996, the BEA introduced the chain-type index as its featured measure of the change in real GDP and in prices. According to the BEA, this approach significantly improved the accuracy of the National Income and Product Accounts (NIPA) estimates. The BEA prepares measures of real GDP and its components in a dollar-denominated form, designated "chained (2005) dollar" estimates.

The two indices (CPI and BEA) differ in formulae, weights, scope of data, and other aspects. Each is thought to address the timeliness and coverage of the data available to the two organizations in the best way possible to meet their reporting responsibilities.

Figure 4-1 shows the CPI and BEA indices over the period 1989-2011. The compound annual growth rate for the consumer price index (CPI) is 2.6 percent, and for the BEA index for the same period is 2.1 percent, a difference of 0.5 percentage points or nearly 20 percent of the CPI compound annual growth rate.

Another way of looking at the CPI and BEA price indices is through their impact on the value of the US dollar over time. Figure 4-2 shows that while $1.00 bought a certain basket of goods in

Figure 4-1: Inflation Indices, 1989-2011

BEA (1989=100)	100.0	103.9	107.5	110.1	112.5	114.9	117.3	119.5	121.6	123.0	124.8	127.5	130.4	132.5	135.3	139.1	143.7	148.4	152.7	156.0	157.7	159.5	162.8
CPI (U) (1989=100)	100.0	105.4	109.8	113.1	116.5	119.5	122.9	126.5	129.4	131.5	134.4	138.9	142.8	145.1	148.4	152.3	157.5	162.6	167.2	173.6	173.0	175.9	181.4

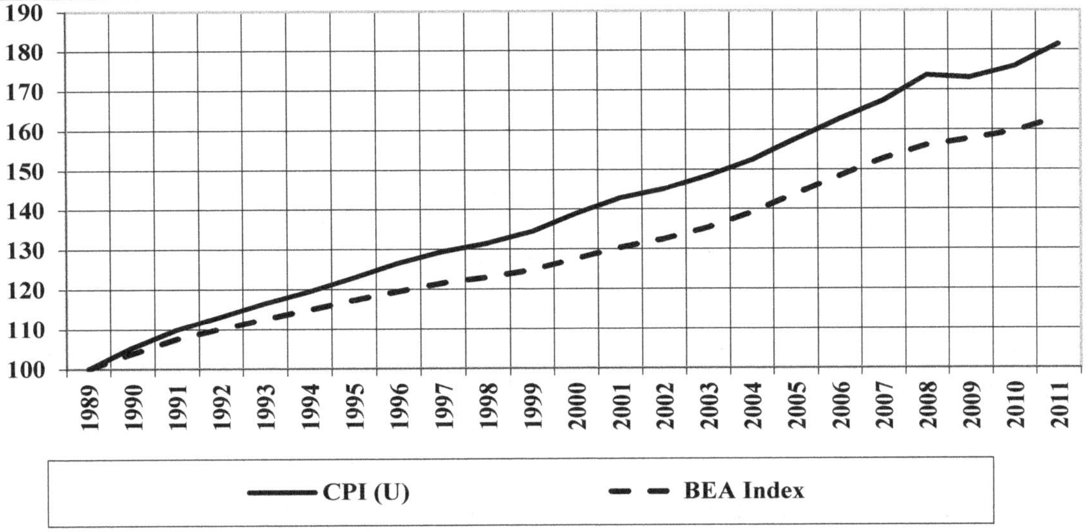

Source: http://www.bea.gov/national/xls/gdplev.xls

1989, that same $1.00 in 2011 could purchase only 58 percent (average of the CPI and BEA index) of the same basket of goods.

Figure 4-2: Value of the Dollar, 1989-2011

BEA (1989=100)	$1.00	$0.96	$0.93	$0.91	$0.89	$0.87	$0.85	$0.84	$0.82	$0.81	$0.80	$0.78	$0.77	$0.75	$0.74	$0.72	$0.70	$0.67	$0.65	$0.64	$0.63	$0.63	$0.61
CPI (U) (1989=100)	$1.00	$0.95	$0.91	$0.88	$0.86	$0.84	$0.81	$0.79	$0.77	$0.76	$0.74	$0.72	$0.70	$0.69	$0.67	$0.66	$0.63	$0.62	$0.60	$0.58	$0.58	$0.57	$0.55

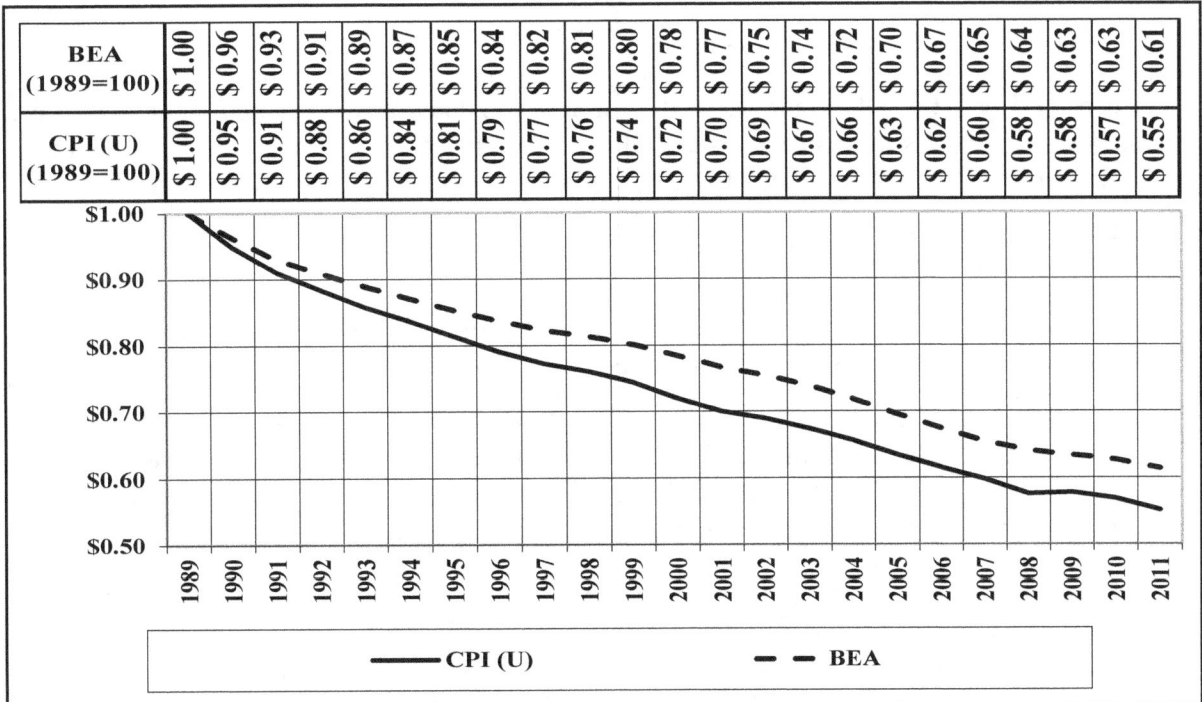

Source: calculated from BEA data in figure 4-1.

4.2   ADJUSTING FOR SEASONAL INFLUENCES

Quarterly and monthly estimates are sometimes seasonally adjusted when the series demonstrates statistically significant seasonal patterns. The seasonal adjustment of data can be illustrated using the treatment of unemployment data by the Bureau of Labor Statistics (BLS) as an example. Unemployment is routinely higher in some months than in others. For example, it is higher in January and February, when it is cold in many parts of the country and work in agriculture, construction, and other seasonal industries is curtailed.

The seasonal fluctuations in the number of unemployed persons reflect not only the normal seasonal weather patterns that tend to be repeated year after year, but also the hiring (and layoff) patterns that accompany regular events such as the winter holiday season and the summer vacation season. These variations make it difficult to tell whether month-to-month changes in unemployment are the result of normal seasonal patterns or changing economic conditions.

Seasonal adjustment uses the past history of the series to identify the seasonal movements and to calculate the size and direction of these movements. A seasonal adjustment factor is then developed and applied to the estimates to eliminate the effects of regular seasonal fluctuations on the data. When a statistical series has been seasonally adjusted, the normal seasonal fluctuations are smoothed out and data for any month can be compared more meaningfully with data from any other month or with an annual average. Many time series that are based on monthly data are seasonally adjusted.

Figure 4-3 illustrates how seasonal adjustment works in practice. The data are monthly unemployment rates during 2010. From January through March when unemployment tends to be higher because of cold weather in much of the country, the unadjusted data are higher. The April through August period is influenced by seasonal jobs entering and leaving the market, and the September through December period also is strongly influenced by seasonal employment.

This is by no means a rigorous explanation of the variations in the seasonal adjustments, but it is suggestive. You should take away two points from this example:

- The annual total of the adjustments is zero. The sum of the upward adjustments exactly equals the sum of the downward adjustments across the year.

- Be careful not to mix the two series. For example, in talking about unemployment during 2010, it would be highly misleading (not to mention intellectually dishonest) to say it was 9.6 in January, 9.4 in May, 9.5 in July, and 9.0 in October. To be consistent, one has to stick with the same series for month-to-month comparisons.

Figure 4-3: Example of Unadjusted versus Seasonally Adjusted Data

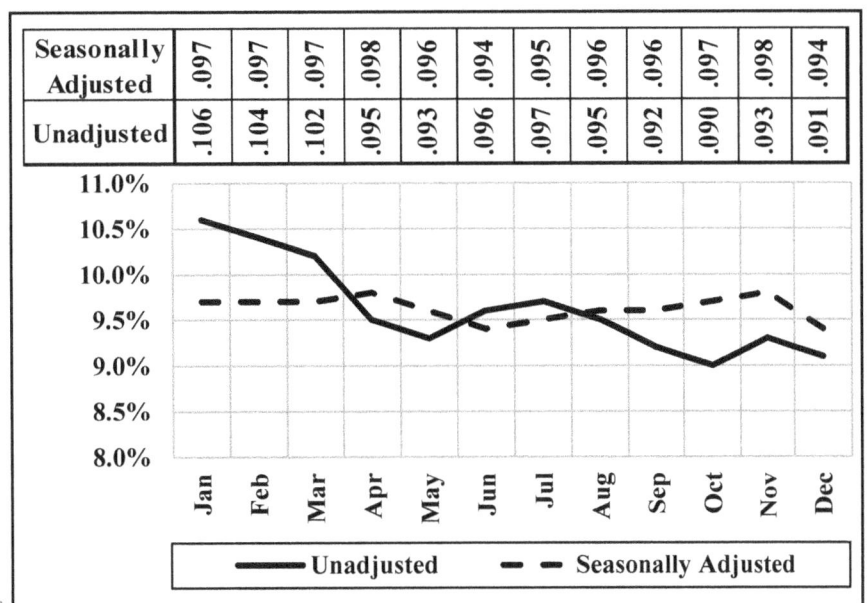

	Jan	Feb	Mar	Apr	May	Jun	Jul	Aug	Sep	Oct	Nov	Dec
Seasonally Adjusted	.097	.097	.097	.098	.096	.094	.095	.096	.096	.097	.098	.094
Unadjusted	.106	.104	.102	.095	.093	.096	.097	.095	.092	.090	.093	.091

5. DATA SOURCES

In the preface, I promised that I would use the most authoritative sources for all the data that I present. That's easy to say, but not so easy to do. For example, the Bureau of Economic Analysis is responsible for the National Income and Product Accounts; the Internal Revenue Service is responsible for tax data, the Census Bureau is responsible for demographic data, and the Federal Reserve is responsible for monetary and flow of funds data, and so on.

On the other hand, the Office of Management and Budget (OMB) publishes much of the above data in the annual budget, sometimes in different form, and often with different values than those published by the originating organizations. Values that are different aren't necessarily wrong. They may represent different things, although they have similar names, or the vintage of the data may be different. For example, the BEA continually updates its data, whereas the OMB publishes its budget once a year. After a few months, even the very same BEA and OMB data series might diverge as the BEA refines its estimates.

Just keep in mind that these and other government organizations have spent decades refining the collection and analysis of these statistics to meet an astounding number and variety of needs of the government, academia, and the public.

There appear to be some types of data, however, that no government organization wants to collect. Data on wealth distribution, illegal immigration, and the cost of federal regulations, for example, are very spotty.

In the following chapters, I will not attempt to reconcile differences among various sources. I will pick the source that appears to be primary, as opposed to derived. As I said earlier, the important thing is to understand what is being presented and feel confident it is consistent. If someone wishes to argue that another source is better for some of the data I present, I probably won't dispute the point, as long as the source is authoritative and what is being presented is well defined. Also, the source should be attempting to measure the same thing as the data presented.

Finally, I gathered all these data from the web, almost exclusively from government sources. If you feel inclined to dig deeper, or to understand relationships among the various data at greater depth than is revealed here, you can pick up where I've left off.

6. WHO'S IN CHARGE?

It's not fair to blame everything that happens to the economy on the White House or Congress or both of them. However, to the extent that they create laws and regulations that impact the economy (and many laws and regulations do), they must share the blame when things go badly. Since I promised to be neutral, I'll leave it to the reader to draw conclusions about who is responsible for the economic effects shown in the various figures in subsequent chapters.

Figure 6-1 shows which political party controlled the White House, the House of Representatives, and the Senate during the period 1989 through 2011. The 107th Congress was uniquely unsettled, and control in the Senate shifted during its term. For more detail on this situation, see the US Senate's website.

As a convenience to the reader, figure 6-1 is condensed into figure 6-2 and inserted in many of the figures that follow so the reader may correlate the political timeline with the timeline of the economic data being presented. Figure 6-2 only will be shown with figures that have timelines that show the appropriate years. Note the color key indicating political party.

Figure 6-1: White House and Congressional Control, by Party, 1989-2011

Year		1989	1990	1991	1992	1993	1994	1995	1996	1997	1998	1999	2000	2001	2002	2003	2004	2005	2006	2007	2008	2009	2010	2011
President		George Bush				William J. Clinton								George W. Bush								Barack Obama		
House	D	260		267		258		204		206		211		212		205		202		233		257		193
	R	175		167		176		230		228		223		221		229		232		202		178		242
	I	0		1		1		1		1		1		2		1		1		0		0		0
Senate	D	55		56		57		48		45		45		50		48		44		49		57		51
	R	45		44		43		52		55		55		49		51		55		49		41		47
	I	0		0		0		0		0		0		1		1		1		2		2		2
Congress		101st		102nd		103rd		104th		105th		106th		107th		108th		109th		110th		111th		112th

| ▨ Democrat control | □ Republican control |

Source: House- http://artandhistory.house.gov/house_history/partyDiv.aspx
Senate- http://www.senate.gov/pagelayout/history/one_item_and_teasers/partydiv.htm

Figure 6-2: White House and Congressional Control, by Party, 1989-2011 (Condensed)

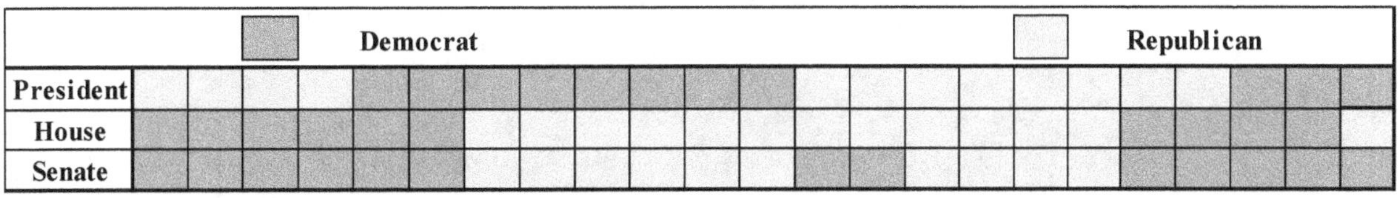

	▨ Democrat	□ Republican
President		
House		
Senate		

PART 2.   THE ECONOMY

7. ECONOMIC PRODUCTION

Economic production is the basis of our national wealth and prosperity. It is the result of private enterprise and the enabler of government activity. Its size and growth affect every aspect of our lives, and it is watched closely by the entire world as a primary indicator of our nation's economic health.

7.1 GROSS DOMESTIC PRODUCT (GDP)

In 1991 the Bureau of Economic Analysis (BEA) began using gross domestic product (GDP) as the primary measure of US economic production. Some of you may recall before that the BEA used gross national product (GNP) as its primary measure. GDP covers the goods and services produced in the US, whether by US citizens or foreign nationals in the US, while GNP covers the goods and services produced by US residents, in the US or overseas.

The BEA deemed GDP to be a more appropriate measure for much of the short-term monitoring and analysis of the US economy, particularly relating to employment, productivity, industry output, and investment in equipment and structures. Moreover, GDP had become more of an international standard.

In the US, GDP and GNP tend to differ little. For example, the difference was between 0.6 and 1.8 percent during the 1980s, just prior to the BEA's decision to use GDP.

7.1.1 Total GDP

In its most complete detail, GDP is impossibly complex. For purposes of understanding the politics of economic production, however, one need understand only that GDP comprises the totality of private consumption, gross private investments, government expenditures, and net foreign trade (exports minus imports). The BEA calls this the "final demand" or "expenditure approach" to measuring GDP. You might recognize it as the Keynesian formulation of GDP:

GDP=Consumption+Investment+Government Expenditures+(Imports-Exports).

Though there are several other ways of looking at or defining GDP, the important point here is to pick a single definition and stick with it over the period of discussion.

7.1.1.1 Annual Data

Figure 7-1 shows GDP in current or non-adjusted dollars and constant or inflation-adjusted dollars annually for the period 1989 through 2011. Note that in current dollars it is 2.8 times as large in 2011 as in 1989. The compound annual growth rate (see chapter 2) for the entire period is 4.7 percent in current dollars. If you choose the period 2007-2011, the compound annual growth rate is 1.8 percent in current dollars. In 2011, US GDP was $15.1 trillion in current dollars.

Note that for purposes of calculating the compound annual growth rate, the number of years used in the formula is the last year of the period minus the first year. For example, the period 2007 through 2011 is a four-year period, because the rate is applied four times. The first year is the base, so it is not counted in the compounding formula.

If we use inflation-adjusted or constant dollars for the period 1989 through 2011, the compound annual growth rate is 2.4 percent. This is what's called the "real growth", and it is significantly less than the growth expressed in current dollars. In 2011, US GDP was $9.3 trillion in 1989 constant dollars (BEA Index with 1989=100 as the base).

Whenever you hear GDP numbers, you need to know whether they are in current or real terms. Whenever you hear GDP growth rates, you need to know whether they are simple or compound growth rates.

Figure 7-1: GDP, Current and Constant Dollars, 1989-2011

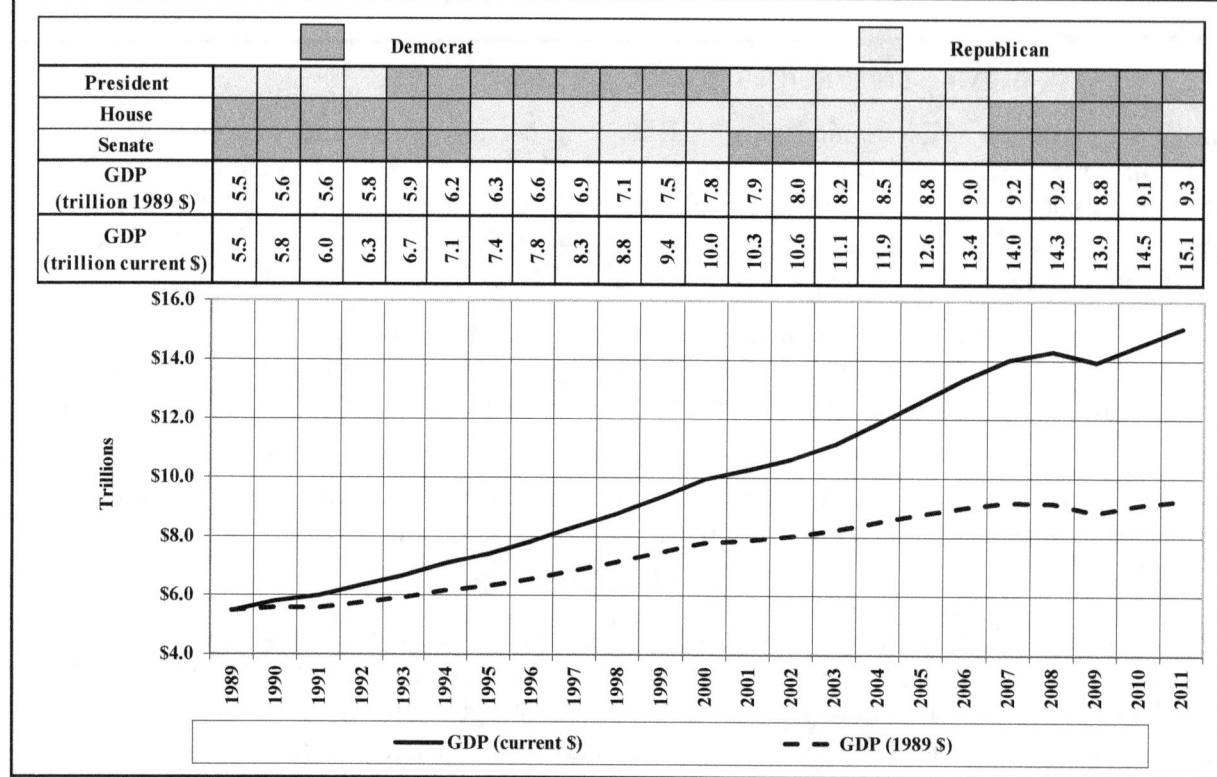

	Democrat																Republican						
President																							
House																							
Senate																							
GDP (trillion 1989 $)	5.5	5.6	5.6	5.8	5.9	6.2	6.3	6.6	6.9	7.1	7.5	7.8	7.9	8.0	8.2	8.5	8.8	9.0	9.2	9.2	8.8	9.1	9.3
GDP (trillion current $)	5.5	5.8	6.0	6.3	6.7	7.1	7.4	7.8	8.3	8.8	9.4	10.0	10.3	10.6	11.1	11.9	12.6	13.4	14.0	14.3	13.9	14.5	15.1

Source: http://www.bea.gov/national/xls/gdplev.xls

7.1.1.2 Quarterly Data

GDP is a key economic indicator, so it is tracked very closely. Annual data are not sufficiently timely for economic decision-making; more current numbers are much in demand. The BEA publishes quarterly GDP estimates, in both current and constant dollars, but they all are seasonally adjusted. Curiously, the BEA says the revision and the publication of unadjusted quarterly estimates of GDP have been suspended because of budget constraints, but estimates through 2004 will continue to be available on BEA's Web site.

Figure 7-2 shows GDP in current and constant dollars quarterly for the period 2006Q1 (2006 quarter 1) through 2011Q4. Note that the data are seasonally adjusted.

7.1.2 Per Capita GDP

Knowing how GDP is changing tells us how the economy as a whole is doing, but it doesn't tell us anything about how individuals are faring. For that, we need to look at the amount of GDP per person, or the per capita GDP (see chapter 3). Simply divide each year's GDP (figure 7-1) by population (figure 3-1) and you get per capita GDP.

Figure 7-3 shows that per capita GDP, or GDP per person, in current dollars is 2.17 times in 2011 what it was in 1989. Per capita GDP growth was slower than GDP growth as a whole because population grew during the period.

Over the entire period, per capita GDP increased in every year except 2009, when it declined by about $1,500. For the entire period, the compound annual growth rate was 3.6 percent in current dollars.

Figure 7-2: GDP, Current and Constant Dollars, Seasonally Adjusted, 2006Q1-2011Q4

GDP (trillion 2005 $)	12.9	12.9	13.0	13.0	13.1	13.2	13.3	13.3	13.3	13.3	13.2	12.9	12.7	12.6	12.7	12.8	12.9	13.1	13.1	13.2	13.2	13.3	13.3	13.4
GDP (trillion current $)	13.2	13.3	13.4	13.6	13.8	14.0	14.1	14.3	14.3	14.4	14.4	14.1	13.9	13.9	13.9	14.1	14.3	14.5	14.6	14.8	14.9	15.0	15.2	15.3

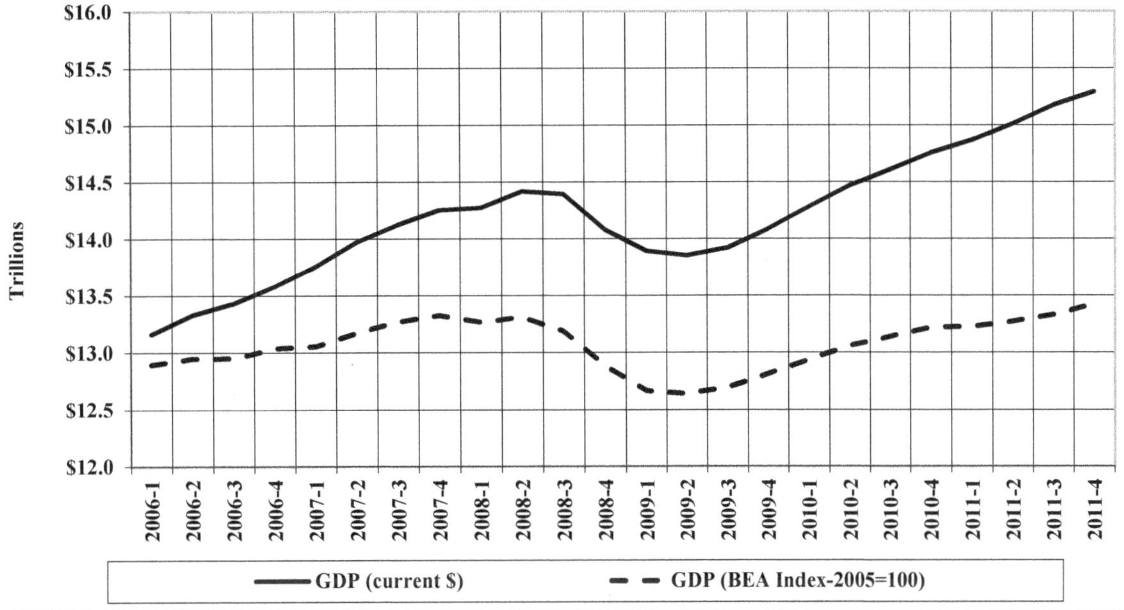

Source: http://www.bea.gov/national/nipaweb/SelectTable.asp?Selected=Y

In constant dollars, per capita GDP grew at a compound annual rate of 1.3 percent. In 2011, per capita GDP was $48,200 in current dollars, and $29,599 in 1989 constant dollars. Real per capita GDP declined at a compound annual rate of -0.7 percent per year over the 2007 through 2011 period. However you look at it, when real GDP grows faster than population, individual average economic circumstances improve.

7.2 ECONOMIC SECTORS

Having seen what GDP as a whole looks like, let's now look at the relative sizes of its four sectors previously mentioned: private consumption, gross private investments, government expenditures, and net foreign trade.

Figure 7-4 shows the relative sizes of the four economic sectors as a percentage of GDP. Note that each vertical bar corresponds to one year and equals 100 percent of GDP for that year. Net imports were mostly negative, however, so the bars fall short of 100 percent by the negative amount of the net exports.

There are no obvious straight-line trends in any of the sectors over the full 23 years of the 1989 through 2011 period. If one chooses shorter time periods, however, one might infer some trends.

7.2.1 Private Consumption

Private consumption averaged 68.4 percent of GDP for the period 1989 through 2011. Its high was 70.8 percent, which occurred in 2009, and its low was 65.6 percent, which occurred in 1989.

Figure 7-3: GDP per Capita, Current and Constant Dollars, 1989-2011

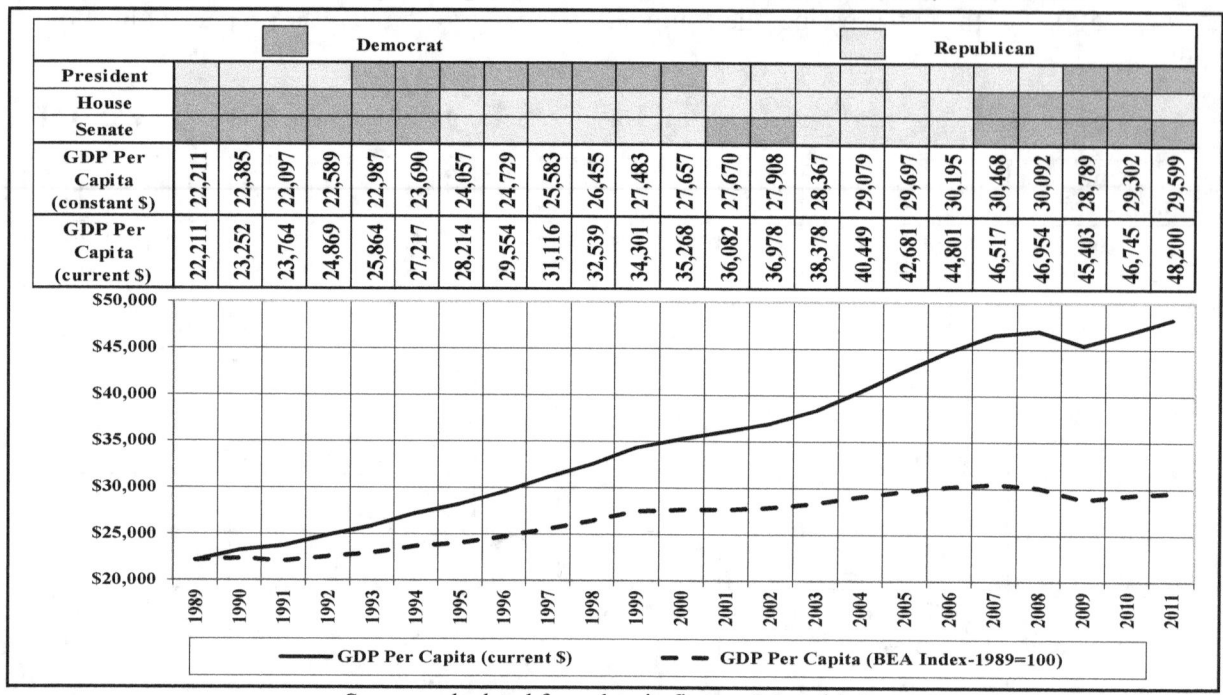

	Democrat																		Republican				
President																							
House																							
Senate																							
GDP Per Capita (constant $)	22,211	22,385	22,097	22,589	22,987	23,690	24,057	24,729	25,583	26,455	27,483	27,657	27,670	27,908	28,367	29,079	29,697	30,195	30,468	30,092	28,789	29,302	29,599
GDP Per Capita (current $)	22,211	23,252	23,764	24,869	25,864	27,217	28,214	29,554	31,116	32,539	34,301	35,268	36,082	36,978	38,378	40,449	42,681	44,801	46,517	46,954	45,403	46,745	48,200

Source: calculated from data in figures 7-1 and 3-1.

Figure 7-4: GDP Sectors as Percentages of GDP, 1989-2011

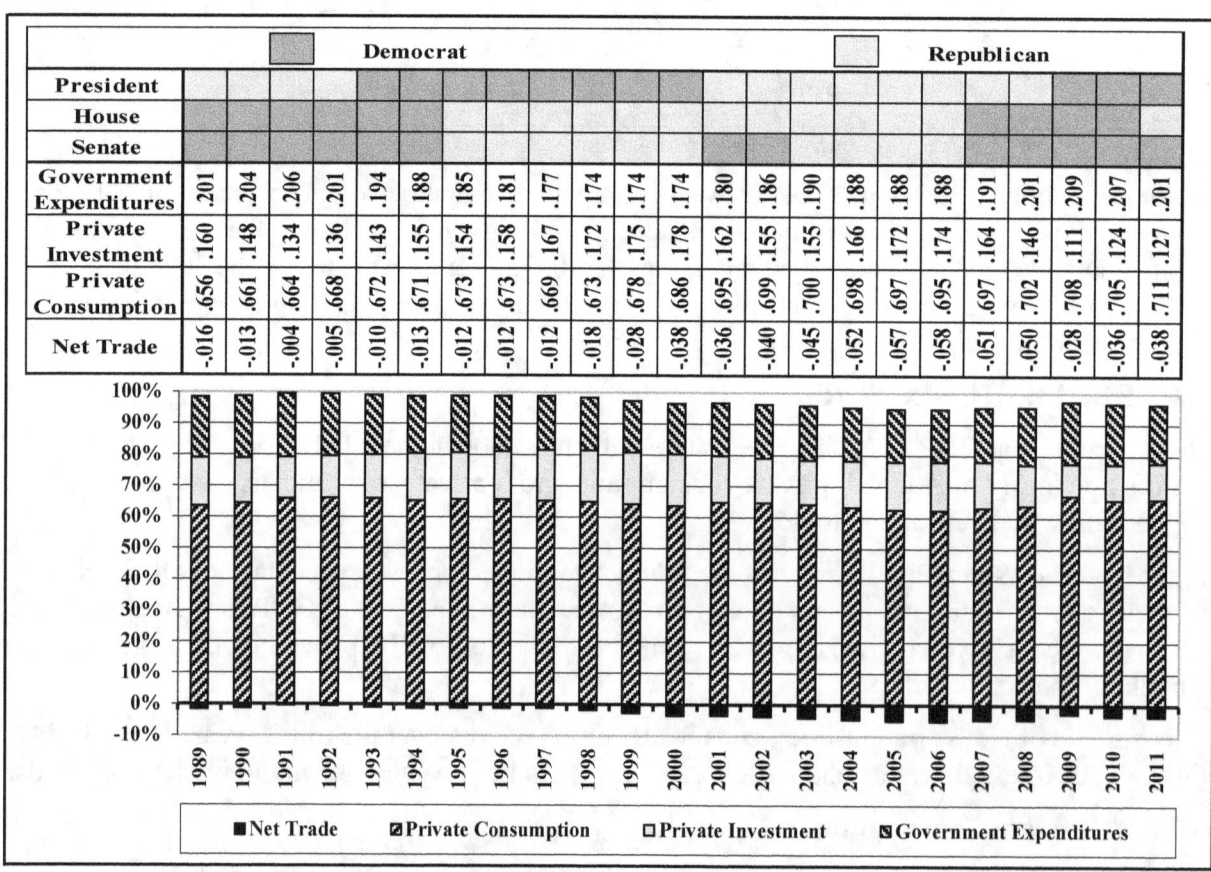

	Democrat																		Republican				
President																							
House																							
Senate																							
Government Expenditures	.201	.204	.206	.201	.194	.188	.185	.181	.177	.174	.174	.174	.180	.186	.190	.188	.188	.188	.191	.201	.209	.207	.201
Private Investment	.160	.148	.134	.136	.143	.155	.154	.158	.167	.172	.175	.178	.162	.155	.155	.166	.172	.174	.164	.146	.111	.124	.127
Private Consumption	.656	.661	.664	.668	.672	.671	.673	.673	.669	.673	.678	.686	.695	.699	.700	.698	.697	.695	.697	.702	.708	.705	.711
Net Trade	-.016	-.013	-.004	-.005	-.010	-.013	-.012	-.012	-.012	-.018	-.028	-.038	-.036	-.040	-.045	-.052	-.057	-.058	-.051	-.050	-.028	-.036	-.038

Source: http://www.bea.gov/national/nipaweb/TableView.asp?SelectedTable=14
&Freq=Qtr&FirstYear=2009&LastYear=2011

7.2.2 Private Investment

Private investment averaged 15.5 percent of GDP for the period 1989 through 2011. Its high was 17.8 percent, which occurred in 2000, and its low was 11.1 percent, which occurred in 2009. Its value in 2011 was 12.7 percent.

7.2.3 Government Expenditures

Government expenditures averaged 19.0 percent of GDP for the period 1989 through 2011. Its high was 20.9 percent, which occurred in 2009; and its low was 17.4 percent, which occurred in 1998-2000. Its value in 2011 was 20.1 percent.

7.2.4 Net Trade

Net trade (exports minus imports) averaged -2.9 percent of GDP for the period 1989 through 2011. Its high was -0.4 percent, which occurred in 1991; and its low was -5.8 percent, which occurred in 2006. Its value in 2011 was -3.8 percent.

7.3 TWO NOTEWORTHY CROSS-SECTOR ACTIVITIES

Two activities cut across the above sectors and deserve a closer look by virtue of their prominence in the political debate: manufacturing and oil and gas extraction.

7.3.1 Manufacturing

Much is made of the state of manufacturing in the US. Figure 7-5 shows gross manufacturing output for the period 1989 through 2010.

Figure 7-5: Manufacturing, 1989-2010

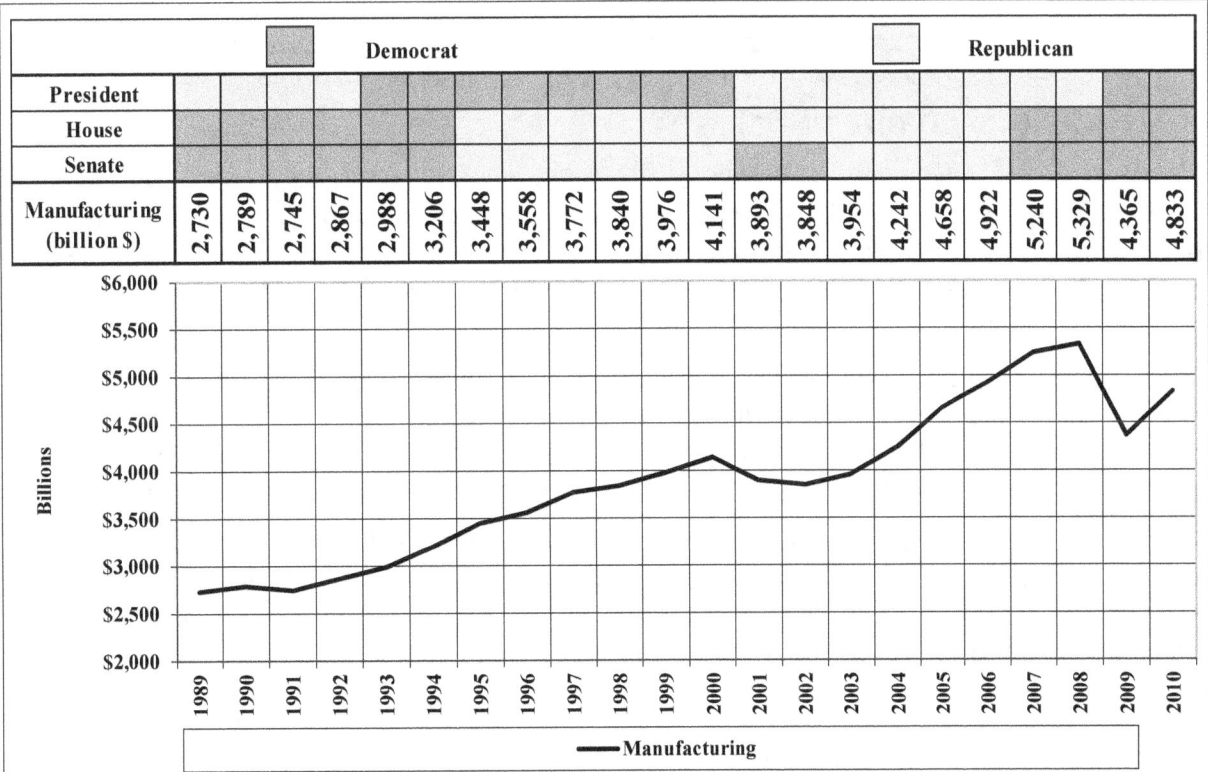

Source: http://www.bea.gov/iTable/iTable.cfm?ReqID=5&step=1

7.3.2 Oil and Gas Extraction

Much also is made of the production of oil and gas in the US. Figure 7-6 shows the value of gas and oil extracted in the US during the period 1989 through 2010.

Figure 7-6: Oil and Gas Extraction, 1989-2010

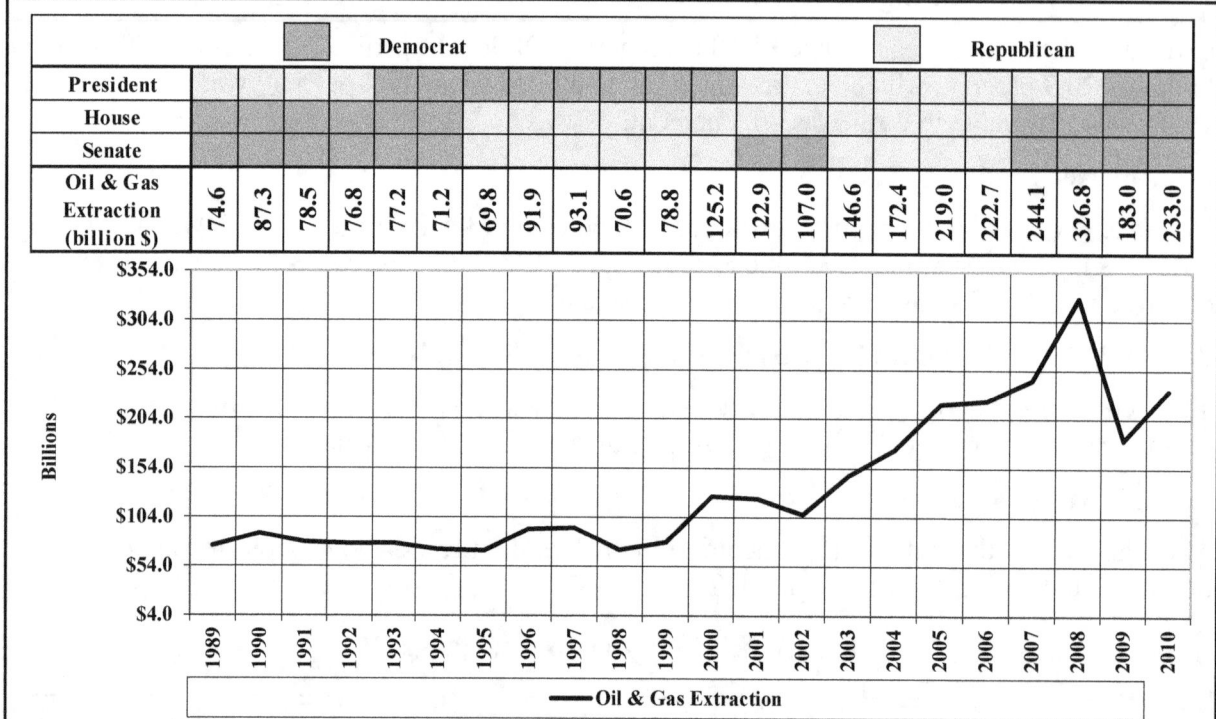

Source: http://www.bea.gov/iTable/iTable.cfm?ReqID=5&step=1

7.4 UNDERGROUND ECONOMY

The BEA goes to great lengths to report economic activity as comprehensively and as accurately as possible, but it recognizes that some income may be underreported or not reported at all. Activities that are characterized by underreporting and non-reporting comprise the underground economy and may include illegal prostitution and gambling, plus some legal cash-based and bartering activities.

In an effort to compensate for this underground income in their national income accounts, the BEA adjusts its income data on the basis of information from the IRS and from household surveys. Adjustments for underreporting ranged between 1.0 and 2.2 percent of GDP from 1984 to 2006, and adjustments for non-reporting are about one-tenth of those for underreporting.

There may be substantial additional income that is not included, either in the direct reporting or in the adjustments. In all likelihood, the higher taxes are or the worse the economy is performing, the larger the underground economy will be as more people attempt to go off the books to save on taxes.

7.5 RECESSION AND DEPRESSION

7.5.1 Recession

The official National Bureau of Economic Research (NBER) definition of recession is as follows:

"A recession is a significant decline in economic activity spread across the economy, lasting more than a few months, normally visible in real GDP, real income, employment, industrial production, and wholesale-retail sales. A recession begins just after the economy reaches a peak of activity and ends as the economy reaches its trough. Between trough and peak, the economy is in an expansion. Expansion is the normal state of the economy; most recessions are brief and they have been rare in recent decades. The start and end dates are determined by the Business Cycle Dating Committee of the National Bureau of Economic Research (NBER). It is a popular misconception that a recession is indicated simply by two consecutive quarters of declining GDP, which is true for most, but not all recessions. NBER uses monthly data to date the start and ending months of recessions."

This official definition relies on a methodology that is far more complex and far less deterministic than the two or three quarters of negative growth that generally is used.

Table 7-1 shows what the NBER calls their business cycle reference dates. Using their definition that a recession begins just after the economy reaches a peak, you can see that for the period 1980 through June 2009, there have been five peaks (January 1980, July 1981, July 1990, March 2001, and December 2007), therefore five recessions. The December 2007 recession was the longest at 18 months; the July 1990 and March 2001 recessions were the shortest at eight months each.

Table 7-1: Recessions, 1980-2010

Peak	Trough	Contraction	Expansion	Cycle	
		Peak to Trough	Previous trough to peak	Trough from Previous Trough	Peak from Previous Peak
Jan-80	Jul-80	6	58	64	74
Jul-81	Nov-82	16	12	28	18
Jul-90	Mar-91	8	92	100	108
Mar-01	Nov-01	8	120	128	128
Dec-07	Jun-09	18	73	91	81
Average		11.2	71	82.2	81.8

Source: NBER

The average duration of the 33 recessions in the 156 years from 1854 to 2009 (inclusive) is 15 months. The average frequency over that period is one recession every 56 months, with an average duration of 16 months. During the period 1980 through 2009 (30 years), the average frequency is one recession every 72 months, with an average duration of 11.2 months.

The most recent decision of the Business Cycle Dating Committee of the NBER is the determination that the last expansion began in June 2009.

Politicians hate recessions. Recessions make it much harder for them to get re-elected. When one hears of quarterly data being adjusted in retrospect, one may wonder about political manipulation. In all fairness, the preparation of economic statistics is a very complex process, and there always is a trade-off between timeliness and accuracy. Statisticians often put out estimates quickly to satisfy the timeliness requirement, then adjust the estimates as additional data come in. This is a perfectly legitimate practice, and in the absence of specific information to the contrary, should be taken at face value.

7.5.2 Depression

In political terms, depressions are even worse than recessions. While the NBER does not separately identify depressions, a particularly severe period of economic weakness may be called a depression. It lasts until economic activity returns close to previous normal levels.

The most recent US depression began in August 1929, and lasted through March 1933, followed by another severe contraction in May 1937 through June 1938. During the 1929 through 1933 contraction, the Bureau of Economic Analysis estimates that real GDP declined 27 percent, making it the worst in US history.

8. UNEMPLOYMENT

Unemployment is a key issue in the 2012 presidential campaign. According to the Bureau of Labor Statistics (BLS), people with jobs are **employed**, and people who do not have jobs and are looking for jobs are **unemployed**. These two groups comprise the **labor force**, while people who are classified neither as employed nor unemployed are **not in the labor force**. In this context, labor force is understood to mean civilian labor force.

Once again, things are not as simple as they appear to be. Read on.

8.1 DEFINITIONS

Let's define some key concepts in more detail, starting with persons not in the labor force. We start here because that's pretty much the way BLS collects its data.

8.1.1 Persons Not in the Labor Force

People who, by BLS definition, are neither employed nor unemployed are not in the labor force. Persons not in the labor force include any person who is in an institution (for example, correctional facilities and residential nursing and mental health care facilities), or on active duty in the armed forces. Also not in the labor force are those persons who have no job and are not looking for one. They may be going to school, be retired, or be out of the labor force for family or other reasons.

Each month, the BLS asks a series of questions of persons not in the labor force to obtain information about their desire for work, the reasons why they had not looked for work in the last four weeks, their prior job search, and their availability for work. These questions include:

1. Do you currently want a job, either full or part time?
2. What is the main reason you were not looking for work during the last four weeks?
3. Did you look for work at any time during the last 12 months?
4. Last week, could you have started a job if one had been offered?

These questions form the basis for estimating the number of persons who are not in the labor force, but who are considered to be "marginally attached to the labor force."

8.1.1.1 Marginally Attached

Marginally attached persons are persons without jobs who are not currently looking for work (and therefore are not counted as unemployed), but have demonstrated some degree of labor force attachment. Specifically, to be counted as "marginally attached to the labor force," individuals must indicate that they currently want a job, have looked for work in the last 12 months (or since they last worked, if they worked within the last 12 months), and are available for work.

8.1.1.2 Discouraged Workers

Discouraged workers are a subset of the marginally attached. Discouraged workers report they are not currently looking for work for one of four reasons:

1. They believe no job is available to them in their line of work or area.
2. They previously had been unable to find work.
3. They lack the necessary schooling, training, skills, or experience.
4. Employers think they are too young or too old, or they face some other type of discrimination.

Additional questions about persons not in the labor force are asked during each household's last month of its four-month tenure in a sample rotation pattern. These questions are designed to collect information about why these people left their previous jobs, when they last worked at a job or business, and whether they intend to look for work in the near future.

8.1.2   Labor Force

According to the BLS, every person age 16 and over who is not excluded (see section 8.1.1, above) is counted in the labor force and classified as either employed or unemployed. Figure 8-1 shows the labor force over the period 1989 through 2011.

Figure 8-1: Labor Force, 1989-2011

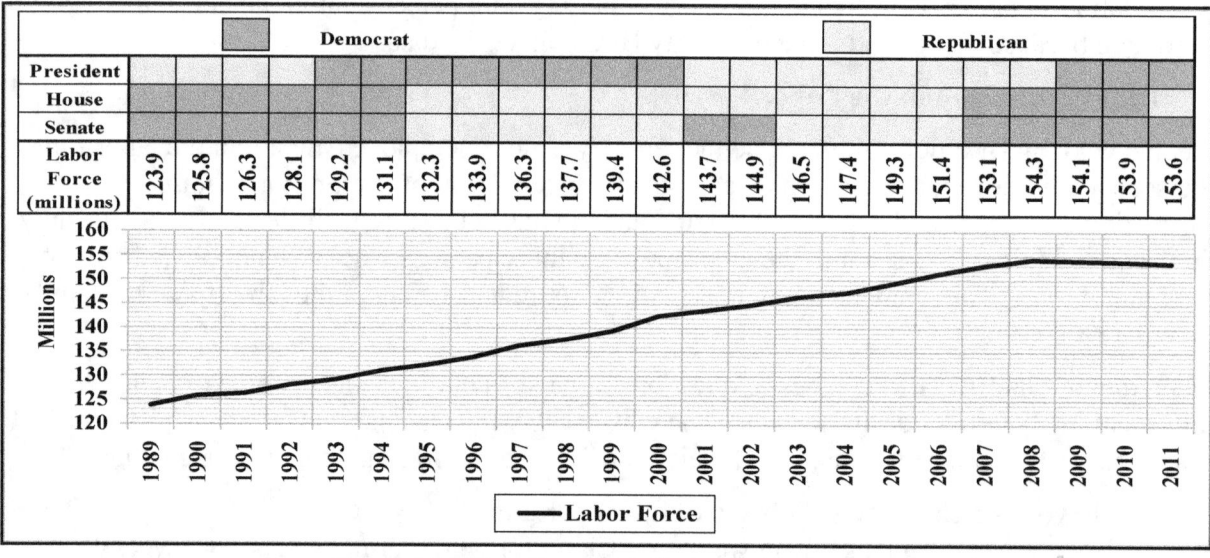

Source: http://data.bls.gov/pdq/SurveyOutputServlet

Figure 8-2 shows that over the 1989 through 2011 period the percentage of the population represented by the labor force remained in the range around 50 percent, but dropped from 50.8 percent in 2007 to 49.1 percent in 2011.

8.1.2.1   Employed

Persons with jobs are employed, including those who did any work for pay or profit during a specific survey week; those who did at least 15 hours of unpaid work in a family-operated enterprise; and those who were temporarily absent from their regular jobs because of illness, vacation, bad weather, industrial dispute, or various personal reasons.

We will deal in more depth with the employed in chapter 9.

8.1.2.2   Unemployed

The BLS standard measure of unemployment is people who are jobless, looking for jobs, and available for work.

8.2   UNEMPLOYMENT MEASURES

8.2.1   BLS Unemployment Rates: U-1 through U-6

The BLS recognizes that their standard measure of unemployment (U-3) is somewhat restricted, and that it is not always an adequate measure of labor market problems. As a result, BLS

Figure 8-2: Labor Force as a Percentage of Population, 1989-2011

Legend: shaded = Democrat (D); unshaded = Republican (R)

	1989	1990	1991	1992	1993	1994	1995	1996	1997	1998	1999	2000	2001	2002	2003	2004	2005	2006	2007	2008	2009	2010	2011
President	R	R	R	R	D	D	D	D	D	D	D	D	R	R	R	R	R	R	R	R	D	D	D
House	D	D	D	D	D	D	R	R	R	R	R	R	R	R	R	R	R	R	D	D	D	D	R
Senate	D	D	D	D	D	D	R	R	R	R	R	R	D	D	R	R	R	R	D	D	D	D	D
Labor Force/ Population	.502	.504	.501	.502	.501	.503	.503	.505	.509	.509	.511	.505	.504	.503	.505	.503	.505	.507	.508	.507	.502	.495	.491

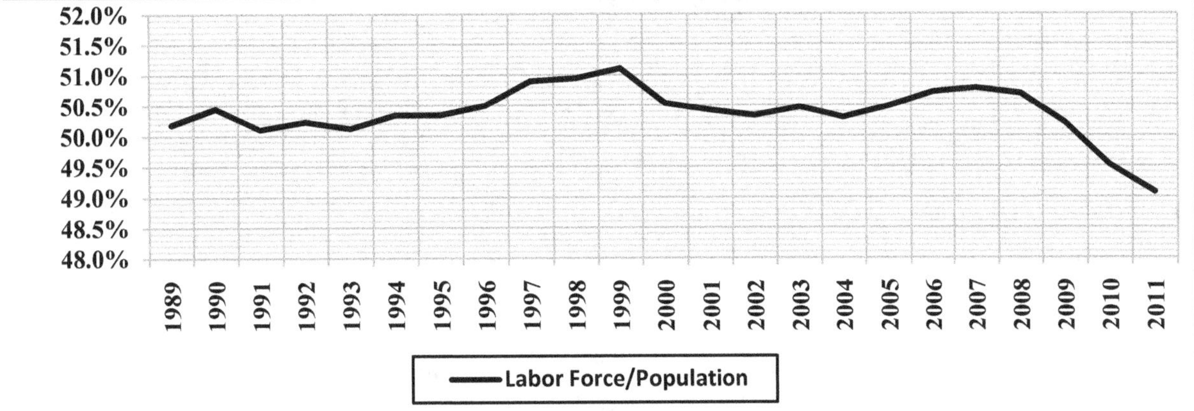

Source: calculated from tables 3-1 and 8-1.

economists in 1994 developed a set of **alternative measures of labor underutilization**. They have defined a total of six measures of unemployment, or labor underutilization, but we will look only at four: U-3 through U-6.

- **U-3 (Official Rate)** - the official rate of unemployment and the one most typically cited in news stories about the economy.
- **U-4** - adds to U-3 discouraged workers who want jobs but have given up the search for work because they believe no jobs are available for them.
- **U-5** - adds to U-4 marginally attached workers who are not discouraged workers.
- **U-6** - the broadest measure of labor underutilization, it includes the unemployed, the marginally attached, and persons who are actually employed but who work fewer hours than they would like (sometimes referred to as underemployed).

Figure 8-3 presents US unemployment over the period 1989 through 2011, using the four selected BLS measures, U-3 through U-6. U-3 numbers are available for the entire period, but U-4 through U-6 are available only from 1994, when these categories were created (actually, redefined).

When you hear a political candidate talk about unemployment, pay attention to the measure he or she is using.

Since unemployment is such a key issues in the 2012 presidential campaign, one might like to know in more recent detail what has been happening. See figure 8-4 for monthly unemployment statistics (U-3 and U-6) for the period January 2009 through December 2011.

Figure 8-3: Unemployment (Four BLS Measures), 1989-2011

	Democrat														Republican								
President																							
House																							
Senate																							
U-6						.109	.101	.097	.089	.080	.074	.070	.081	.096	.101	.096	.089	.082	.083	.105	.162	.167	.159
U-5						.074	.067	.065	.059	.054	.050	.048	.056	.067	.070	.065	.061	.055	.055	.068	.105	.111	.104
U-4						.065	.059	.057	.052	.047	.044	.042	.049	.060	.063	.058	.054	.049	.049	.061	.097	.103	.095
U-3	.053	.056	.068	.075	.069	.061	.056	.054	.049	.045	.042	.040	.047	.058	.060	.055	.051	.046	.046	.058	.093	.096	.089

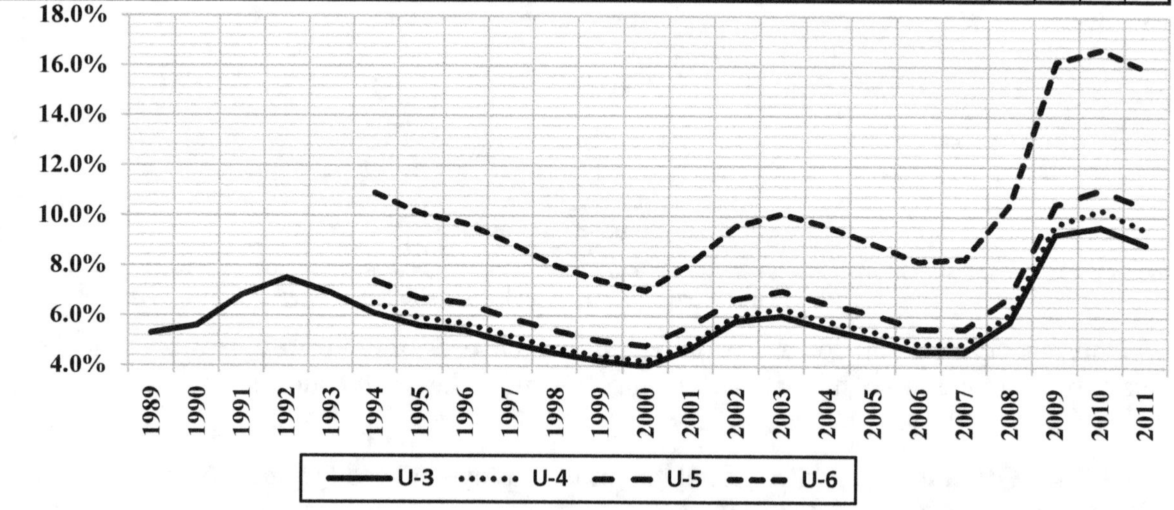

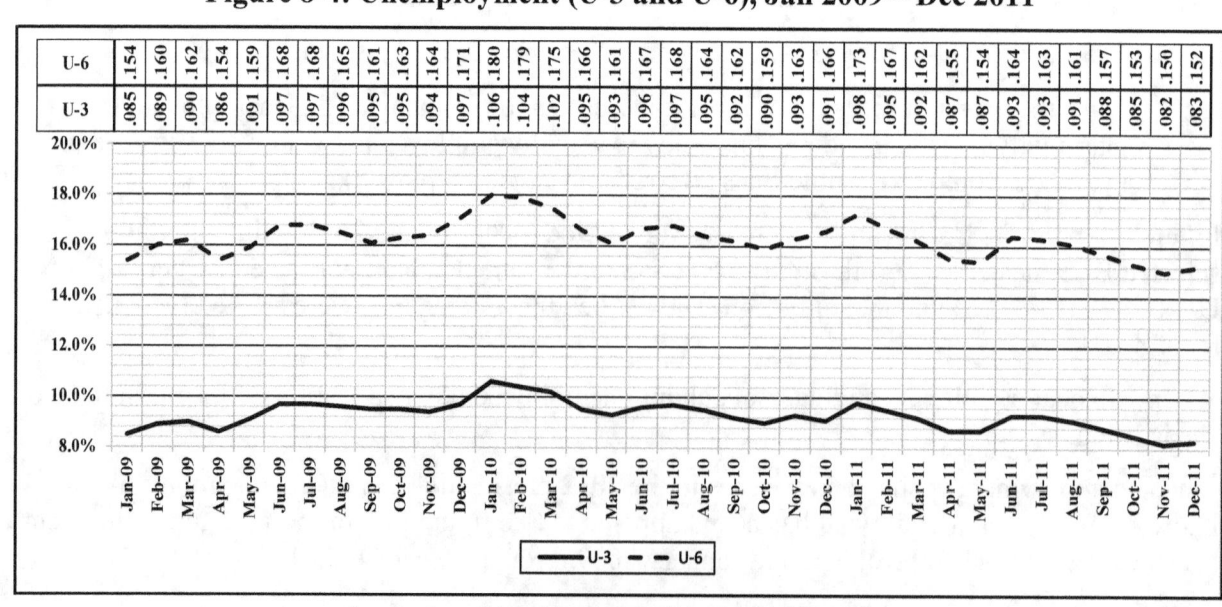

Source: http://data.bls.gov/pdq/SurveyOutputServlet

Figure 8-4: Unemployment (U-3 and U-6), Jan 2009 – Dec 2011

	Jan-09	Feb-09	Mar-09	Apr-09	May-09	Jun-09	Jul-09	Aug-09	Sep-09	Oct-09	Nov-09	Dec-09	Jan-10	Feb-10	Mar-10	Apr-10	May-10	Jun-10	Jul-10	Aug-10	Sep-10	Oct-10	Nov-10	Dec-10	Jan-11	Feb-11	Mar-11	Apr-11	May-11	Jun-11	Jul-11	Aug-11	Sep-11	Oct-11	Nov-11	Dec-11
U-6	.154	.160	.162	.154	.159	.168	.168	.165	.161	.163	.164	.171	.180	.179	.175	.166	.161	.167	.168	.164	.162	.159	.163	.166	.173	.167	.162	.155	.154	.164	.163	.161	.157	.153	.150	.152
U-3	.085	.089	.090	.086	.091	.097	.097	.096	.095	.095	.094	.097	.106	.104	.102	.095	.093	.096	.097	.095	.092	.090	.093	.091	.098	.095	.092	.087	.087	.093	.093	.091	.088	.085	.082	.083

Source: http://data.bls.gov/pdq/SurveyOutputServlet

8.2.2 An Unconventional Measure of Unemployment

Let's take "labor force" out of the picture. Subtract employment from total population and divide by total population and you will have the fraction of the population that is not employed. While there are some obvious shortcomings with this as a metric, its index is revealing. Figure 8-5 shows the index of people not working for the period January 2009 through December 2011. Note the presence of the seasonal dips in June and July of each year. We address these and other seasonal variations in the next section.

Figure 8-5: Index of People Not Working, Jan 2009-Dec 2011

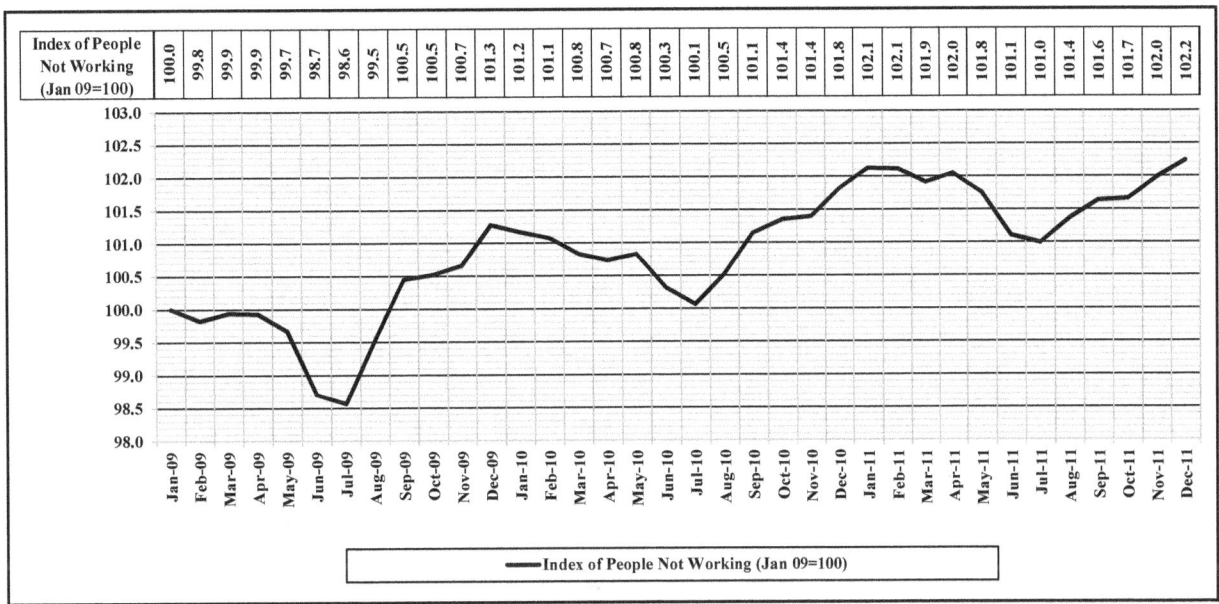

Source: figure 3-1 and figure 9-1

8.3 SEASONALLY ADJUSTED RATES

We looked at seasonally adjusting data in section 4.2, where we saw that quarterly and monthly estimates could be adjusted seasonally to remove the average effect of variations that normally occur at about the same time and in about the same magnitude each year. Unemployment is routinely higher in some months than in others. For example, it is higher in January and February, when it is cold in many parts of the country and work in agriculture, construction, and other seasonal industries is curtailed.

Figure 8-4 showed U-3 and U-6 monthly over the period January 2009 through December 2011. Those figures are unadjusted. Figure 8-6 shows the same data for unadjusted U-3, and adds the data for seasonally adjusted U-3 for comparison.

The two points I made in section 4.2 bear repeating:

- The annual total of the seasonal adjustments is zero. The sum of the upward adjustments exactly equals the sum of the downward adjustments across the year.

- Do not mix the two series. For example, in talking about unemployment during 2011, it would be highly misleading (not to mention intellectually dishonest) to say it was 7.8 in January 09, 8.6 in April 09, 9.8 in February 10, and 9.0 in October 10. To be consistent, one has to stay with the same series for month-to-month comparisons.

8.4 OTHER UNEMPLOYMENT TYPES

One doesn't seem to hear the terms much today in the popular press, but unemployment can be divided into two classes: structural and cyclical. There are still other types, but generally speaking, total unemployment is a combination of cyclical and structural unemployment.

The distinction between the two types of unemployment is important, because curing each type requires a different remedy. For example, educational programs can address some long term

Figure 8-6: U-3 Unadjusted and Seasonally Adjusted, Jan 2009-Dec 2011

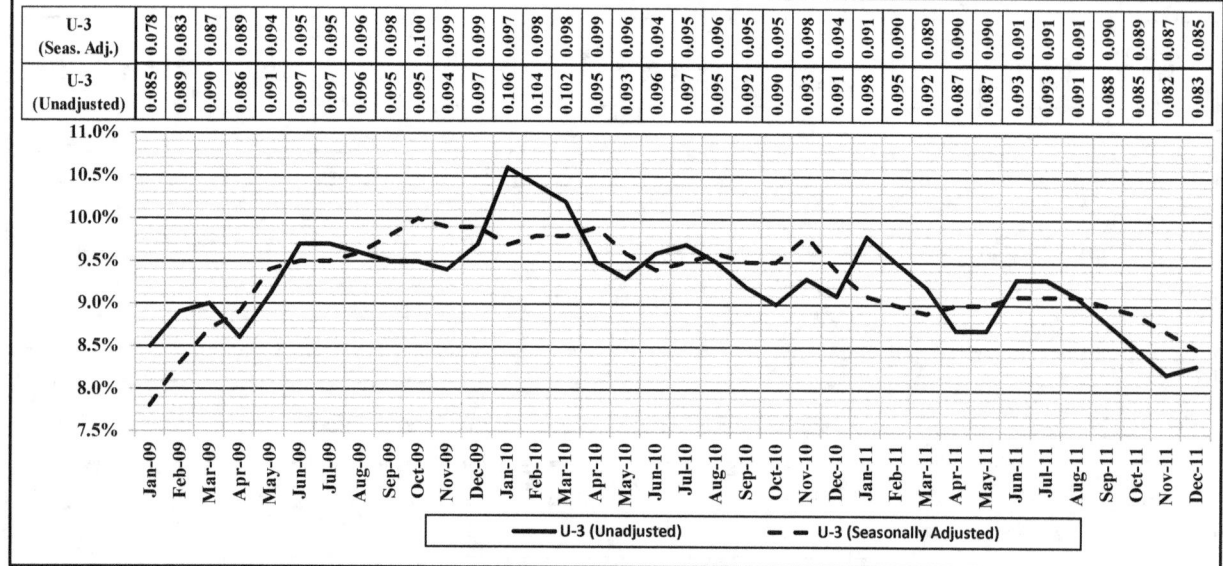

http://data.bls.gov/pdq/SurveyOutputServlet

structural problems, whereas programs that stimulate demand might address only short term cyclical problems.

8.4.1 Structural

Structural unemployment results from long term conditions in the economy and the workforce. For example, the mechanization of agriculture led to structural unemployment among farmers. More generally, obsolescence of technology, and a related obsolescence of job skills among the labor force, causes structural unemployment.

The structurally unemployed may not have the skill required to find jobs in the current economy, even though they would like to have work and there is work available. Or the structurally unemployed may be in one area while jobs are in another, resulting in a geographical form of structural unemployment. These people represent a level of unemployment below which the economy will not go even if it is booming.

Economists disagree on the level of structural unemployment in the US economy. Estimates range from 4 percent to 7 percent, though unemployment rates during the 2000 through 2007 period seem to suggest that it's closer to 4 than to 7.

The reason one doesn't hear much about it today may be that we are so far from bumping into the structural limit of employment, that people don't even mention it.

8.4.2 Cyclical

Cyclical unemployment is a function of the business cycle. During periods of high economic activity and growth, people with appropriate skills find jobs and cyclical unemployment tends to be low. During periods of low economic activity and growth, such as in recessions, even appropriately skilled people have difficulty finding jobs, and cyclical unemployment increases. Workers have the skills and experience that employers need, but demand is lacking and economic activity supports fewer jobs. As economic activity improves, the cyclically unemployed increasingly are able to find jobs.

9. EMPLOYMENT

9.1 TOTAL EMPLOYMENT

In chapter 8, we defined employment in the context of the labor force and unemployment. In this chapter, we'll look again at employment and some of its components, including civilian and federal employment, and active-duty military personnel.

9.1.1 Civilian Employment

Total US civilian employment includes everyone employed according to the BLS, except for active-duty military personnel. It includes government workers at the federal, state, and local levels. Figure 9-1 shows total civilian employment for the period 1989 through 2011.

Figure 9-1: Total Civilian Employment, 1989-2011

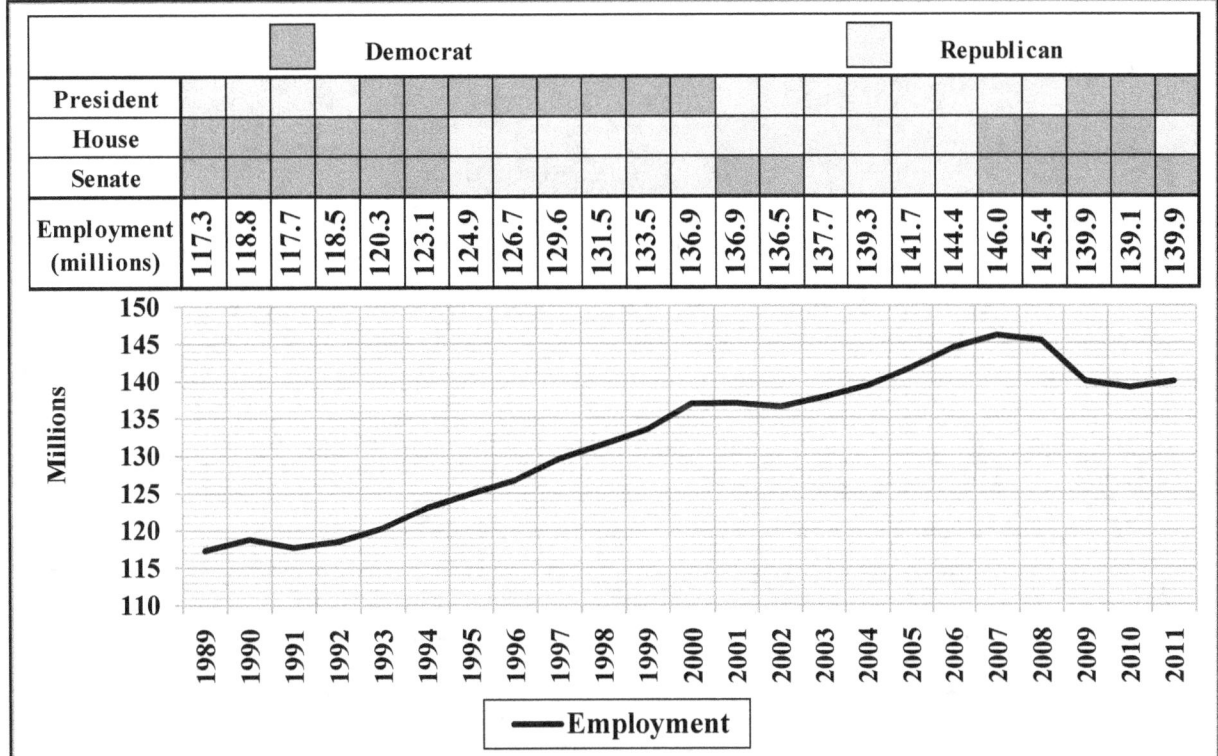

Source: http://data.bls.gov/pdq/SurveyOutputServlet

One should recognize that population grew over the 1989 through 2011 period, and that the composition of the population may have changed. For example, with an increasing average age of the population, it would be reasonable to assume that a higher percentage of the population is retired, therefore not employed. That said, the simple percentage of the population that is employed is shown in figure 9-2.

9.1.2 Federal Employment

Direct employees of the federal government are considered federal employees; contractors who work for civilian firms under contract to the federal government are not considered federal employees. Figure 9-3 shows the number of federal employees, excluding active-duty military personnel, for the period 1989 through 2010.

Figure 9-2: Total Civilian Employment as a Percentage of Population, 1989-2011

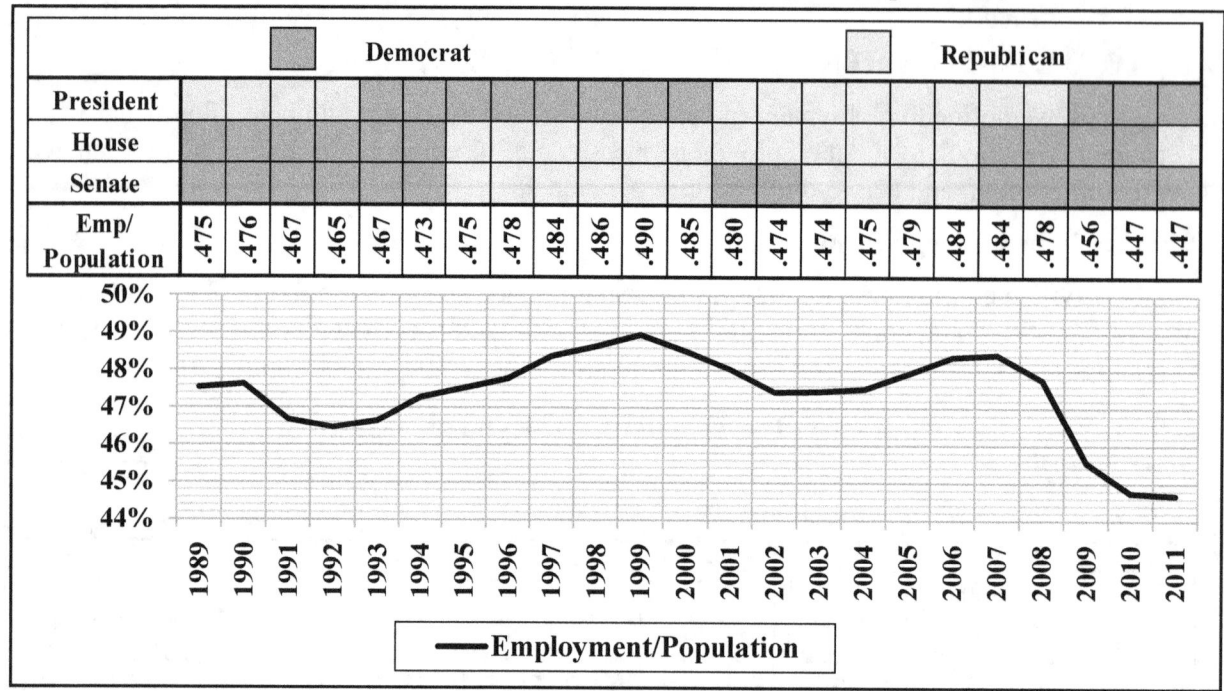

Source: figure 3-1 and figure 9-1

Figure 9-3: Non-Military Federal Employment, 1989-2010

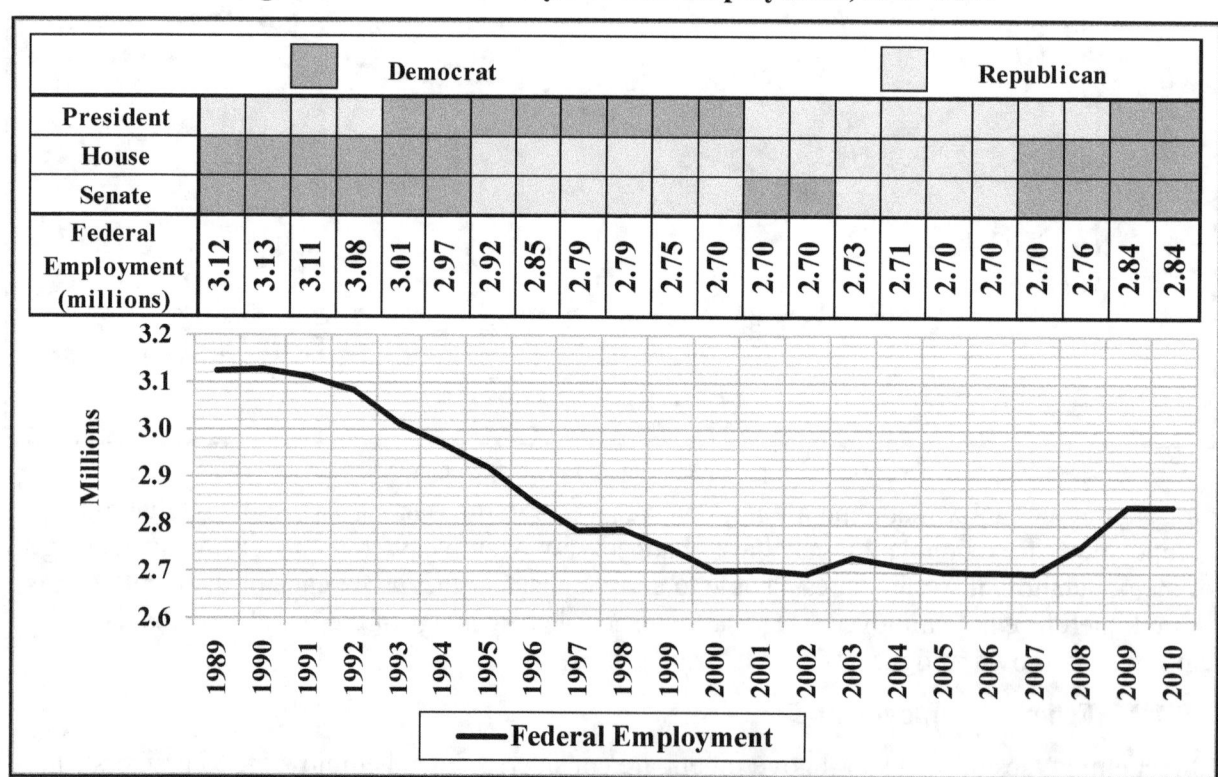

Source: http://www.opm.gov/feddata/HistoricalTables/TotalGovernmentSince1962.asp

---

9.1.3 Active-Duty Military

Active-duty military personnel are not included in the civilian employment numbers. However, civilian contractors working for the Department of Defense are included in the civilian employment numbers, not in the military numbers, and not in the federal workforce. Figure 9-4 shows the numbers of active-duty military personnel for the period 1989 through 2011.

9.1.4 Employment by Age

The BLS is definitive about whom they include in their employment figures at the youngest age. You must be 16 or above to be included. There is no such cutoff at the upper ages. One can leave the workforce at any age, whether by retirement or otherwise.

Figure 9-5 shows the age distribution of US employment over the period 1989 through 2011.

Figure 9-4: Active-Duty Military Personnel, 1989-2011

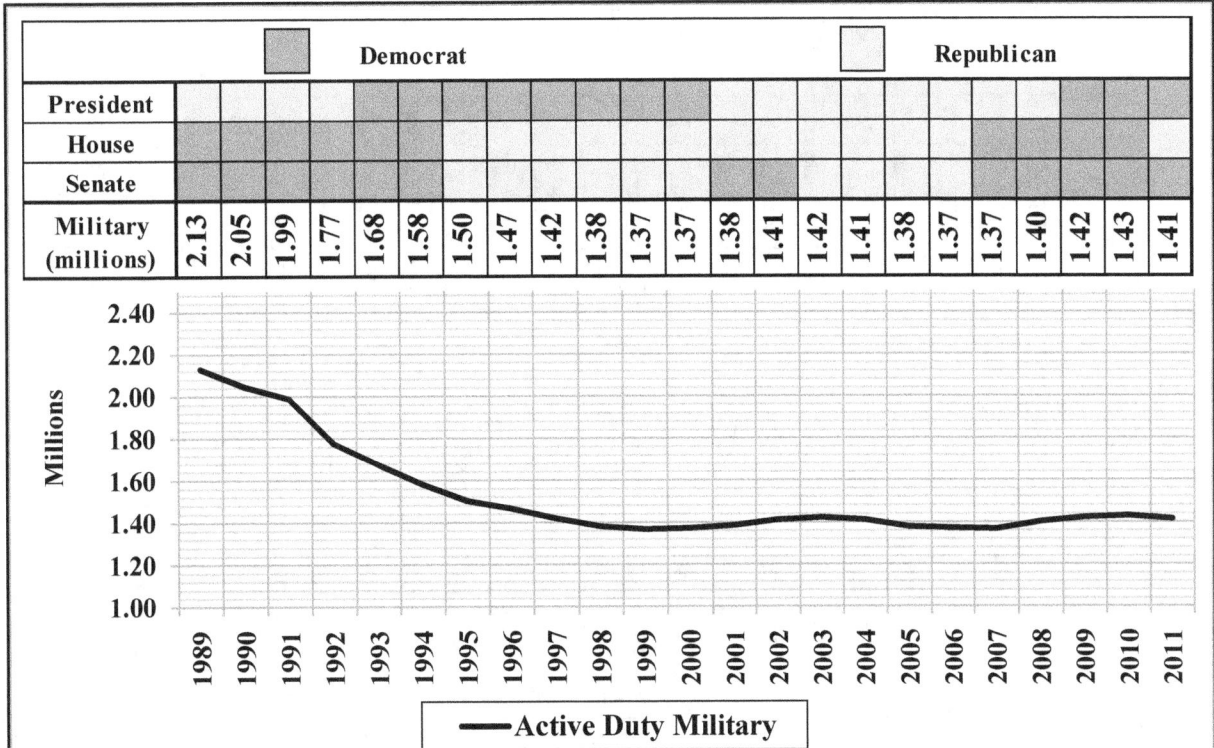

Source: http://siadapp.dmdc.osd.mil/personnel/MILITARY/miltop.htm

9.1.5 Employment by Education

One of the most important determinants of employment and income is education. We will talk in the next chapter about the impact of education on income, but for now, let's see what employment looks like by level of education.

Figure 9-6 shows the educational distribution of US employment over the period 1992 through 2011. The BLS time series for education only goes back to 1992.

9.2 "CLASSES"

Much is made during election campaigns of classes, in particular the working class and the middle class. Classes come not from economics, per se, but rather from political economics and

Figure 9-5: Employment by Age Group, 1989-2011

	Democrat											Republican										
President																							
House																							
Senate																							
65 and Over	.028	.028	.028	.029	.028	.030	.030	.030	.030	.029	.029	.031	.032	.031	.034	.035	.037	.038	.039	.042	.045	.046	.047
55-64	.099	.095	.094	.092	.091	.092	.093	.093	.097	.099	.101	.103	.110	.119	.123	.127	.131	.135	.140	.146	.152	.156	.158
45-54	.166	.166	.172	.181	.189	.192	.198	.203	.208	.212	.217	.224	.228	.231	.233	.233	.234	.236	.237	.239	.242	.238	.234
35-44	.254	.264	.271	.271	.272	.274	.276	.278	.277	.276	.275	.266	.262	.256	.252	.248	.242	.238	.233	.229	.224	.220	.215
25-34	.291	.285	.280	.274	.267	.261	.258	.252	.244	.237	.230	.229	.225	.221	.220	.218	.217	.215	.217	.216	.216	.219	.218
16-24	.161	.162	.156	.153	.151	.151	.146	.144	.145	.147	.148	.148	.144	.142	.138	.140	.138	.137	.133	.128	.120	.121	.128

Legend: ■ 16-24 ▨ 25-34 ▢ 35-44 ⊞ 45-54 ◪ 55-64 ▢ 65 and Over

Source: http://data.bls.gov/pdq/querytool.jsp?survey=l

sociology. Individuals who use classes in political discourse purporting to address economic issues often do so to confuse and alienate, rather than inform.

9.2.1 Working Class

In an economic sense, anyone who works would be in the working class. Politicians, however, use the phrase "working class" as a badge for honor for people at the lower end of the economic scale, whether they work or not. The objective is to differentiate those at the lower end of the economic scale from those at the upper end by implying that those at the upper end somehow don't work for their pay. This is largely the Marxian approach to labor, which was to differentiate between those who worked for wages and those who did not. When you hear "working class" in an economic context, the speaker most likely is invoking class warfare rather than reason.

Figure 9-6: Employment by Educational Level, 1992-2011

Bachelors and Up	.273	.277	.281	.287	.291	.294	.302	.308	.309	.312	.320	.326	.328	.330	.335	.342	.348	.356	.359	.366
Some College	.255	.265	.276	.280	.278	.274	.272	.275	.277	.279	.275	.274	.276	.276	.274	.274	.278	.277	.277	.277
High School	.353	.348	.337	.330	.327	.327	.322	.318	.313	.309	.306	.303	.300	.298	.295	.292	.286	.282	.281	.276
Less Than High School	.118	.110	.106	.103	.105	.104	.104	.100	.100	.100	.099	.097	.095	.096	.096	.091	.088	.085	.083	.081

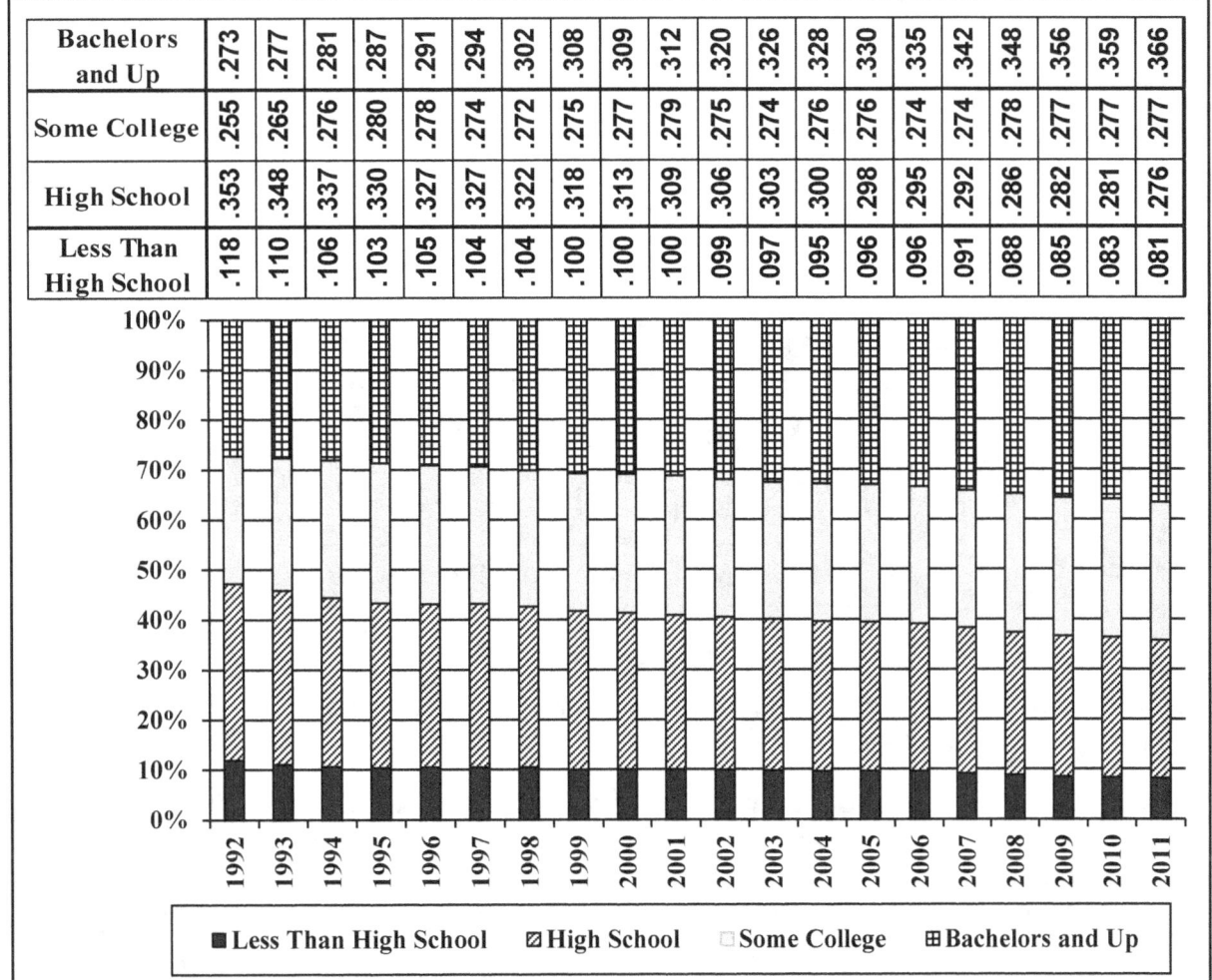

Source: http://www.bls.gov/webapps/legacy/cpsatab4.htm

9.2.2   Middle Class

"Middle class" is another phrase that has little economic meaning. One can define middle class to mean the group of income earners around the national US income average or median, but how inclusive the class might be is entirely arbitrary. One also could use any arbitrarily selected income range to define the middle class. A speaker who uses the phrase in a political debate about the economy is playing on the largely positive connotations that the phrase has for most Americans, but is conveying little of economic consequence.

9.3   UNIONS

Much is made about the power of unions to sway the outcome of US elections. Campaign finance laws and practices are not the subject of this book, so we will look at only a few statistics concerning unions.

Figure 9-7 shows the percentages of US workers who are in unions and those who are not union members but are represented by or affiliated with unions.

Figure 9-7: Percentage of US Employees in or Affiliated with Unions, 2000-2011

Affiliated, not Union	.015	.014	.012	.014	.013	.012	.011	.012	.013	.013	.012	.012
Union Members	.134	.133	.133	.129	.125	.125	.120	.121	.124	.123	.119	.118

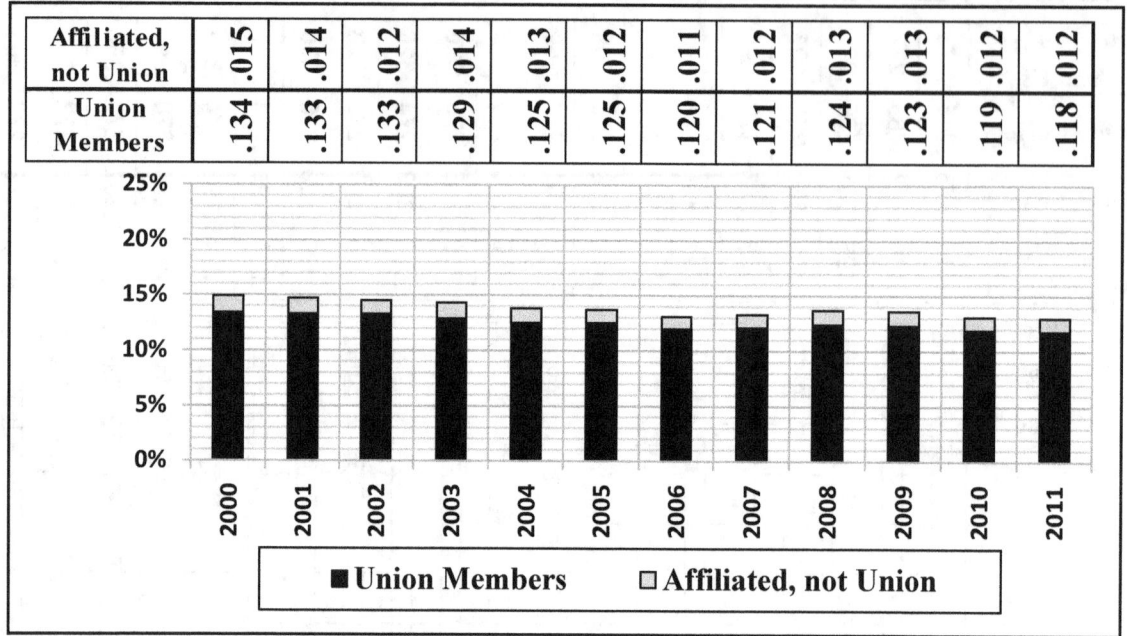

Source: http://data.bls.gov/pdq/SurveyOutputServlet

Figure 9-8 shows the percentages of government workers (federal, state, and local) who belong to unions or are affiliated with unions.

Figure 9-8: Percentage of Government Employees in or Affiliated with Unions, 2000-2011

Affiliated, not Union	.049	.046	.041	.044	.043	.041	.039	.039	.040	.037	.037	.037
Union Members	.369	.368	.373	.372	.364	.365	.362	.359	.368	.374	.362	.370

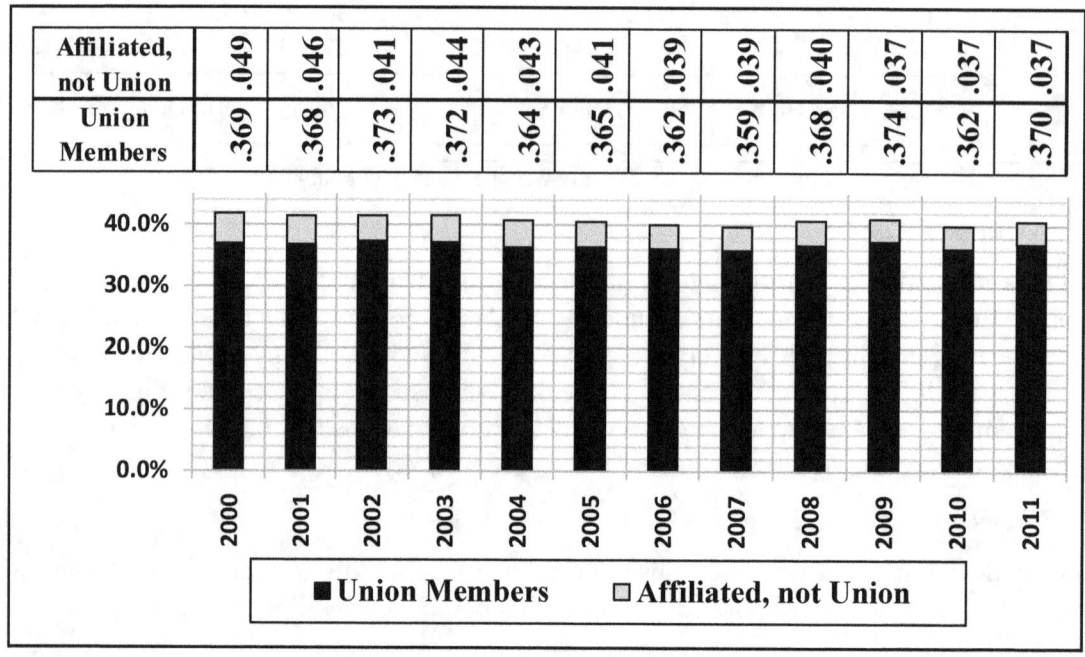

Source: http://data.bls.gov/pdq/SurveyOutputServlet

10. INCOME DISTRIBUTION

In this chapter, we will use a concept of income called **money income** by the US Census Bureau. Money income is defined as income received on a regular basis (exclusive of certain money receipts such as capital gains), before payments for personal income taxes, social security, union dues, and Medicare deductions, among other things.

The Census Bureau does not count the following receipts as income: (1) capital gains people received (or losses they incurred) from the sale of property, including stocks, bonds, a house, or a car (unless the person was engaged in the business of selling such property, in which case the Census Bureau counts the net proceeds as income from self-employment); (2) withdrawals of bank deposits; (3) money borrowed; (4) tax refunds; (5) gifts; and (6) lump-sum inheritances or insurance payments.

Money income does not reflect the fact that some families receive part of their income in the form of noncash benefits, such as food stamps, health benefits, subsidized housing, and goods produced and consumed on the farm. In addition, money income does not reflect the fact that noncash benefits also are received by some nonfarm residents, which may take the form of the use of business transportation and facilities, or full or partial payments by business for retirement programs, medical, and educational expenses. Moreover, for many different reasons there is a tendency in household surveys for respondents to underreport their income. (See section 7-4 on the underground economy.)

Figure 10-1 shows the median and mean incomes of US households for the period 1989 through 2010. Median income is the income at the center of the income distribution. That is, the same number of households earned more than the median as earned less than the median income. Mean income is the average income earned by all the households, calculated by dividing total household income by the number of households.

Figure 10-1: Median and Mean Household Incomes, 1989-2010

Democrat | Republican

President	R	R	R	R	D	D	D	D	D	D	D	D	R	R	R	R	R	R	R	R	D	D
House	D	D	D	D	D	D	R	R	R	R	R	R	R	R	R	R	R	R	D	D	D	D
Senate	D	D	D	D	D	D	R	R	R	R	R	R	D	D	R	R	R	R	D	D	D	D
Mean ($)	36,520	37,403	37,922	38,840	41,428	43,133	44,938	47,123	49,692	51,855	54,737	57,135	58,208	57,852	59,067	60,466	63,344	66,570	67,609	68,424	67,976	67,530
Median ($)	28,906	29,943	30,126	30,636	31,241	32,264	34,076	35,492	37,005	38,885	40,696	41,990	42,228	42,409	43,318	44,334	46,326	48,201	50,233	50,303	49,777	49,445

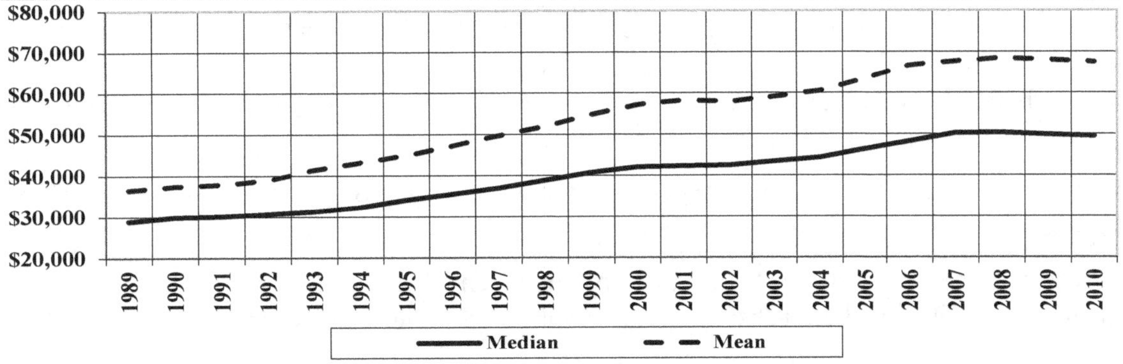

Source: http://www.census.gov/hhes/www/income/data/historical/household/

Figure 10-2 shows the shares of US income by income level (lowest fifth, second-lowest fifth, and so forth) for the period 1989 through 2010.

Figure 10-2: Income Shares by Income Level, 1989-2010

	Democrat											Republican									

	1989	1990	1991	1992	1993	1994	1995	1996	1997	1998	1999	2000	2001	2002	2003	2004	2005	2006	2007	2008	2009	2010
President																						
House																						
Senate																						
Highest Fifth	.468	.466	.465	.469	.489	.491	.487	.490	.494	.492	.494	.498	.501	.497	.498	.501	.504	.505	.497	.500	.503	.502
4th Fifth	.240	.240	.242	.242	.235	.234	.233	.233	.232	.232	.232	.230	.230	.233	.234	.232	.230	.229	.234	.233	.232	.234
3rd Fifth	.158	.159	.159	.158	.151	.150	.152	.151	.150	.150	.149	.148	.146	.148	.148	.147	.146	.145	.148	.147	.146	.146
2nd Fifth	.095	.096	.096	.094	.090	.089	.091	.090	.089	.090	.089	.089	.087	.088	.087	.087	.086	.086	.087	.086	.086	.085
Lowest Fifth	.038	.038	.038	.038	.036	.036	.037	.036	.036	.036	.036	.036	.035	.035	.034	.034	.034	.034	.034	.034	.034	.033

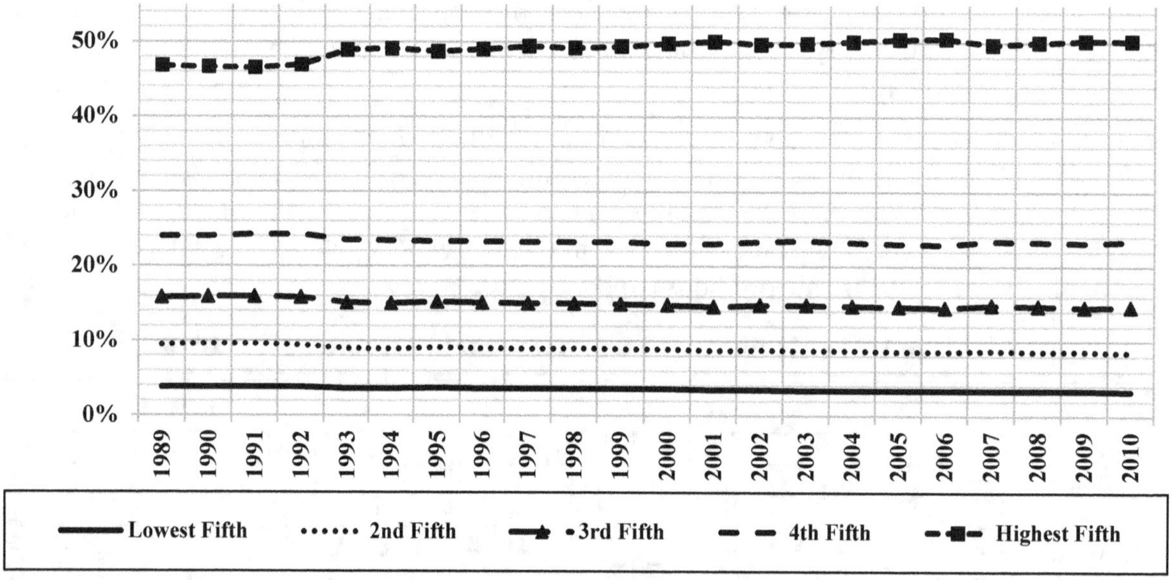

Lowest Fifth ...... 2nd Fifth ●3rd Fifth – – 4th Fifth –■– Highest Fifth

Source: http://www.census.gov/hhes/www/income/data/historical/household/

10.1 EDUCATION

Education is one of the most important determinants of an individual's ability to earn income. There are many exceptions, and we all can point to self-made individuals who have succeeded without benefit of commensurate formal education. However, the general rule holds that the greater the education, the higher the income.

We've already seen the relationship of employment to education (figure 9-6). Figure 10-3 shows the relationship between income and education.

Finally, nothing demonstrates the relationship between education and employment, and education and income, better than the BLS graphic reproduced in figure 10-4.

Figure 10-3: Annual Earnings by Educational Level, 1989-2010

	Democrat																Republican					
President																						
House																						
Senate																						
Year	1989	1990	1991	1992	1993	1994	1995	1996	1997	1998	1999	2000	2001	2002	2003	2004	2005	2006	2007	2008	2009	2010
Advanced Degree (AD)	41,019	41,458	46,039	48,652	55,789	56,105	56,667	61,317	63,229	63,473	67,697	71,194	72,869	72,824	74,602	78,224	79,946	82,320	80,977	83,144	85,818	83,841
Bachelors Degree (BD)	30,736	31,112	31,323	32,629	35,121	37,224	36,980	38,112	40,478	43,782	45,678	49,595	50,623	51,194	51,206	51,568	54,689	56,788	57,181	58,613	56,665	57,621
Some College (SC)	20,255	20,694	20,551	20,867	21,539	22,226	23,862	25,181	26,235	27,566	28,403	29,939	30,782	31,046	31,498	32,010	33,496	34,650	35,138	34,808	34,773	34,366
High School (HS)	17,594	17,820	18,261	18,737	19,422	20,248	21,431	22,154	22,895	23,594	24,572	25,692	26,795	27,280	27,915	28,631	29,448	31,071	31,286	31,283	30,627	31,003
Less Than High School (LTHS)	12,242	12,582	12,613	12,809	12,820	13,697	14,013	15,011	16,124	16,053	16,121	17,738	18,793	18,826	18,734	19,182	19,915	20,873	21,484	21,023	20,241	20,911

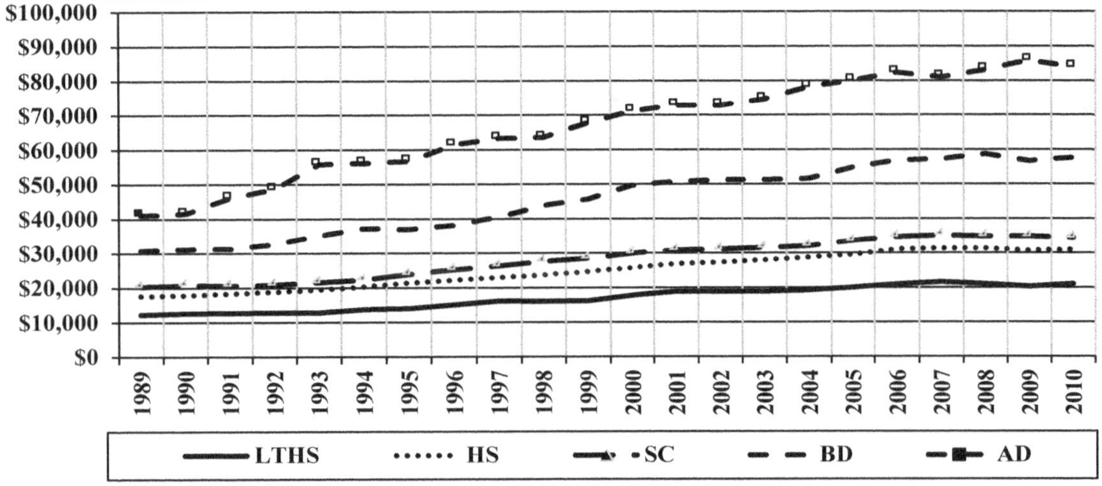

Source: www.census.gov/population/socdemo/education/cps2008/tabA-3.xls

Figure 10-4: Education versus Employment and Earnings, 2010

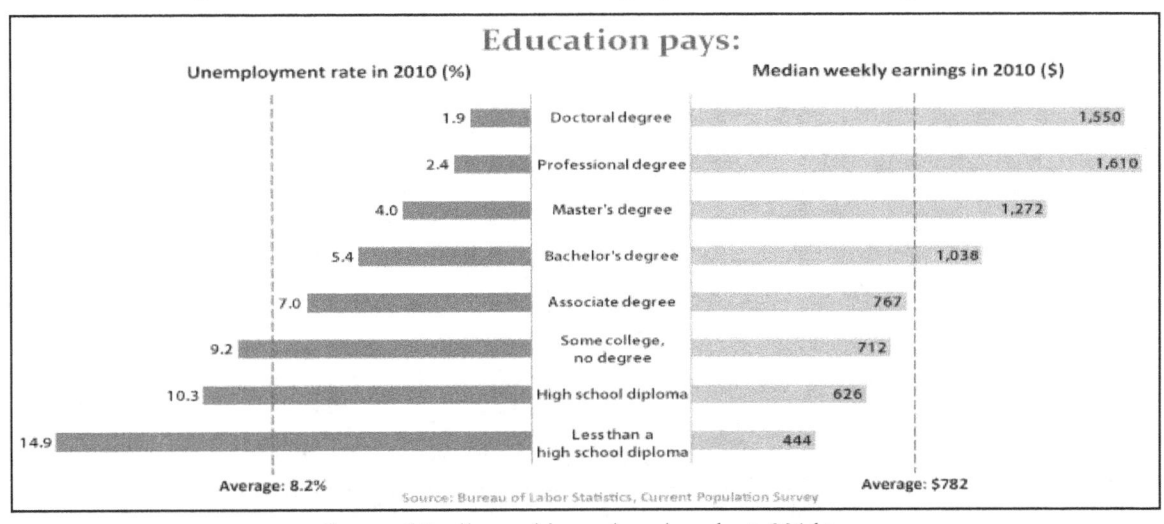

Source: http://www.bls.gov/emp/ep_chart_001.htm

11. WEALTH DISTRIBUTION

Wealth distribution and income distribution are closely related. Our purpose here is not to establish causality, but to look at the distribution of wealth over time.

In political discourse, wealth distribution often is linked to fairness. Fairness is not an economic concept. It is a political concept whose purpose is to justify the redistribution of wealth based on political, rather than economic, grounds.

Wealth is not tracked explicitly and rigorously by the government. The Federal Reserve Board does a Survey of Consumer Finances every three years, and it is data from those surveys that you will see below. The last survey for which data are available was done in 2007. Data from the 2010 survey are to be published in the first half of 2012.

Federal Reserve analysts reported on the 2007 survey results in *Changes in US Family Finances from 2004 to 2007: Evidence from the Survey of Consumer Finances*, published in the *Federal Reserve Bulletin*, February 2009. They summarized the economic background of the survey period, and evaluated mean and median family net worth, which we will use to help explain wealth distribution. Also in 2011, Federal Reserve analysts estimated in *Surveying the Aftermath of the Storm: Changes in Family Finances from 2007 to 2009* that median and net worth fell by 23.2 and 18.8 percent, respectively, from 2007 to 2009. In figure 11-1, the 2009 figures are the 2007 figures reduced by these percentages.

11.1 NET WORTH

Figure 11-1 shows the median and mean net worth (assets minus liabilities) of families for selected years during the period 1989 through 2009.

Household wealth declined between 1989 and 1992, but recovered by 1995. It increased modestly between 1995 and 2001, then more quickly between 2004 and 2007, the last year of the survey data. Federal Reserve analysts estimate that net worth plunged in 2007 through 2009, when the median net worth was only a bit higher than in 1995, and the mean value was between 1998 and 2001 levels. The declines are attributed primarily to the drop in prices of primary residences, privately held businesses, and publicly traded equities.

11.2 NET WORTH DISTRIBUTION

While the Federal Reserve only presents wealth data for every third year, they provide sufficient detail to determine the distribution of wealth across both net worth levels and income levels.

Figure 11-2 shows the percentage of net worth held by individuals in each of the five net worth levels for selected years during the period 1989 through 2007. The percentage of net worth held over the period stayed the same for the lower half of net worth holders, while the upper 1 percent increased their share from 30 percent to 34 percent.

Figure 11-3 shows the percentage of net worth held by individuals in each of the five income levels for selected years during the period 1989 through 2007. The percentage of net worth held over the period declined by 2 percent for the lower half of income earners, while the upper 1 percent increased their share from 22 percent to 26 percent.

Figure 11-1: Median and Mean Family Net Worth, Selected Years, 1989-2009

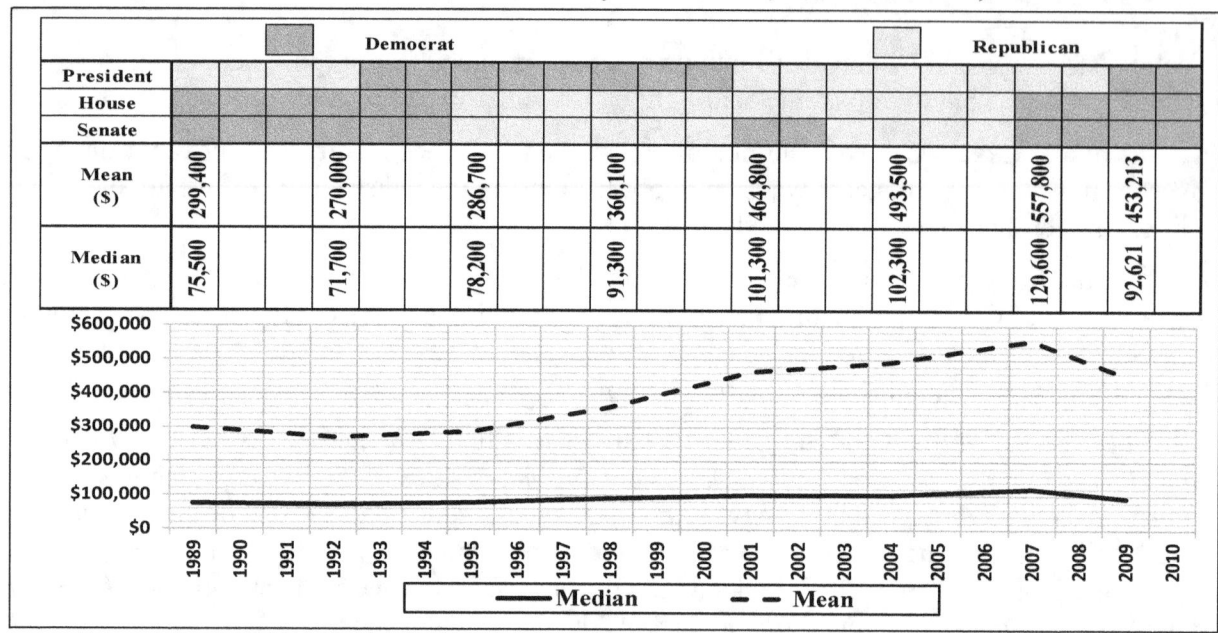

	1989	1992	1995	1998	2001	2004	2007	2009
Mean ($)	299,400	270,000	286,700	360,100	464,800	493,500	557,800	453,213
Median ($)	75,500	71,700	78,200	91,300	101,300	102,300	120,600	92,621

Legend: Democrat / Republican (President, House, Senate)

— Median   - - Mean

Source: http://www.federalreserve.gov/econresdata/scf/scf_2007.htm

Figure 11-2: Percentage of Net Worth by Level of Net Worth, Selected Years 1989-2007

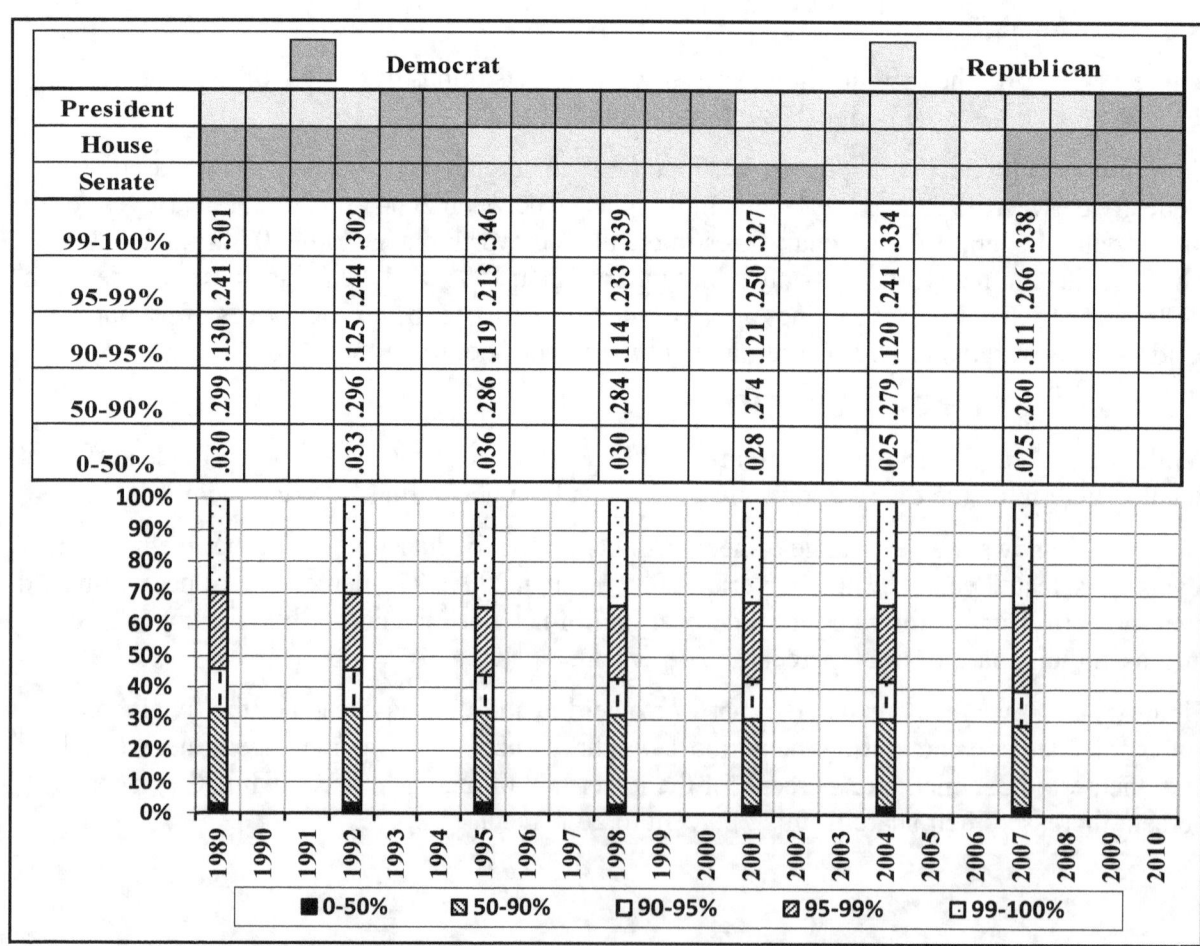

	1989	1992	1995	1998	2001	2004	2007
99-100%	.301	.302	.346	.339	.327	.334	.338
95-99%	.241	.244	.213	.233	.250	.241	.266
90-95%	.130	.125	.119	.114	.121	.120	.111
50-90%	.299	.296	.286	.284	.274	.279	.260
0-50%	.030	.033	.036	.030	.028	.025	.025

Legend: Democrat / Republican (President, House, Senate)

■ 0-50%   ▨ 50-90%   ☐ 90-95%   ▨ 95-99%   ☐ 99-100%

Source: http://www.federalreserve.gov/pubs/feds/2009/200913/200913pap.pdf

Presentational Note

Figure 11-2 is called a stacked bar chart. It shows selected characteristics of a population that is divided into segments or levels. Two examples of segments are quartiles/fourths and quintiles/fifths. Figure 11-2 breaks its population up into the groups 0-50%, 50-90%, 90-95%, 95-99% and the top 1%. These charts can be confusing, so I'll go through an example that I hope will make reading this figure and subsequent ones of this type easier.

In the example table below, we have a population of 10 people identified in column (1). We want to look at their net worth by income levels, in this case by quintiles or fifths. Because we have 10 people, each quintile or fifth of the population will have two people in it. To figure out who is in which quintile, we sort the people according to their income, then we identify the lowest fifth (persons A and B), the second lowest fifth (persons C and D), and so on. The results are in column (4).

Next we calculate the total net worth of people in each quintile (5), and divide each quintile total into the total net worth of all the people ($8.66 million). That produces column (6).

Person (1)	Income (2)	Net Worth (3)	Fifths or Quintiles (4)	Net Worth per Quintile (5)	% of Net Worth by Income Quartile (6)
J	$ 500,000	$5,000,000	Highest Fifth	$6,200,000	71.6%
I	$ 120,000	$1,200,000			
H	$ 75,000	$ 750,000	4th Fifth	$1,250,000	14.4%
G	$ 50,000	$ 500,000			
F	$ 29,000	$ 290,000	3rd Fifth	$ 540,000	6.2%
E	$ 25,000	$ 250,000			
D	$ 22,000	$ 220,000	2nd Fifth	$ 420,000	4.8%
C	$ 20,000	$ 200,000			
B	$ 15,000	$ 150,000	Lowest Fifth	$ 250,000	2.9%
A	$ 10,000	$ 100,000			
			Total Net Worth:	$8,660,000	100.0%

This exercise is for a single year, and it corresponds to one column of data in a figure like 11- 2 or 11-3, for example. Note that the segments or levels can be labeled in various ways.

Highest Fifth	.716
4th Fifth	.144
3rd Fifth	.062
2nd Fifth	.048
Lowest Fifth	.029

80-100%	.716
60-80%	.144
40-60%	.062
20-40%	.048
0-20%	.029

Figure 11-3: Percentage of Net Worth by Level of Income, Selected Years 1989-2007

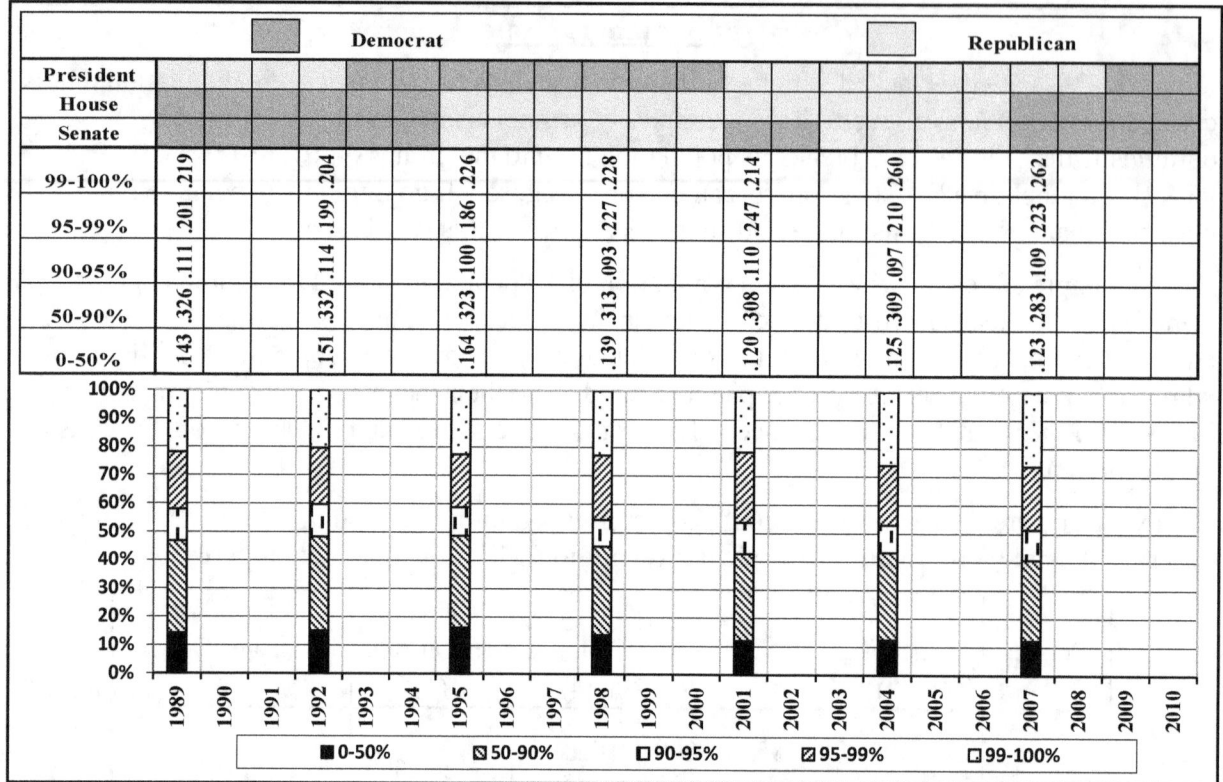

12.1 INTRODUCTION

No topic is more contentious in the 2012 campaign than taxes. Much of the discussion revolves around the concept of fairness. As I pointed out in chapter 11, fairness is not an economic concept, but a political one. The discussion that follows is about what taxes have been and what they are now, not on what they should be.

As if we need to be told what taxes are, the Bureau of Economic Analysis (BEA) defines taxes as compulsory, unrequited payments, in cash or in kind, received by the government from other sectors. They are described as unrequited because the government provides nothing in return to the payer, except that the government *may* use the money to provide goods, services and benefits to individuals and society at large. (The emphasis on *may* is mine.)

We will talk about taxes in terms of how much we pay and how much tax compliance costs, but first let's take a look at the code that creates and sustains our taxes.

12.2 TAX CODE

There appears to be no authoritative government source of information about some aspects of the tax code, so I refer you to *The Rising Cost of Complying with the Federal Income Tax*, Special Report No. 138, by J. Scott Moody, Wendy P. Warcholik, and Scott A. Hodge of the Tax Foundation. The report was published in December 2005 and includes the following information:

- The number of words in income tax law grew from 172,000 in 1955 to 1,286,000 in 2005.

- The number of words in federal income tax regulations grew from 547,000 in 1955 to 5,778,000 in 2005.

- The Internal Revenue Code and IRS Regulations grew from 1,396,000 words in 1955 to 9,097,000 words in 2005.

12.3 TAX REVENUE

Tax revenue is the amount of taxes collected by the US government. The cost to US individuals, businesses, and other entities is in the form of the tax liabilities each entity incurs and pays to the government.

Figure 12-1 shows total US taxes collected at the federal level during the period 1989 through 2010, and Figure 12-2 shows them as a percentage of GDP. Total taxes consist of personal current taxes, taxes on production and imports, taxes on corporate income, and taxes from the rest of the world. Definitions for these taxes are from the BEA's Methodology Paper, *Government Transactions*, dated September 2005.

12.3.1 Personal Current Taxes

Personal current taxes are tax payments (net of refunds) by US residents that are not chargeable to business expense. They includes taxes on income (including realized net capital gains), taxes on personal property, and personal license taxes. Personal taxes do not include residential real estate taxes, estate and gift taxes, or personal contributions for social insurance (Social Security, for example).

12.3.2 Taxes on Production and Imports

Taxes on production and imports include taxes payable on goods and services when they are produced, delivered, sold, transferred, or otherwise disposed of (such as sales taxes and excise taxes); customs duties; and other taxes on production, consisting mainly of taxes on the ownership or use by business of land, buildings, or other assets.

Figure 12-1: Total Federal Taxes Collected, 1989-2010

	Democrat																			Republican	
President																					
House																					
Senate																					
Total tax receipts (billion $)	621.1	642.1	635.6	659.9	713.1	781.3	844.6	932.0	1,030.1	1,115.8	1,195.3	1,309.6	1,249.5	1,073.5	1,070.3	1,153.8	1,383.8	1,558.3	1,637.6	1,447.8	1,170.3	1,340.8

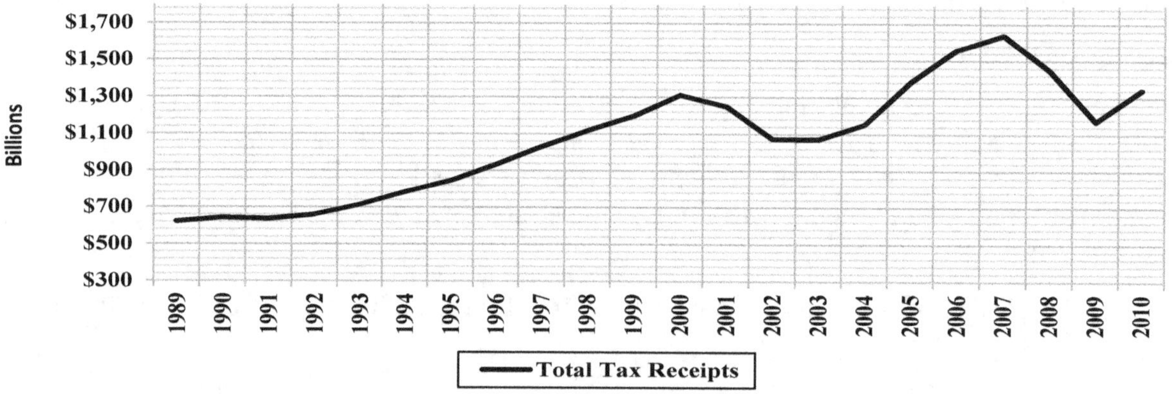

Source: http://www.bea.gov/national/nipaweb/SelectTable.asp?Selected=N

Figure 12-2: Total Federal Taxes Collected as Percentage of GDP, 1989-2010

	Democrat																			Republican	
President																					
House																					
Senate																					
Total Taxes/ GDP	.113	.111	.106	.104	.107	.110	.114	.119	.124	.127	.128	.132	.121	.101	.096	.097	.110	.116	.117	.101	.084	.092

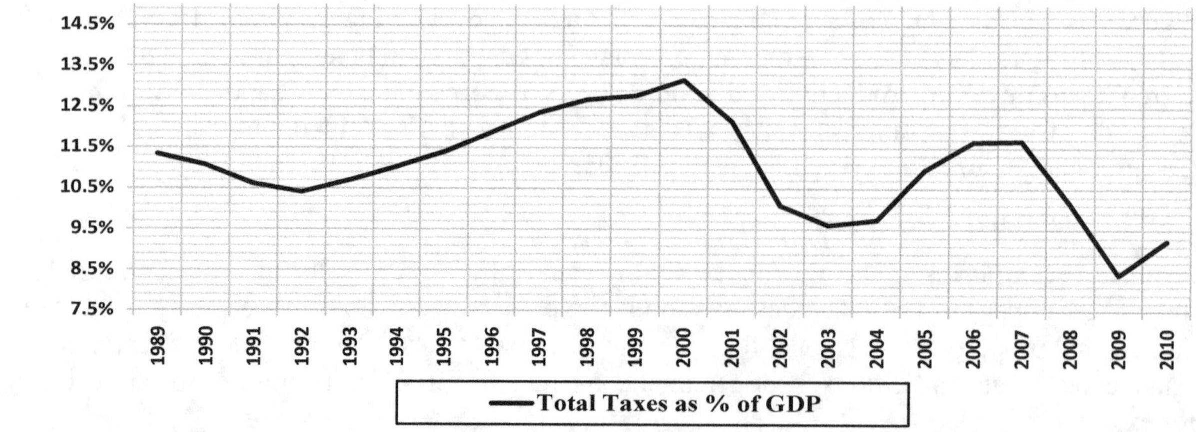

Source: figure 7-1 and figure 12-1

12.3.3 Taxes on Corporate Income

Taxes on corporate income are income tax liabilities on all corporate earnings, including realized net capital gains and net of applicable tax credits. They also include payments of net earnings by the Federal Reserve System to federal government accounts.

12.3.4 Taxes from the Rest of the World

Taxes from the rest of the world are income taxes received by the federal government from the rest of the world. The published estimates also include some taxes on production and some current transfers because the source data do not permit the reliable separation of the taxes on income.

Figure 12-3 shows the relative share of total taxes represented by each of the four tax components over the period 1989 through 2010.

Figure 12-3: Total Federal Taxes by Type, 1989-2010.

	1989	1990	1991	1992	1993	1994	1995	1996	1997	1998	1999	2000	2001	2002	2003	2004	2005	2006	2007	2008	2009	2010
Rest of the World	.004	.005	.004	.004	.004	.004	.005	.006	.005	.005	.005	.006	.006	.007	.008	.009	.009	.009	.009	.013	.013	.010
Corporate Income	.189	.184	.173	.180	.194	.201	.212	.205	.197	.183	.178	.168	.132	.140	.185	.217	.246	.253	.222	.161	.172	.246
Production and Imports	.080	.079	.097	.096	.093	.101	.090	.078	.076	.072	.070	.067	.068	.081	.083	.082	.071	.064	.058	.065	.083	.076
Personal	.727	.732	.726	.720	.709	.694	.694	.712	.722	.740	.747	.760	.794	.772	.723	.693	.673	.674	.712	.761	.732	.669

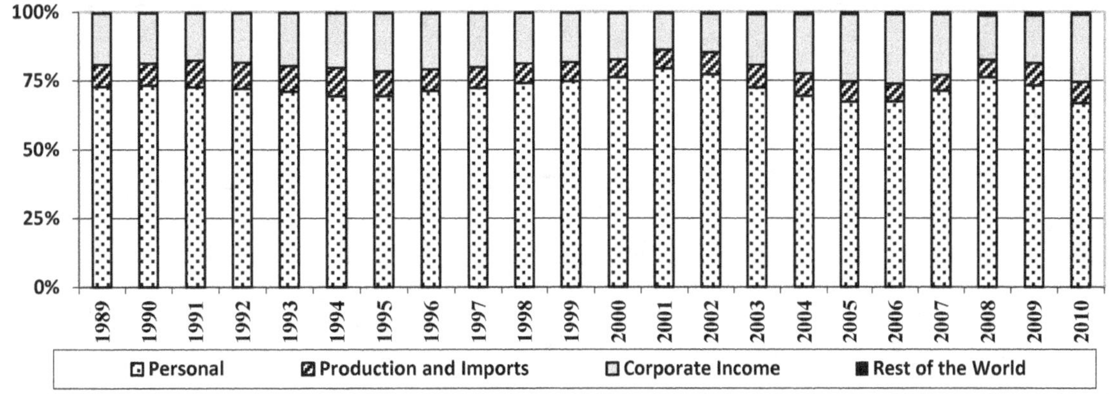

Source: http://www.bea.gov/national/nipaweb/SelectTable.asp?Selected=N

12.4 TAX BURDEN

12.4.1 Incidence

Figure 12-4 shows household total tax rates by income level for the period 1989 through 2007.

Figure 12-5 shows the share of total taxes by income level for the period 1989 through 2007.

Figure 12-6 shows individual income tax rates by income level for the period 1989 through 2007.

Figure 12-7 shows the share of income taxes by income level for the period 1989 through 2007.

Figure 12-4: Household Total Tax Rates by Income Level, 1989-2007

	Democrat																		Republican			
President																						
House																						
Senate																						
Top 1%	.289	.288	.299	.306	.345	.358	.361	.360	.349	.334	.335	.330	.328	.328	.317	.314	.316	.313	.295			
Top 5%	.272	.270	.276	.281	.305	.313	.318	.320	.316	.308	.312	.310	.300	.295	.285	.287	.292	.291	.279			
Top 10%	.263	.261	.266	.269	.286	.294	.298	.301	.299	.293	.297	.296	.285	.279	.268	.271	.276	.276	.267			
Top 20%	.252	.251	.253	.256	.268	.274	.278	.280	.280	.276	.280	.280	.267	.260	.250	.252	.258	.258	.251			
61%-80%	.205	.206	.205	.202	.202	.204	.205	.203	.205	.204	.205	.205	.189	.183	.174	.173	.175	.175	.174			
41%-60%	.179	.179	.176	.174	.173	.173	.173	.173	.174	.168	.169	.166	.153	.148	.138	.141	.142	.142	.143			
21%-40%	.139	.146	.142	.137	.135	.131	.134	.132	.136	.130	.133	.130	.115	.108	.098	.099	.101	.102	.106			
0%-20%	.079	.089	.084	.082	.080	.066	.063	.056	.058	.058	.061	.064	.051	.047	.046	.043	.043	.045	.040			

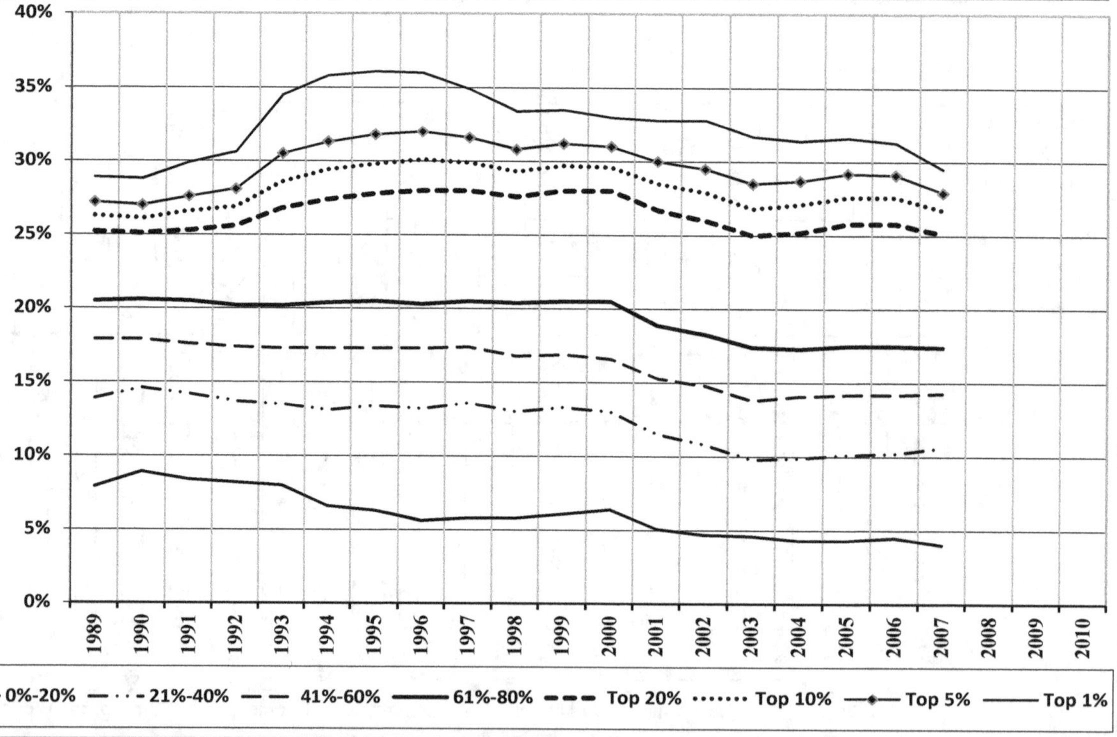

Source: http://www.cbo.gov/publications/collections/collections.cfm?collect=13

12.4.2 Compliance Cost

Not only does there not seem to be much interest in reporting on the size of the tax code, there appears to be nobody in the US government comprehensively looking at the cost of complying with US tax regulations. *The Rising Cost of Complying with the Federal Income Tax*, while dated, provides the following useful information:

- In 2005, US taxpayers paid about $1.2 trillion in federal income taxes and spent an estimated 6 billion hours filling out their taxes. The estimated cost of the hours is over $265.1 billion. The 6 billion hours are equivalent to 3 million work-years at 2,000 hours per year.

Figure 12-5: Share of Total Taxes by Income Level, 1989-2007

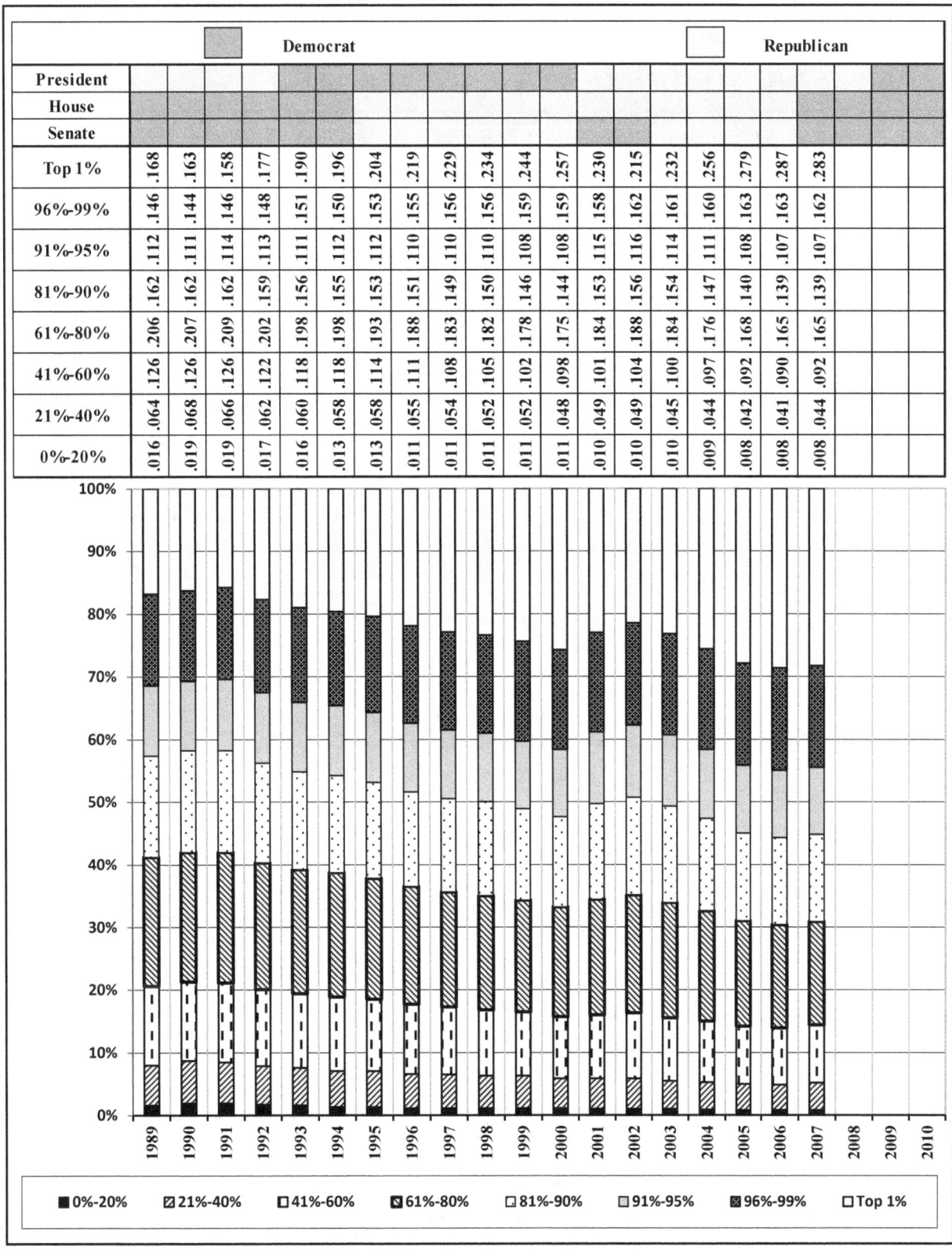

	Democrat																	Republican	
President																			
House																			
Senate																			
Top 1%	.168	.163	.158	.177	.190	.196	.204	.219	.229	.234	.244	.257	.230	.215	.232	.256	.279	.287	.283
96%-99%	.146	.144	.146	.148	.151	.150	.153	.155	.156	.156	.159	.159	.158	.162	.161	.160	.163	.163	.162
91%-95%	.112	.111	.114	.113	.111	.112	.112	.110	.110	.110	.108	.108	.115	.116	.114	.111	.108	.107	.107
81%-90%	.162	.162	.162	.159	.156	.155	.153	.151	.149	.150	.146	.144	.153	.156	.154	.147	.140	.139	.139
61%-80%	.206	.207	.209	.202	.198	.198	.193	.188	.183	.182	.178	.175	.184	.188	.184	.176	.168	.165	.165
41%-60%	.126	.126	.126	.122	.118	.118	.114	.111	.108	.105	.102	.098	.101	.104	.100	.097	.092	.090	.092
21%-40%	.064	.068	.066	.062	.060	.058	.058	.055	.054	.052	.052	.048	.049	.049	.045	.044	.042	.041	.044
0%-20%	.016	.019	.019	.017	.016	.013	.013	.011	.011	.011	.011	.011	.010	.010	.010	.009	.008	.008	.008

Legend: ■ 0%-20% ▨ 21%-40% ▫ 41%-60% ▧ 61%-80% ▫ 81%-90% ▨ 91%-95% ▨ 96%-99% ▫ Top 1%

Source: http://www.cbo.gov/publications/collections/collections.cfm?collect=13

The Rising Cost of Complying with the Federal Income Tax has a number of detailed charts of the sort that appear in this report. In deference to the authors' extensive work, I refer you to the report for further information (http://www.taxfoundation.org/news/show/1281.html).

Figure 12-6: Individual Tax Rates by Income Level, 1989-2007

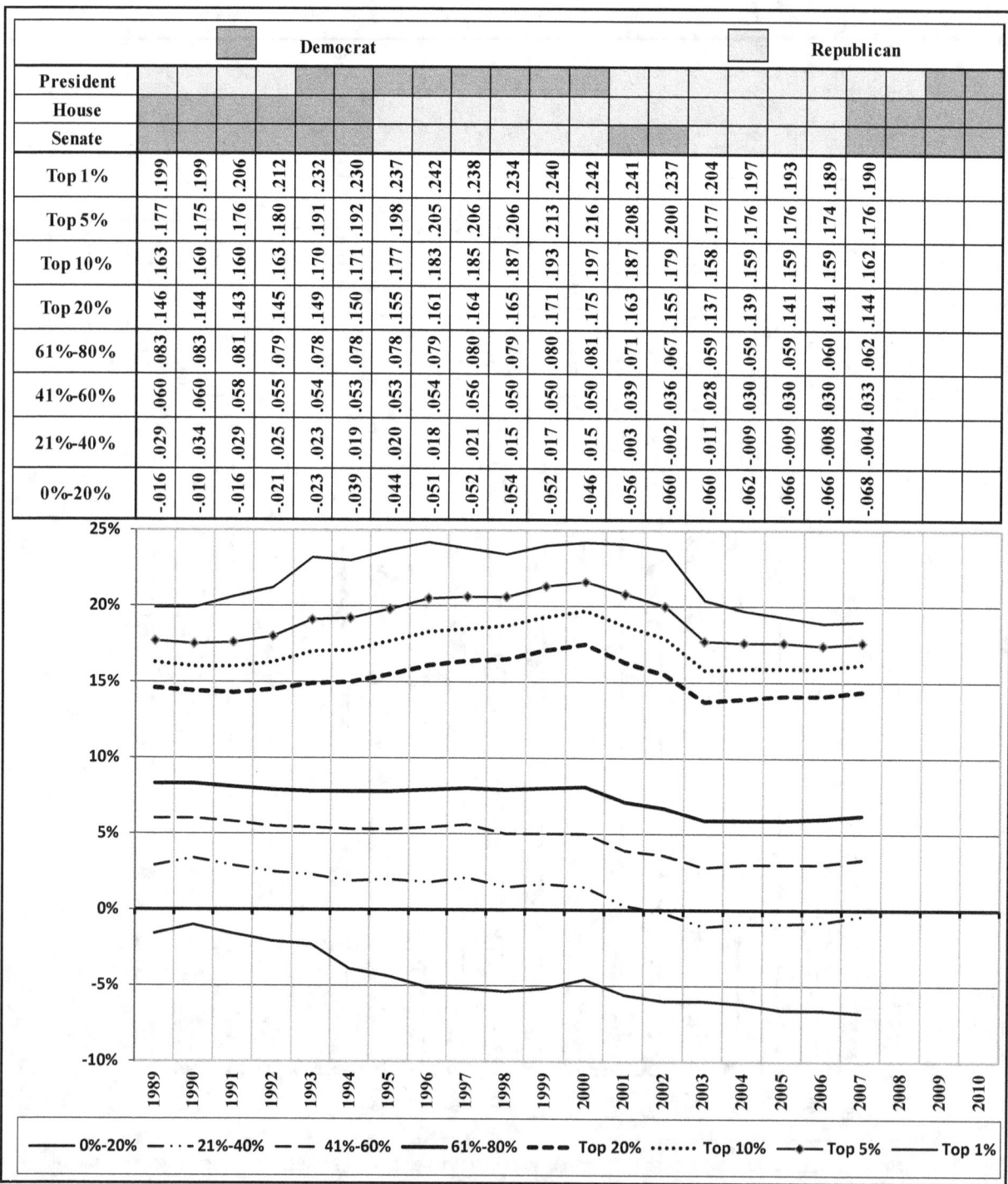

	1989	1990	1991	1992	1993	1994	1995	1996	1997	1998	1999	2000	2001	2002	2003	2004	2005	2006	2007	2008	2009	2010
Top 1%	.199	.199	.206	.212	.232	.230	.237	.242	.238	.234	.240	.242	.241	.237	.204	.197	.193	.189	.190			
Top 5%	.177	.175	.176	.180	.191	.192	.198	.205	.206	.206	.213	.216	.208	.200	.177	.176	.176	.174	.176			
Top 10%	.163	.160	.160	.163	.170	.171	.177	.183	.185	.187	.193	.197	.187	.179	.158	.159	.159	.159	.162			
Top 20%	.146	.144	.143	.145	.149	.150	.155	.161	.164	.165	.171	.175	.163	.155	.137	.139	.141	.141	.144			
61%-80%	.083	.083	.081	.079	.078	.078	.078	.079	.080	.079	.080	.081	.071	.067	.059	.059	.059	.060	.062			
41%-60%	.060	.060	.058	.055	.054	.053	.053	.054	.056	.050	.050	.050	.039	.036	.028	.030	.030	.030	.033			
21%-40%	.029	.034	.029	.025	.023	.019	.020	.018	.021	.015	.017	.015	.003	-.002	-.011	-.009	-.009	-.008	-.004			
0%-20%	-.016	-.010	-.016	-.021	-.023	-.039	-.044	-.051	-.052	-.054	-.052	-.046	-.056	-.060	-.060	-.062	-.066	-.066	-.068			

Democrat Republican

President, House, Senate

Legend: 0%-20% ··· 21%-40% — 41%-60% — 61%-80% ■■■ Top 20% ······ Top 10% ♦ Top 5% — Top 1%

Source: http://www.cbo.gov/publications/collections/collections.cfm?collect=13

Figure 12-7: Share of Income Taxes by Income Level, 1989-2007

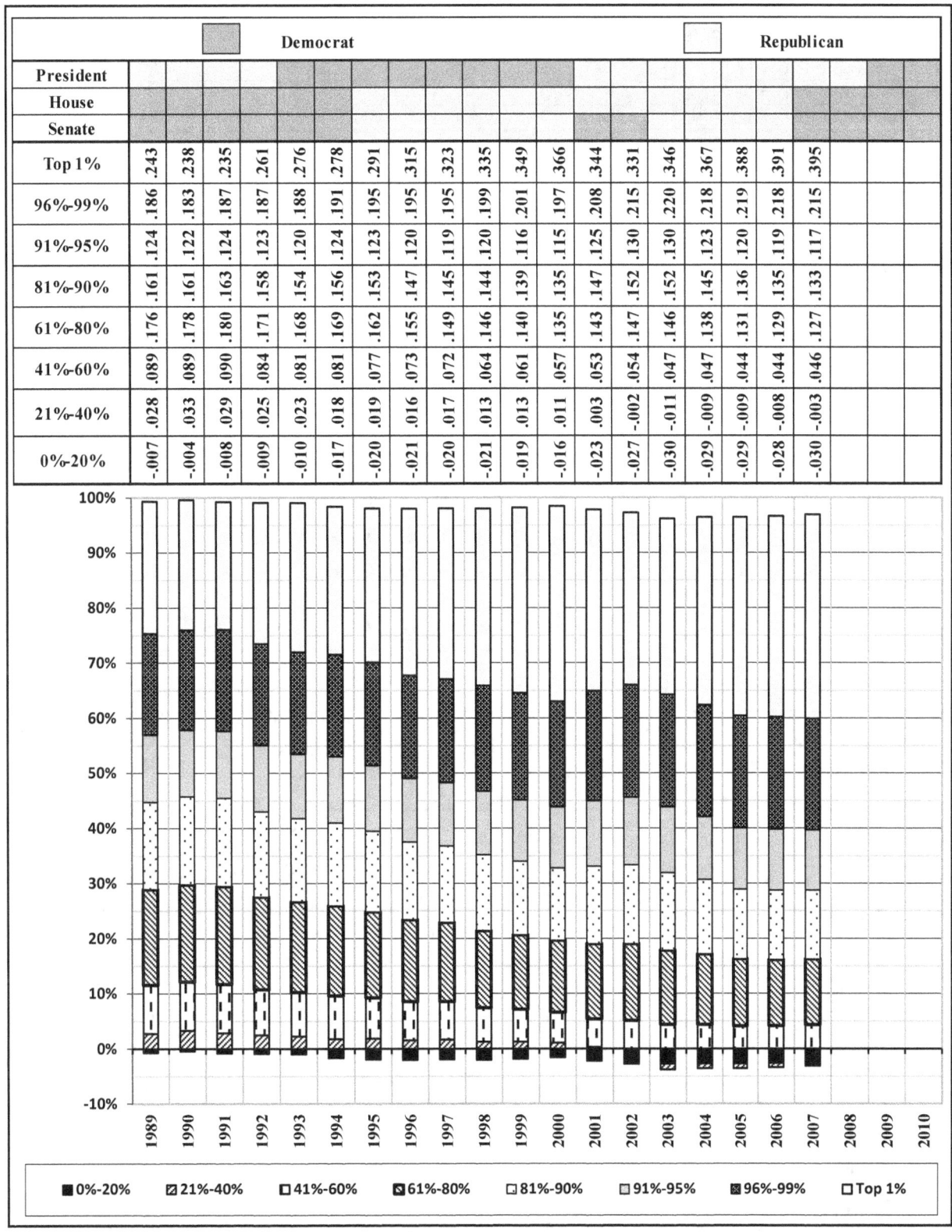

	1989	1990	1991	1992	1993	1994	1995	1996	1997	1998	1999	2000	2001	2002	2003	2004	2005	2006	2007
Top 1%	.243	.238	.235	.261	.276	.278	.291	.315	.323	.335	.349	.366	.344	.331	.346	.367	.388	.391	.395
96%-99%	.186	.183	.187	.187	.188	.191	.195	.195	.195	.199	.201	.197	.208	.215	.220	.218	.219	.218	.215
91%-95%	.124	.122	.124	.123	.120	.124	.123	.120	.119	.120	.116	.115	.125	.130	.130	.123	.120	.119	.117
81%-90%	.161	.161	.163	.158	.154	.156	.153	.147	.145	.144	.139	.135	.147	.152	.152	.145	.136	.135	.133
61%-80%	.176	.178	.180	.171	.168	.169	.162	.155	.149	.146	.140	.135	.143	.147	.146	.138	.131	.129	.127
41%-60%	.089	.089	.090	.084	.081	.081	.077	.073	.072	.064	.061	.057	.053	.054	.047	.047	.044	.044	.046
21%-40%	.028	.033	.029	.025	.023	.018	.019	.016	.017	.013	.013	.011	.003	-.002	-.011	-.009	-.009	-.008	-.003
0%-20%	-.007	-.004	-.008	-.009	-.010	-.017	-.020	-.021	-.020	-.021	-.019	-.016	-.023	-.027	-.030	-.029	-.029	-.028	-.030

Source: http://www.cbo.gov/publications/collections/collections.cfm?collect=13

12.4.3 IRS Operating Costs

Figure 12-8 shows the annual operating cost of the IRS for the period 1989 through 2010.

Figure 12-8: IRS Operating Costs, 1989-2010

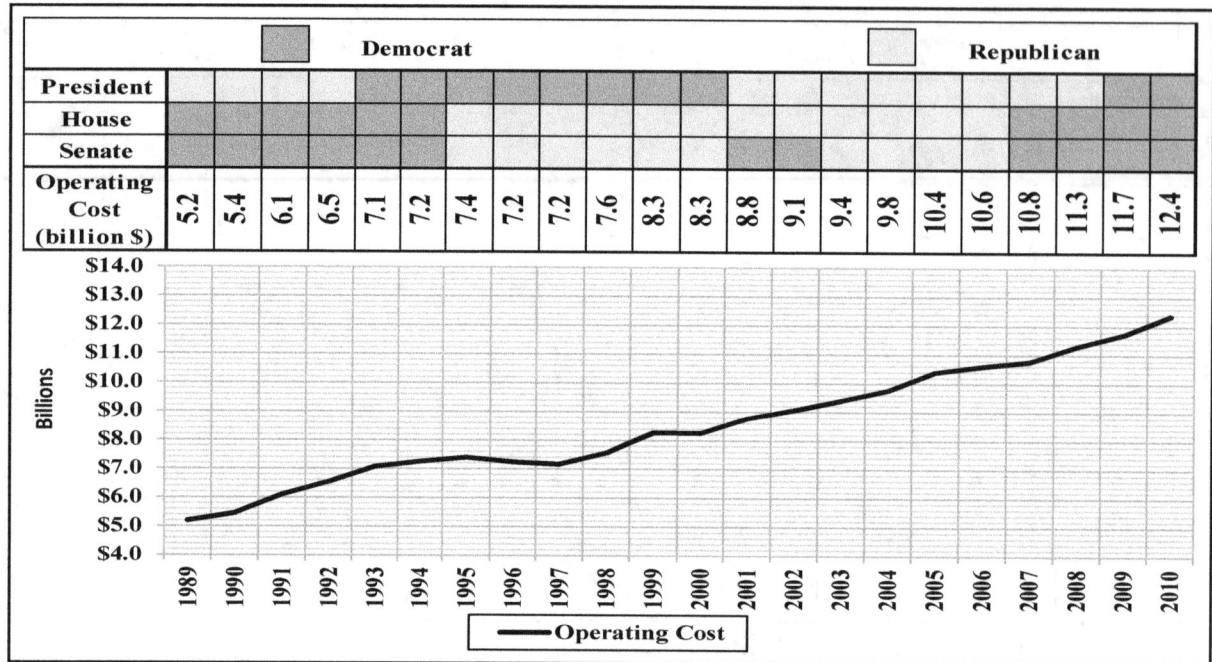

Source: http://www.irs.gov/taxstats/article/0,,id=207706,00.html

Figure 12-9 shows the number of people employed by the IRS for the period 1989 through 2010.

Figure 12-9: IRS Full-Time Equivalent Employees, 1989-2010

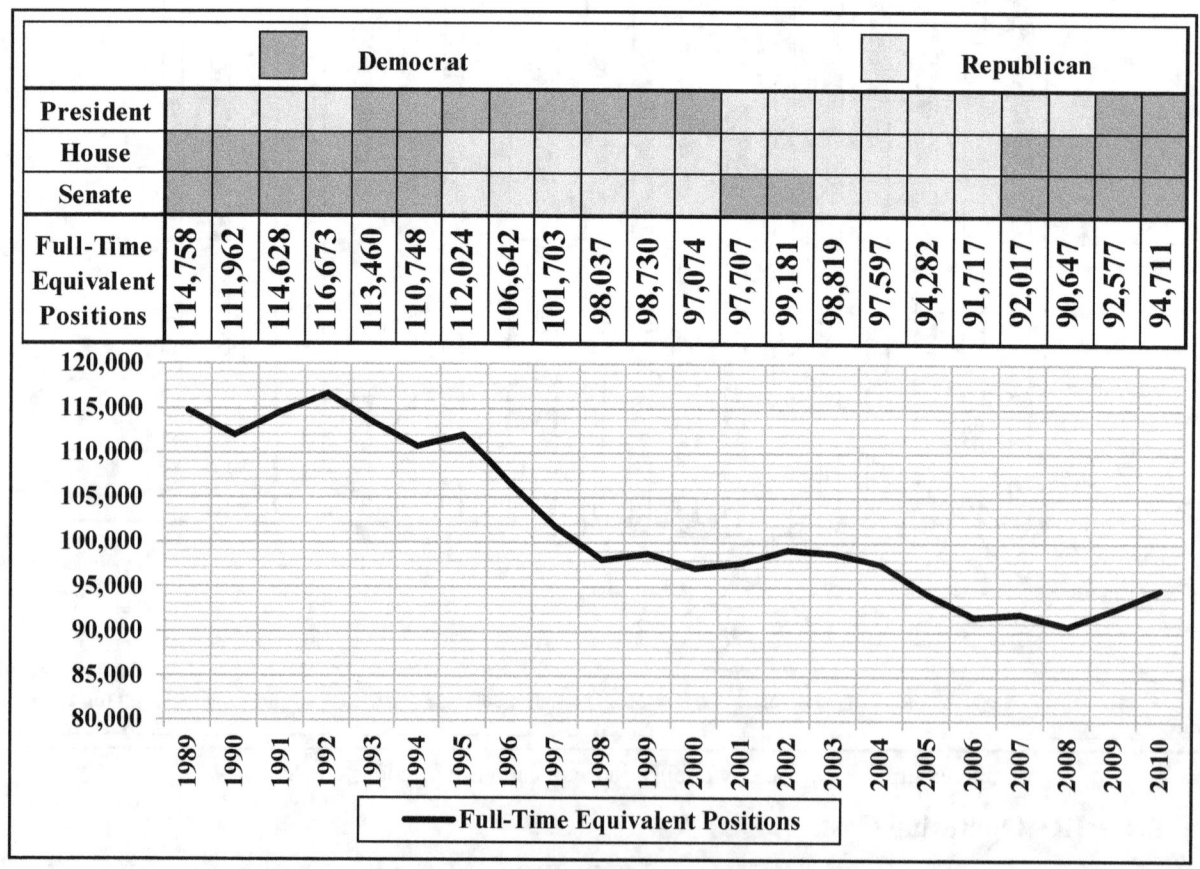

Source: http://www.irs.gov/taxstats/article/0,,id=207706,00.html

PART 3.   FEDERAL SPENDING

13. THE BUDGET

In this chapter, we turn from estimation and recordation to speculation and exaggeration, with a healthy dose of obfuscation and manipulation. We are going to talk about the federal budget, and I apologize in advance to the tens of thousands of federal workers who labor every year to support this system. This description and critique is not meant to impugn your efforts in any way, but to describe a corrupt, dysfunctional process as objectively as possible.

What follows is how the process is supposed to work. It's ironic that Congress decided in 1976 that they needed to shift the federal government's fiscal year from July through June, to October through September, so they would have more time to prepare and pass the budget. They incurred massive expense and untold confusion by creating a transitional quarter of July through September 1976 to effect this change. Their record of delivering budgets on time since then can be characterized only as shameful.

Much of what follows comes from *A Citizen's Guide to the Budget*, published in 2002.

13.1 DEFINITIONS

Here are a few words and phrases used in discussion of the budget process that you need to understand.

13.1.1 Mandatory Spending

Mandatory or direct spending is characterized by a lack of annual discretion to establish spending levels. Instead, it usually involves a binding legal obligation by the federal government to provide funding for an individual, program, or activity. Congress and the President may act to change the spending that current laws require for mandatory programs.

Mandatory spending sometimes is referred to as entitlement spending, but entitlement spending actually is the largest component of mandatory spending.

13.1.2 Discretionary Spending

Discretionary spending is what the President and Congress must decide to spend each year through annual appropriations bills. Congress and the President must act each year to provide spending authority for discretionary programs.

13.1.3 Authorization

Authorizing legislation, proposed by a committee of jurisdiction other than the House or Senate Appropriations Committees, establishes and continues the operation of a federal program or agency either indefinitely or for a specific period, or sanctions a particular type of obligation or expenditure within a program. Authorization is used in two different ways: (1) to describe legislation enacting new program authority, that is, authorizing the program; and (2) to describe legislation authorizing an appropriation.

In some instances, authorizing legislation may contain an appropriation or provide other forms of budget authority, such as contract authority, borrowing authority, or entitlement authority

13.1.4 Appropriation

An appropriation statute, under the jurisdiction of the House and Senate Committees on Appropriations, generally provides legal authority for federal agencies to incur obligations and to make payments out of the Treasury for specified purposes. An appropriation act fulfills the requirement of Article I, Section 9, of the US Constitution, which provides that "no money shall be drawn from the Treasury, but in Consequence of Appropriations made by Law."

Under the rules of both houses, an appropriation act should follow enactment of authorizing legislation. Major types of appropriation acts are regular, supplemental, deficiency, and continuing. Regular appropriation acts are all appropriation acts that are not supplemental, deficiency, or continuing. Currently, regular annual appropriation acts that provide funding for the continued operation of federal departments, agencies, and various government activities are considered by Congress annually. From time to time, supplemental appropriation acts also are enacted.

13.1.5 Continuing Resolution (CR)

A continuing resolution (CR) is an appropriation act that provides budget authority for federal agencies, specific activities, or both to continue in operation when Congress and the President have not completed action on the regular appropriation acts by the beginning of the fiscal year.

Enacted in the form of a joint resolution, a CR is passed by both houses of Congress and signed into law by the President. It may be enacted for the full year, up to a specified date, or until regular appropriations are enacted and it usually specifies a maximum rate at which the obligations may be incurred based on levels specified in the resolution. For example, the resolution may state that obligations may not exceed the current rate or must be the lower of the amounts provided in the appropriation bills passed in the House or Senate. If enacted to cover the entire fiscal year, the resolution will usually specify amounts provided for each appropriation account.

13.1.6 "Baseline" Budgeting

Baseline budgeting originally was established as a tool to facilitate the formulation of annual budgets. Twice a year, generally in January and August, the Congressional Budget Office (CBO) prepares baseline projections of federal revenues, outlays, and the surplus or deficit. Those projections are designed to show what would happen if current budgetary policies were continued as is--that is, they serve as a benchmark for assessing possible changes in policy. They are not forecasts of actual budget outcomes, since the Congress undoubtedly will enact legislation that will change revenues and outlays. Similarly, they are not intended to represent the appropriate or desirable levels of federal taxes and spending.

The genesis of baseline budget can be found in the Congressional Budget Act of 1974. That act required the Office of Management and Budget (OMB) to prepare projections of federal spending for the upcoming fiscal year based on a continuation of the existing level of governmental services. It also required the newly established CBO to prepare five-year projections of budget authority, outlays, revenues, and the surplus or deficit. OMB published its initial current-services budget projections in November 1974, and CBO's five-year projections first appeared in January 1976. Today's baseline budget projections are very much like those prepared more than two decades ago, although they now span 10 years instead of five.

The Budget Act was silent on whether to adjust estimates of discretionary appropriations for anticipated changes in inflation. Until 1989, OMB's projections excluded inflation adjustments for discretionary programs. CBO's projections, however, assumed that appropriations would keep pace with inflation, although CBO also has published projections without these so-called discretionary inflation adjustments. The CBO baseline has been used in every year since 1981 for developing budget resolutions and measuring compliance with reconciliation instructions.

The Deficit Control Act of 1985 provided the first legal definition of the baseline. For the most part, the act defined the baseline in conformity with previous usage. If appropriations had not been enacted for the upcoming fiscal year, the baseline was to assume the previous year's level without any adjustment for inflation. In 1987, however, Congress amended the definition of the baseline so that discretionary appropriations would be adjusted to keep pace with inflation.

Baseline budget projections increasingly became the subject of political debate and controversy during the late 1980s and early 1990s. Some critics contended that baseline projections create a bias in favor of spending by assuming that federal spending keeps pace with inflation, increases in caseloads, and other factors that drive the growth of entitlement programs. Those critics also observed that entitlement spending continued to rise, even as eligibility rules were tightened and payment rates reduced. Changes that merely slowed the growth of federal spending programs, they argued, should not be described as cuts in spending.

Baseline budget projections depend critically on the economic and other estimating assumptions on which they are based. CBO typically illustrates the sensitivity of the budget to the economy in two different ways. One way is through rules of thumb that involve changes in individual economic variables taken in isolation. Another approach is to prepare complete alternative economic forecasts, such as one marked by a recession. In addition, budget projections depend on a host of factors that are not included in the economic forecast. For example, budget estimators must take account of the expected effects on future spending of such factors as birth rates, mortality, disability, and changes in the circumstances of individuals and families. They must also make assumptions about how individual taxpayers, beneficiaries, state and local governments, and providers of health care and other services respond to federal legislation.

13.2 FORMULATING THE BUDGET

Table 13-1 shows the timeline for federal budget preparation each year. The President and Congress both play major roles in developing the federal budget. The annual budget process formally begins when the President submits his budget request to Congress (typically the first Monday in February). The budget takes effect after the requisite authorization and appropriation bills are passed by both the House and Senate and signed by the President, but not before October 1, the beginning of the fiscal year.

13.3 MONITORING THE BUDGET

Once the President and Congress approve the budget, it is monitored by several entities:

- Agency program managers and budget officials, including the Inspectors General, or IGs;
- The Office of Management and Budget;
- Congressional committees; and
- The Government Accountability Office, an auditing arm of Congress.

This oversight is designed to do the following:

- Ensure that agencies comply with legal limits on spending, and that they use budget authority only for the purposes intended;
- See that programs are operating consistently with legal requirements and existing policy;
- Ensure that programs are well managed and achieving the intended results.

Table 13-1: Federal Budget Formulation Process and Timeline

Date	Action
Calendar Year Prior to Fiscal Year Start	
Spring	OMB issues planning guidance to executive agencies.
Spring and Summer	Agencies send budget requests to the Office of Management and Budget (OMB).
July	OMB issues annual update to Circular A-11, providing detailed instructions for submitting budget data and material for agency budget requests.
September	Agencies submit initial budgets to OMB.
October-November	OMB reviews agency budget requests in relation to President's priorities, program performance, and budget constraints; modifies; and sends back to agencies.
November-December	President, based on recommendations by the OMB director, makes decisions on agency requests. OMB informs agencies of decisions.
December	Agencies may appeal these decisions to the OMB director or even the President.
Calendar Year in Which Fiscal Year Begins	
First Monday in February	President submits budget to Congress.
February 15	Congressional Budget Office submits economic and budget outlook report to Budget Committees.
Six weeks after President submits budget	Committees submit views and estimates to Budget Committees.
April 1	Senate Budget Committee reports budget resolution.
April 15	Congress completes action on budget resolution.
May 15	Annual appropriations bills may be considered in the House, even if action on budget resolution has not been completed.
June 10	House Appropriations Committee reports last annual appropriations bill.
June 15	Congress completes action on reconciliation legislation (if required by budget resolution).
June 30	House completes action on annual appropriations bills
July 15	President submits mid-session review of his budget to Congress.
September 10 (or within 30 days of spending bill approval)	OMB apportions available funds to agencies by time period, program, project, or activity.
	Congress passes continuing resolutions for agencies without appropriations bills passed and signed by the beginning of the fiscal year.
Calendar Years in Which Fiscal Year Begins and Ends	
October 1	Fiscal year begins.
October-September	Agencies make allotments, obligate funds, conduct activities, and request supplemental appropriations, if necessary. President may propose supplemental appropriations and impoundments (i.e., deferrals or rescissions) to Congress.
September 30	Fiscal year ends.

Source: Congressional Research Service

13.4 A DISMAL RECORD

Congress in recent years has a dismal record of passing its budget resolutions on time (May 15 for 1980 through 1984, and April 15 thereafter). In the 32 years from 1980 through 2011, Congress passed budget resolutions on time only 4 times, was late 23 times, and in 5 of the years, didn't pass budget resolutions at all. In the years in which the budget was passed late or not at all, Congress passed and the White House signed continuing resolutions that funded government operations, thereby avoiding shutting down the federal government. In one case, however, they failed even to pass a continuing resolution on time and the federal government shut down intermittently between November 1995 and April 1996. See figure 13-1.

Figure 13-1: Dates of Final Adoption of Annual Budget Resolution, 1980-2010

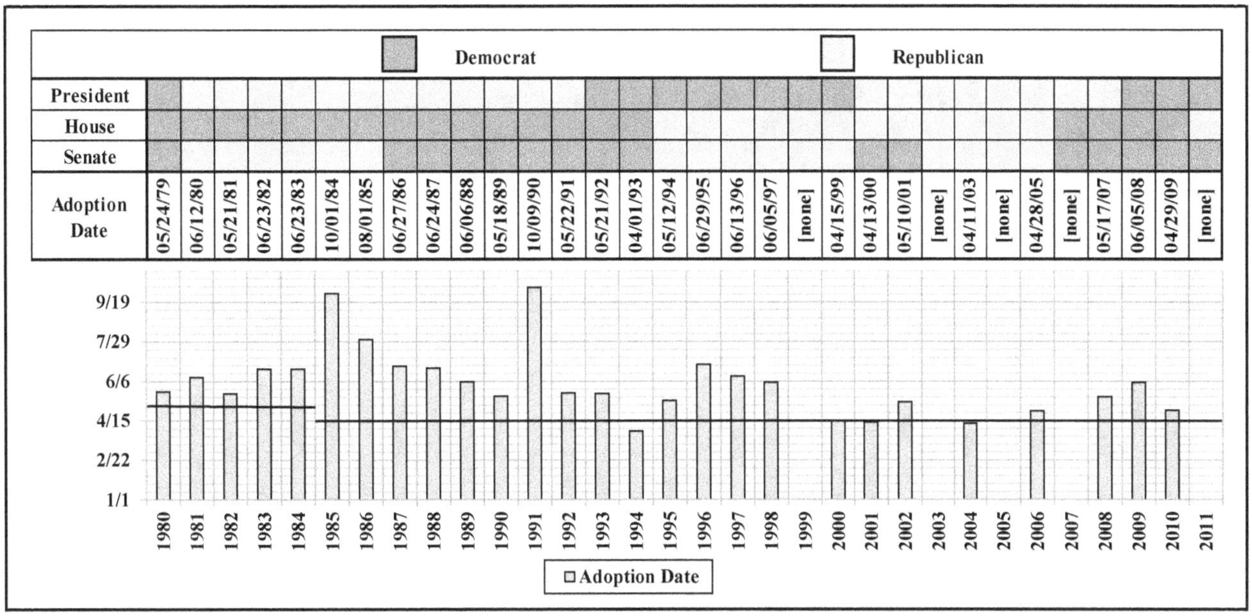

	Democrat		Republican
President			
House			
Senate			

Adoption Date: 05/24/79, 06/12/80, 05/21/81, 06/23/82, 06/23/83, 10/01/84, 08/01/85, 06/27/86, 06/24/87, 06/06/88, 05/18/89, 10/09/90, 05/22/91, 05/21/92, 04/01/93, 05/12/94, 06/29/95, 06/13/96, 06/05/97, [none], 04/15/99, 04/13/00, 05/10/01, [none], 04/11/03, [none], 04/28/05, [none], 05/17/07, 06/05/08, 04/29/09, [none]

Chart (Adoption Date) — vertical axis: 1/1, 2/22, 4/15, 6/6, 7/29, 9/19; horizontal axis years 1980 through 2011.

□ Adoption Date

Source: http://www.senate.gov/CRSReports/crs-publish.cfm?pid='0E%2C*PLS2%23%20%20%20%0A

The record is even worse than figure 13-1 indicates. For example, as of March 2012 no official budget has been passed for over three years. The figure shows only that for the three-year period 2008 through 2010 the appropriations bills finally were signed, some in the form of continuing resolutions.

14. RECEIPTS AND EXPENDITURES

US federal government receipts and expenditures are among the most obscure, contentious, and misleading concepts in this book. Part of the problem is the varied constituencies these data serve, from economists, econometricians, and statisticians, to politicians. The average voter is pretty much stuck when it comes to getting understandable numbers.

That said, the Bureau of Economic Analysis (BEA) does an unbelievably good job collecting and massaging the data into usable form, and publishing them on a regular schedule. They are the source of the receipts and expenditure data presented in the rest of this chapter.

For those of you who would like to reconcile the receipts and expenditure numbers in this chapter with the government consumption figures in the previous chapter—don't even try it. The government consumption in the last chapter includes federal, state, and local government consumption, and the receipts and expenditure numbers in this chapter are for the federal government alone. In addition, the concept of consumption has a specific and limited meaning, and it does not translate directly to the concept of expenditures. This is not to say that you can't get from one to the other. You can, but how to do that is way beyond the scope of this modest book.

14.1 RECEIPTS

The closest thing we have to revenue numbers for the US government is what the BEA calls "receipts", and there are two types: current and total. See figure 14-1 for current and total receipts for the period 1989 through 2010.

14.1.1 Current Receipts

Current receipts consist of current tax receipts, contributions for government social insurance, income from assets, current transfer receipts, and the current surplus from the operation of government enterprises. See figure 14-2 for current receipts by source for the period 1989 through 2010. The BEA defines the sources as follows:

14.1.1.1 Current taxes

Current taxes are tax payments made by persons or businesses: income taxes, sales taxes, property taxes, excise taxes, customs duties, severance taxes, documentary and stamp taxes, and special assessments such as license fees. See chapter 12 for more on taxes.

14.1.1.2 Social insurance contributions

Social insurance contributions finance the provision of certain social benefits to qualified persons, including contributions for Social Security, Medicare, unemployment insurance, and a number of smaller programs.

14.1.1.3 Income receipts from government assets

Income receipts from government assets include interest, dividends, and rental income, such as royalties paid on drilling on the outer continental shelf.

14.1.1.4 Current transfer receipts

Current transfer receipts include grants from other levels of government, fines, fees, donations, unclaimed bank deposits, deposit insurance premiums, and tobacco settlements. Also included are net insurance settlements, certain penalty taxes, miscellaneous transfers, and excise taxes paid by nonprofit institutions serving households.

14.1.1.5 Current surplus of government enterprises

Current surplus of government enterprises receipts represent the net profit for government enterprises.

14.1.2 Total Receipts

Total receipts consist of current receipts and capital transfer receipts.

Figure 14-1: Federal Current and Total Receipts, 1989-2010

Democrat   Republican

President																						
House																						
Senate																						
Total Receipts (billion $)	1,047	1,094	1,113	1,159	1,237	1,337	1,423	1,544	1,677	1,803	1,924	2,085	2,048	1,885	1,907	2,039	2,315	2,552	2,681	2,531	2,253	2,445
Current Receipts (billion $)	1,038	1,083	1,102	1,148	1,224	1,322	1,408	1,526	1,656	1,778	1,895	2,057	2,020	1,859	1,885	2,014	2,290	2,525	2,655	2,502	2,233	2,430

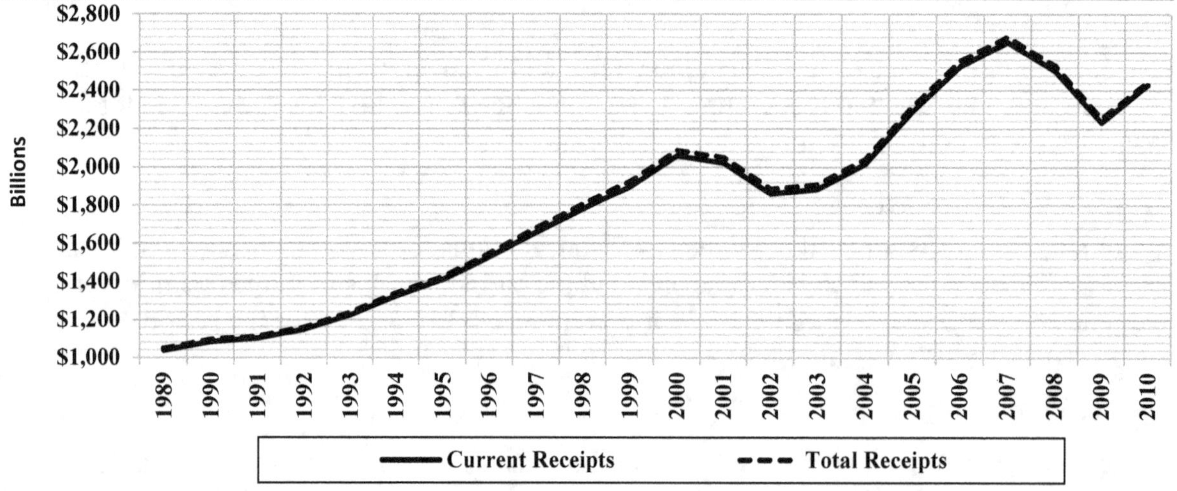

Billions
$2,800
$2,600
$2,400
$2,200
$2,000
$1,800
$1,600
$1,400
$1,200
$1,000
1989
1990
1991
1992
1993
1994
1995
1996
1997
1998
1999
2000
2001
2002
2003
2004
2005
2006
2007
2008
2009
2010
Current Receipts
Total Receipts

Source: http://www.bea.gov/national/nipaweb/SelectTable.asp?Selected=N

14.2 EXPENDITURES

The BEA also is the source of our US federal expenditure numbers. See figure 14-3 for current and total expenditures for the period 1989 through 2010.

Current expenditures include government consumption expenditures, current transfer payments, interest payments, and subsidies, but exclude wage accruals less disbursements. Current expenditures exclude capital investment but include consumption of fixed capital. See figure 14-4 for current expenditures by type for the period 1989 through 2010.

Total expenditures consists of current expenditures, capital transfer payments, gross investment (structures plus equipment and software), and net purchases of non-produced assets, less consumption of fixed capital.

Figure 14-2: Federal Current Receipts by Source as Percentage of Current Receipts, 1989-2010

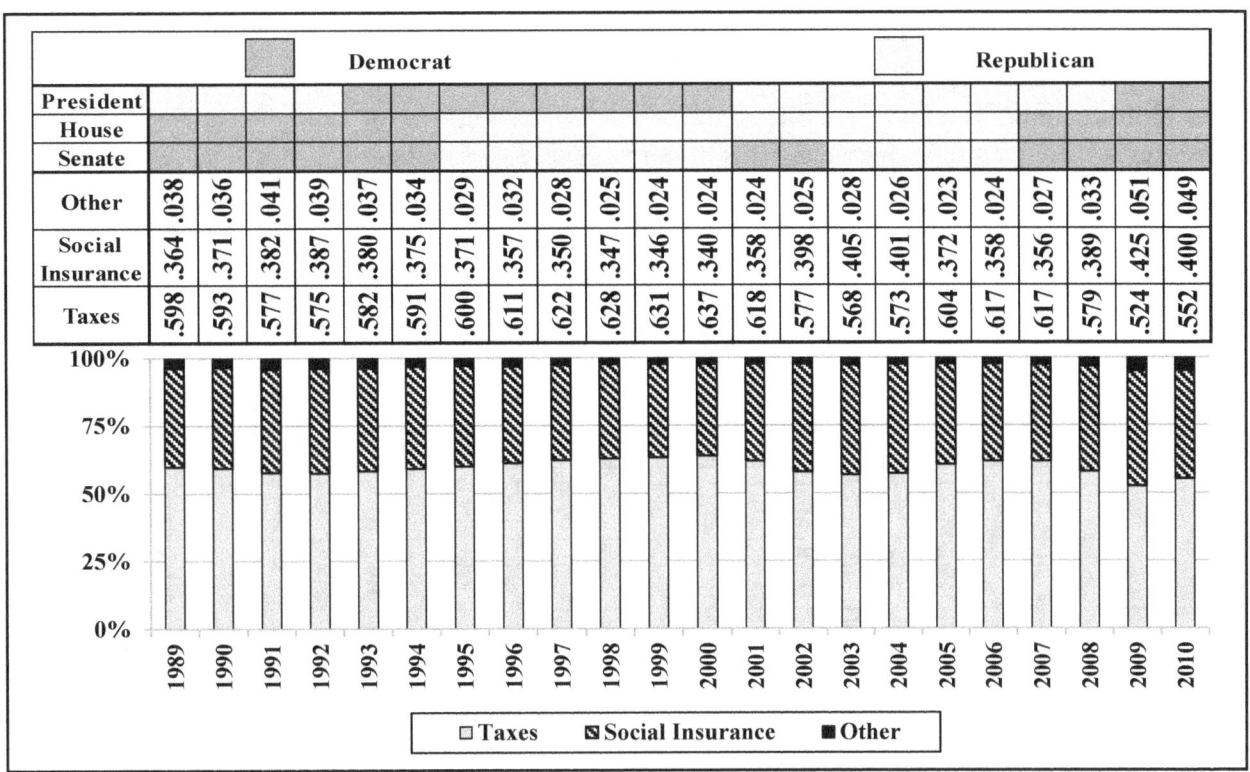

Source: http://www.bea.gov/national/nipaweb/SelectTable.asp?Selected=N

Figure 14-3: Federal Current and Total Expenditures, 1989-2010

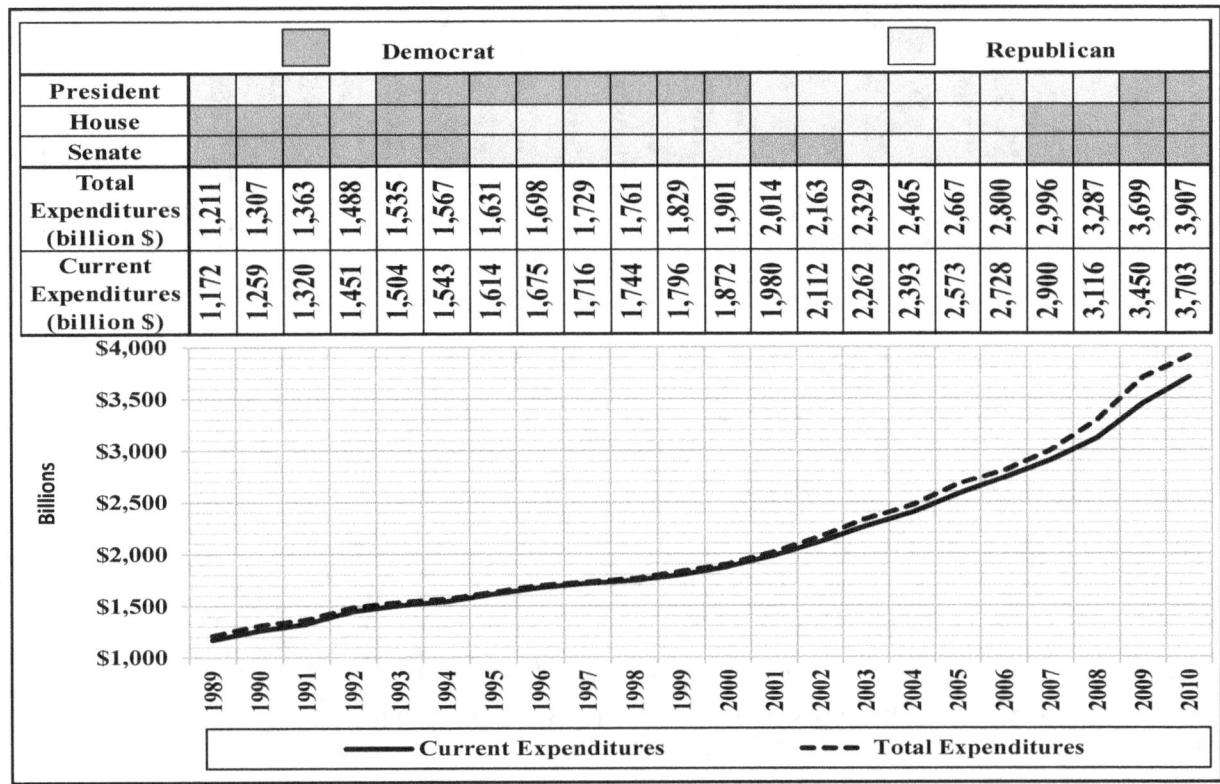

Source: http://www.bea.gov/national/nipaweb/SelectTable.asp?Selected=N

14.3 NET SAVING, AND NET LENDING OR BORROWING

Net saving is the difference between current receipts and current expenditures. It can be thought of as a measure of the extent to which the government is covering its current operations from current receipts.

Net lending or borrowing is the difference between total receipts and total expenditures. It represents the government's cash surplus or borrowing requirement.

Figure 14-4: Federal Current Expenditures by Type as Percentage of Current Expenditures, 1989-2010

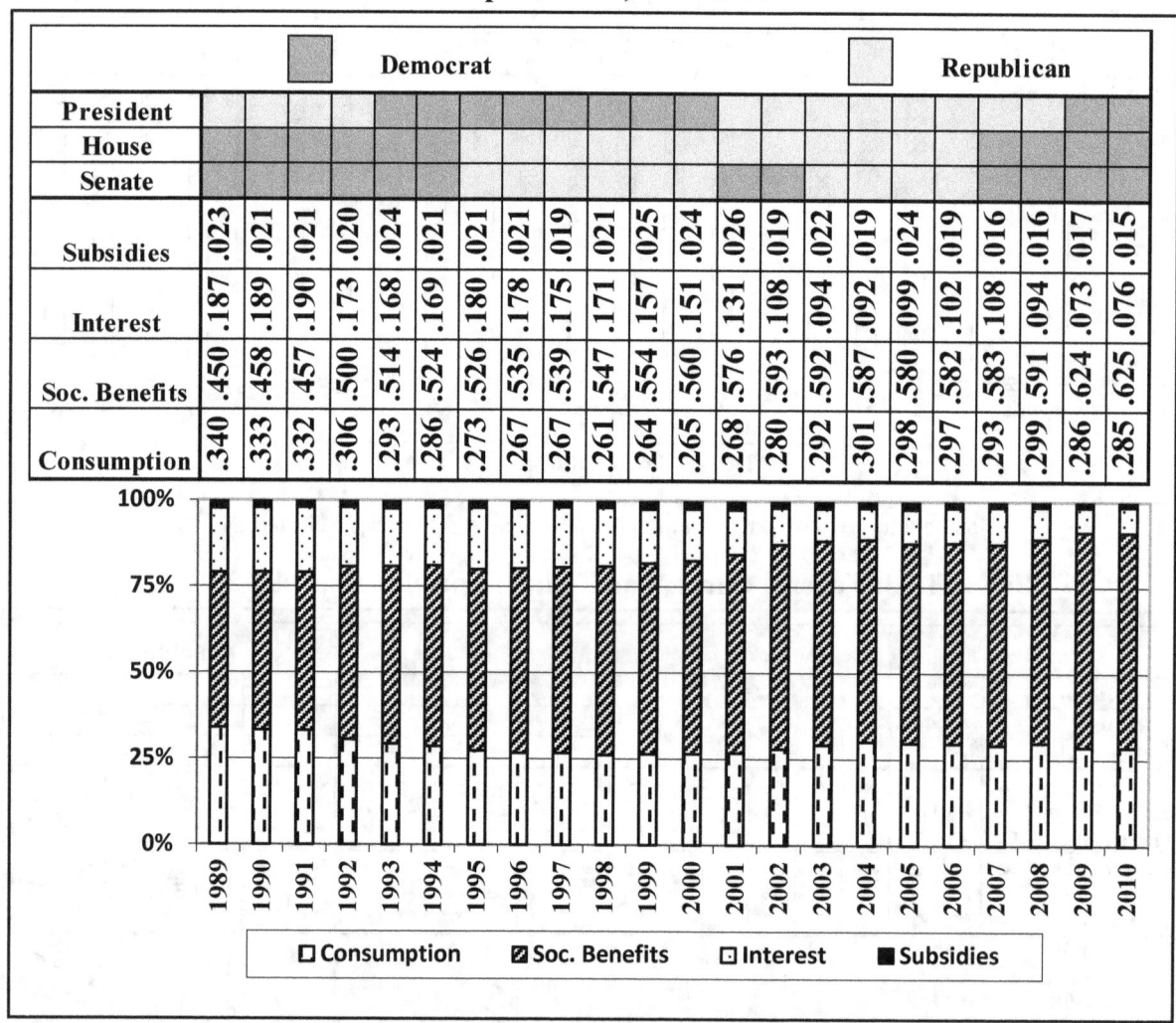

	Democrat																			Republican
Subsidies	.023	.021	.021	.020	.024	.021	.021	.021	.019	.021	.025	.024	.026	.019	.022	.019	.024	.019	.016	.016	.017	.015
Interest	.187	.189	.190	.173	.168	.169	.180	.178	.175	.171	.157	.151	.131	.108	.094	.092	.099	.102	.108	.094	.073	.076
Soc. Benefits	.450	.458	.457	.500	.514	.524	.526	.535	.539	.547	.554	.560	.576	.593	.592	.587	.580	.582	.583	.591	.624	.625
Consumption	.340	.333	.332	.306	.293	.286	.273	.267	.267	.261	.264	.265	.268	.280	.292	.301	.298	.297	.293	.299	.286	.285

Source: http://www.bea.gov/national/nipaweb/SelectTable.asp?Selected=N

14.4 DEFICITS AND SURPLUSES

Here's where things begin to get interesting. If US net saving is negative and/or total receipts minus total expenditures are negative, the budget is in deficit. Conversely, if US net saving is positive and/or total receipts minus total expenditures are positive, the budget is in surplus.

Figure 14-5 shows the differences between receipts and expenditures (both current and total) for the period 1989-2010. Only during the four-year period 1998 through 2001 were there surpluses, and they were on both the current and total measures.

Figure 14-5: Federal Net Saving, Lending or Borrowing, 1989-2010

	Democrat														Republican						
President																					
House																					
Senate																					
Net Lending or Borrowing (billion $)	-164	-213	-250	-328	-298	-229	-209	-154	-52	42	95	185	34	-278	-422	-427	-352	-247	-315	-756	-1,446	-1,462
Net Saving (billion $)	-134	-176	-218	-303	-280	-220	-206	-148	-60	34	99	185	41	-253	-376	-380	-283	-204	-245	-614	-1,218	-1,274

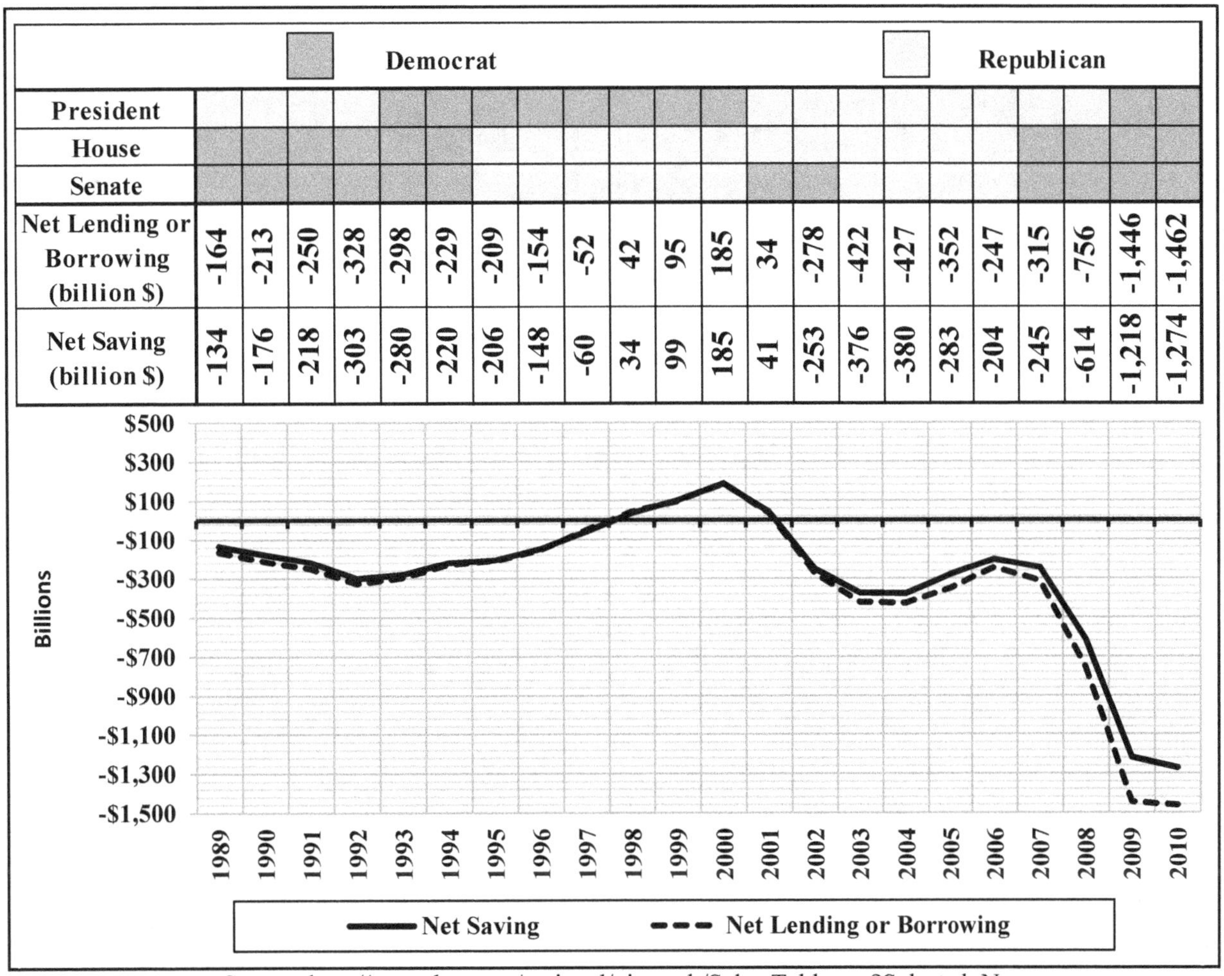

Source: http://www.bea.gov/national/nipaweb/SelectTable.asp?Selected=N

Budget deficits are important because they largely determine the amount of funds the government must borrow from the private economy to pay for excess spending during a fiscal year. Any funds the government borrows from the private economy are not available for private investment. This fact has significant implications for interest rates, inflation, and the long-run performance of the economy.

So far, we've dealt only with receipts and expenditures. In a given year, if we are in deficit because we spend more than we take in, the amount of the deficit increases our national debt by the same amount. Similarly, if we are in surplus, national debt decreases by that amount. Or so it would seem from the accounting described to this point.

In chapter 15, we address debt explicitly, and see if we can relate annual surpluses or deficits to annual changes in debt.

15. DEBT

The federal government issues debt securities mainly for two reasons: to finance the federal deficit; and to convert surpluses in federal government accounts, primarily trusts funds, into securities. By law, trust fund surpluses generally must be invested in federal securities. Gross federal debt is defined to include both the debt held by the public and the debt held by government accounts. Nearly all federal debt has been issued by the Treasury and is called "public debt", but a small portion has been issued by other government agencies and is called "agency debt".

15.1 TOTAL DEBT

The federal debt is the accumulated debt of the federal government. It is the largest legally and contractually binding obligation of the federal government.

As we saw in chapter 14, total debt relates to total federal spending and total revenues under what is known as the unified budget concept. Figure 15-1 shows total or gross US debt over the period 1989 through 2011.

Figure 15-1: Debt, 1989-2011

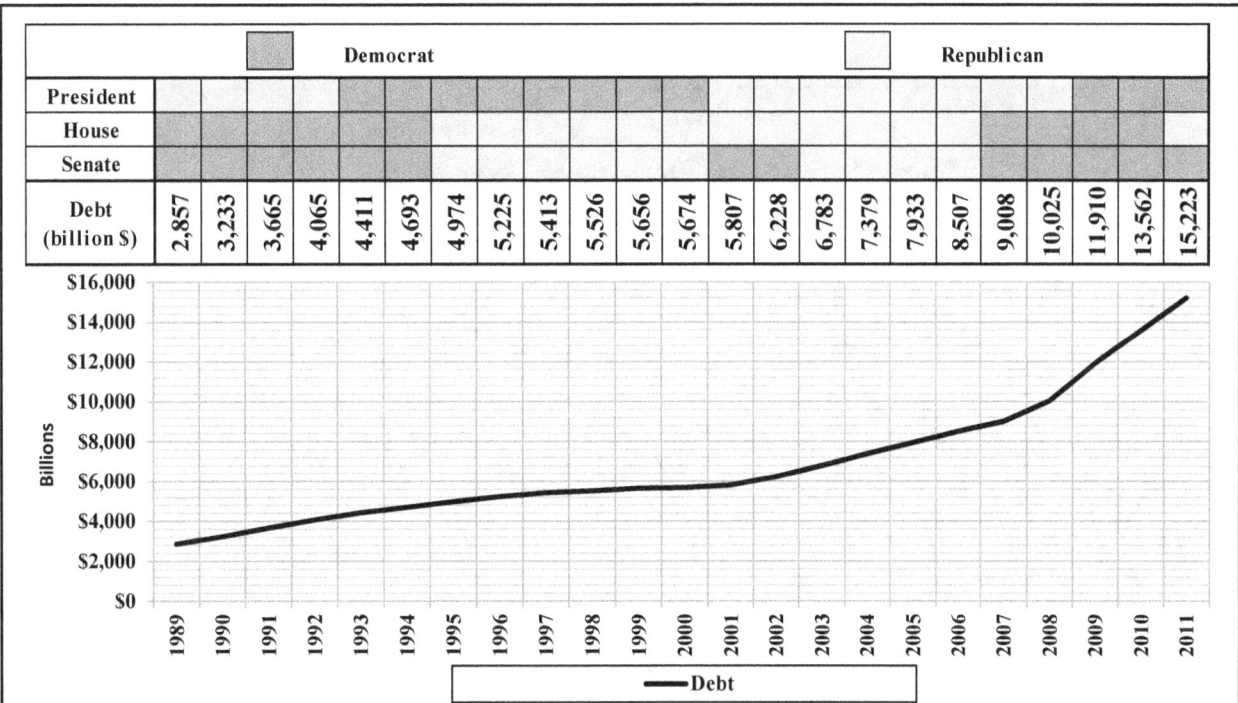

Source: treasurydirect.gov/govt/reports/pd/histdebt/histdebt_histo4.htm

Figure 15-2 shows the gross US debt as a percentage of GDP over the period 1989 through 2011.

Figure 15-3 shows the annual increases in gross US debt over the period 1989 through 2011. Note that the debt increases in every year of the period.

Figure 15-4 compares the unified budget deficits and surpluses we saw in chapter 14 with the annual changes in gross US debt. The two differ, sometimes by a wide margin. Why the difference? Read on.

Figure 15-2: Debt as a Percentage of GDP, 1989-2011

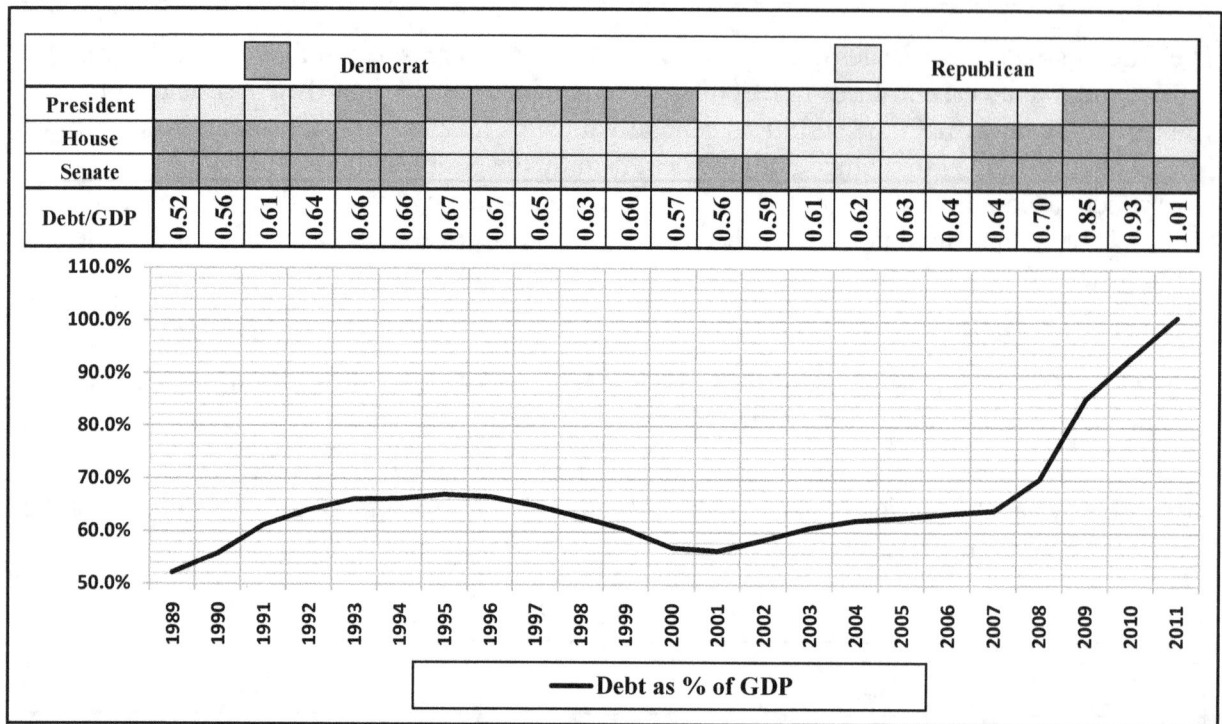

	Democrat		Republican	

Year	1989	1990	1991	1992	1993	1994	1995	1996	1997	1998	1999	2000	2001	2002	2003	2004	2005	2006	2007	2008	2009	2010	2011
President																							
House																							
Senate																							
Debt/GDP	0.52	0.56	0.61	0.64	0.66	0.66	0.67	0.67	0.65	0.63	0.60	0.57	0.56	0.59	0.61	0.62	0.63	0.64	0.64	0.70	0.85	0.93	1.01

Source: tables 7-1 and 15-1

Figure 15-3: Annual Increases in US Debt, 1989-2011

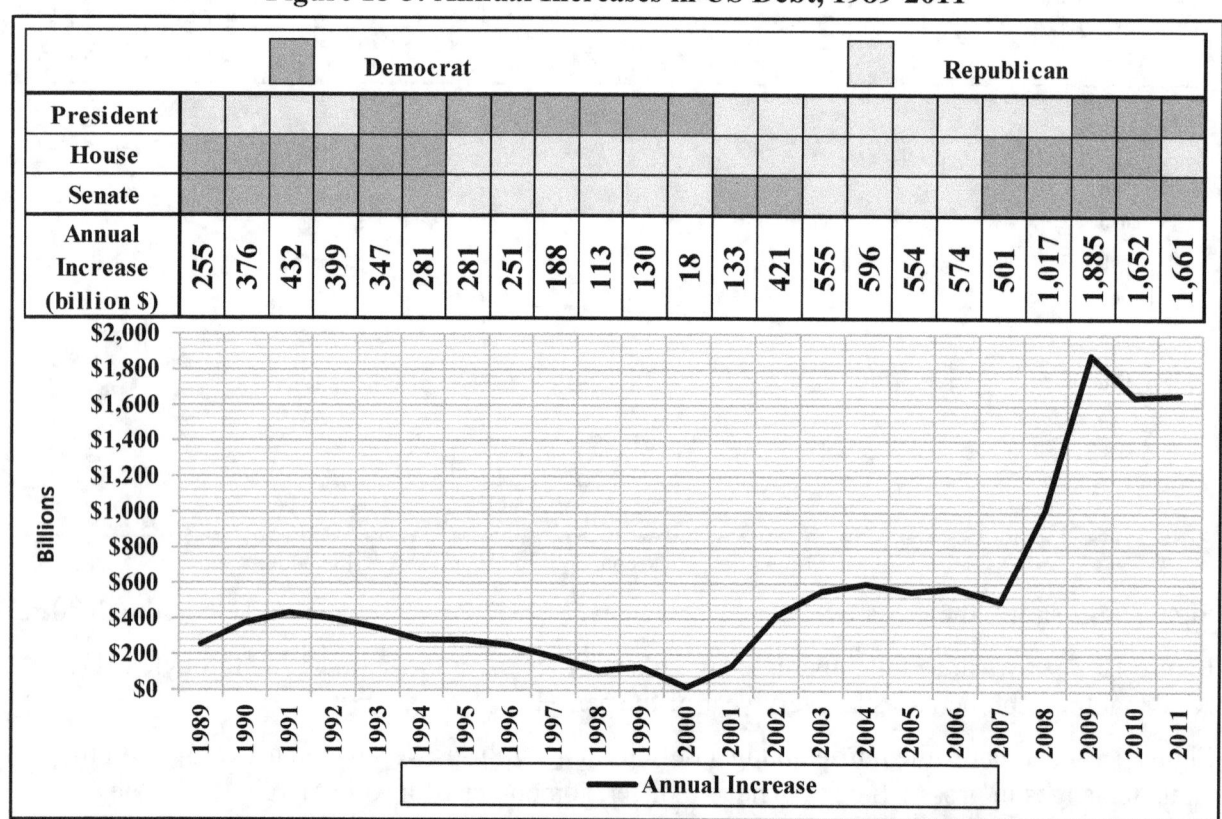

	Democrat		Republican	

Year	1989	1990	1991	1992	1993	1994	1995	1996	1997	1998	1999	2000	2001	2002	2003	2004	2005	2006	2007	2008	2009	2010	2011
President																							
House																							
Senate																							
Annual Increase (billion $)	255	376	432	399	347	281	281	251	188	113	130	18	133	421	555	596	554	574	501	1,017	1,885	1,652	1,661

Source: treasurydirect.gov/govt/reports/pd/histdebt/histdebt_histo4.htm

Figure 15-4: Deficits versus Changes in Debt, 1989-2010

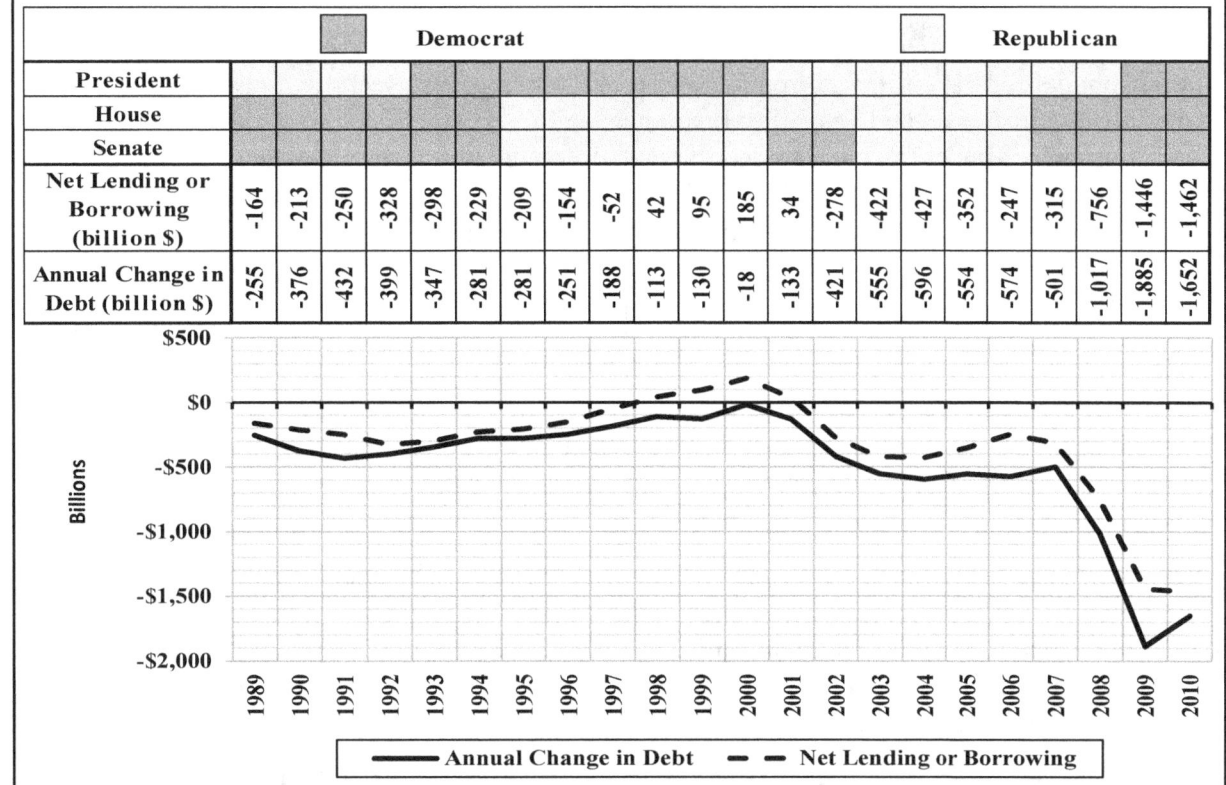

Source: see figures 14-4 and 15-2

15.2 DEFICITS AND CHANGES IN THE DEBT

This section repeats some of the material on the US budget presented in chapter 13, and provides additional insight into the US receipts and expenditures presented in chapter 14.

15.2.1 On-and Off-Budget

The US in reality keeps three sets of books. The first is the current budget, consisting of on-budget items only. The second is the unified budget, consisting of both on- and off-budget items. There is a legal distinction between ''on-budget'' and ''off-budget'', and we'll take a brief detour from our debt discussion to clarify it, then go on to the third set of books.

The outlays and receipts for on- and off-budget entities must be shown separately, but there is no conceptual difference between the two. The off-budget federal entities engage in the same basic activities of government as the on-budget entities, and the programs of off-budget entities result in the same kind of spending and receipts as on-budget entities. The ''unified budget'' reflects the conceptual similarity between on-budget and off-budget entities by showing combined totals of outlays and receipts for both types of entities.

The federal government has used the unified budget concept as the foundation for its budgetary analysis and presentation since the 1969 budget. This concept was developed by the President's Commission on Budget Concepts in 1967. It calls for the budget to include all the federal government's programs and all the financial transactions of these programs with the public.

Every year since 1971, however, at least one federal entity that would otherwise be included in the budget has been declared to be off-budget by law. Such off-budget federal entities are federally owned and controlled, but their transactions are excluded from the on-budget totals by law. When a federal entity is off-budget by law, its receipts, outlays, and surplus or deficit are separated from the on-budget receipts, outlays, and surplus or deficit, and its budget authority is also separated from the total budget authority for the on-budget federal entities.

The off-budget federal entities currently consist of the two Social Security Trust Funds: Old-Age and Survivors Insurance and Disability Insurance; and the Postal Service Fund. Social Security was classified off-budget as of 1986 and the Postal Service Fund was classified off-budget in 1989. A number of other entities that had been declared off-budget by law at different times before 1986 have been classified on-budget by law since at least 1985.

In principle, the on- and off-budget surpluses or deficits are added together to determine the Government's financing needs. If you compare the deficits in figure 14-5 with debt changes in figure 15-3, you will see they are not the same. Why not?

Enter the third set of books. It turns out that the Government's need to borrow in any year depends on several factors besides the unified budget surplus or deficit. These other factors, **other transactions affecting borrowing from the public**, either can increase or decrease the Government's need to borrow and their impact can vary considerably in size from year to year.

These other factors include a change in Treasury operating cash balances, net financing disbursements of the direct loan and guaranteed loan financing accounts, and net purchases of non-federal securities by the National Railroad Retirement Investment Trust (NRRIY). (Anyone interested in the detailed rationale for this fascinating accounting approach should read *2012 Analytical Approaches* by the OMB.)

In the 22 years from 1989 through 2010, deficits totaled $7.248 trillion while debt grew by $10.959 trillion. "Other factors" added a total of $3.711 trillion of borrowing to that reported by the Bureau of Economic Analysis (BEA) over that period. In other words, the deficits were 51 percent greater over that period than was reported. See figure 15-5.

15.2.2 Public and Intra-Governmental Debt Holdings

Yet another distinction without a difference when considering US debt is that between publicly held and intra-government debt.

Public debt, or debt held by the public, is federal debt held by all investors outside of the federal government, including individuals, corporations, state or local governments, the Federal Reserve banking system, and foreign governments. When debt held by the Federal Reserve is excluded, the remaining amount is referred to as privately-held debt.

Intra-governmental debt, or debt held by government accounts, is federal debt held by the federal government itself. Most of this debt is held by trust funds, such as Social Security.

Gross debt is the total amount of outstanding federal debt, whether issued by the Treasury or other agencies and held by the public or federal government accounts.

15.3 FINANCING THE DEBT

One of the most troubling aspects of the national debt is the amount of interest paid to service it. Figure 15-6 shows the gross and net annual interest that the US Treasury paid on the national debt each year for the period 1989 through 2010. Net interest is gross or total interest payments minus interest receipts.

Figure 15-5: Difference between Deficits and Debt Changes ("Other Factors"), 1989-2010

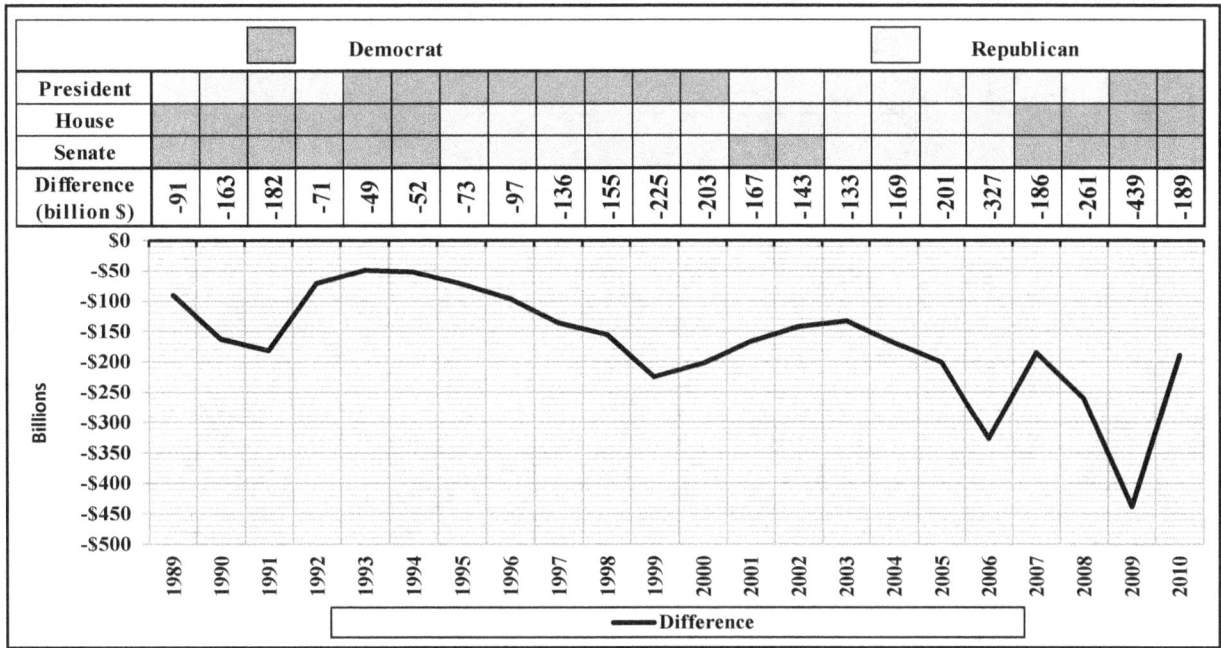

	1989	1990	1991	1992	1993	1994	1995	1996	1997	1998	1999	2000	2001	2002	2003	2004	2005	2006	2007	2008	2009	2010
President																						
House																						
Senate																						
Difference (billion $)	-91	-163	-182	-71	-49	-52	-73	-97	-136	-155	-225	-203	-167	-143	-133	-169	-201	-327	-186	-261	-439	-189

Source: see figure 15-3

Figure 15-6: Interest Payments on National Debt, 1989-2010

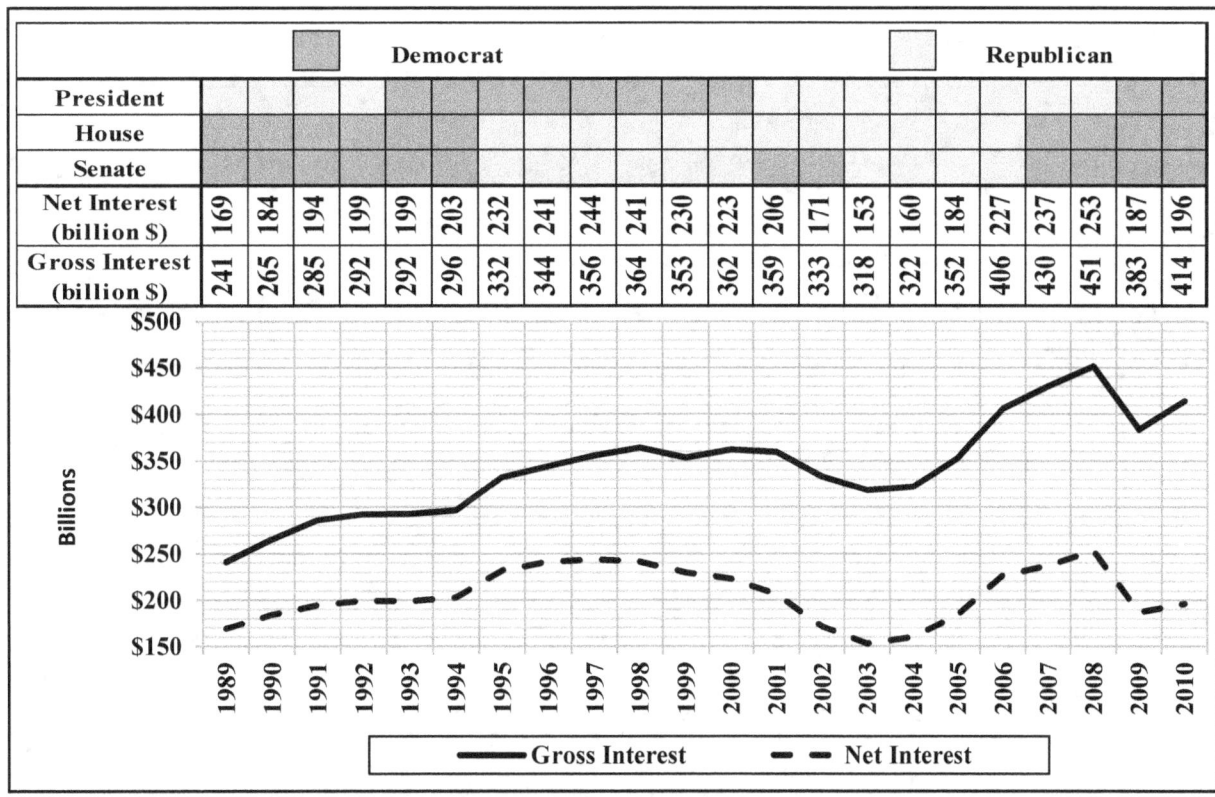

	1989	1990	1991	1992	1993	1994	1995	1996	1997	1998	1999	2000	2001	2002	2003	2004	2005	2006	2007	2008	2009	2010
President																						
House																						
Senate																						
Net Interest (billion $)	169	184	194	199	199	203	232	241	244	241	230	223	206	171	153	160	184	227	237	253	187	196
Gross Interest (billion $)	241	265	285	292	292	296	332	344	356	364	353	362	359	333	318	322	352	406	430	451	383	414

Source: www.whitehouse.gov/sites/default/files/omb/budget/.../hist08z5.xls

Note that if the average interest rate paid on the debt were to rise from the 2010 level of around 3 percent to a more historically normal 5 percent, interest payments would rise by $264 billion to around $680 billion annually.

Figure 15-7 shows gross interest on the debt as a percentage of GDP, and 15-8 shows it as a percentage of federal spending, both over the period 1989 through 2010.

Figure 15-7: Gross Debt Interest as Percentage of GDP, 1989-2010

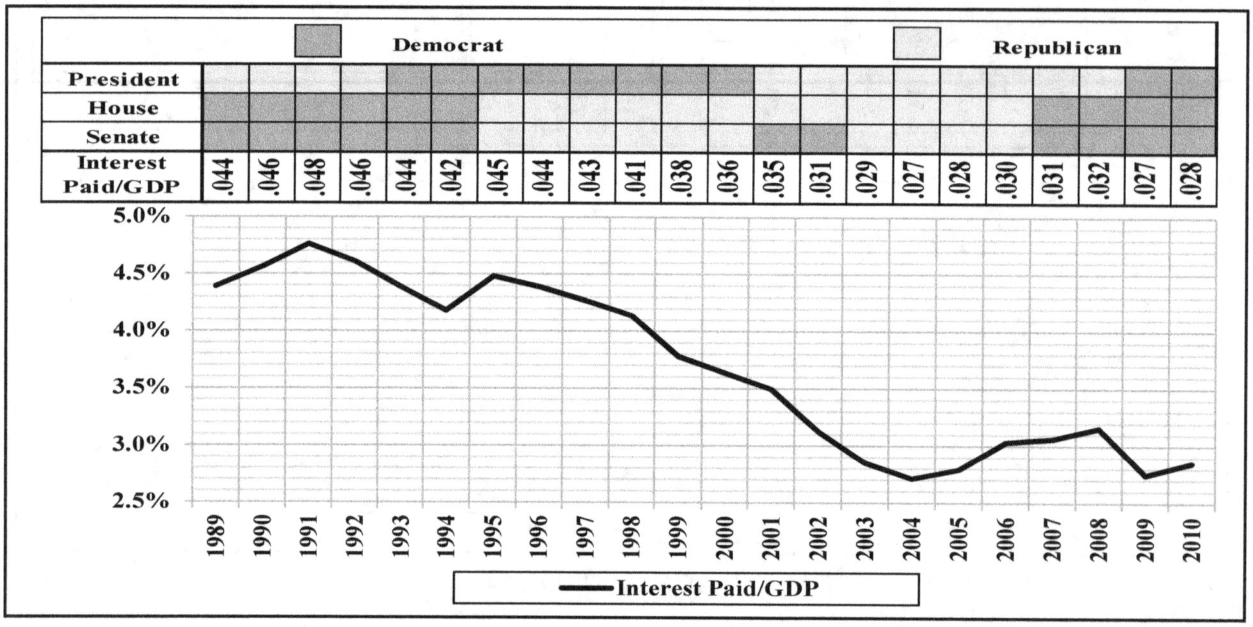

	Democrat													Republican							
President																					
House																					
Senate																					
Interest Paid/GDP	.044	.046	.048	.046	.044	.042	.045	.044	.043	.041	.038	.036	.035	.031	.029	.027	.028	.030	.031	.032	.027	.028

Source: calculated from figures 7-1 and 15-5

Figure 15-8: Gross Debt Interest as Percentage of Federal Expenditures, 1989-2010

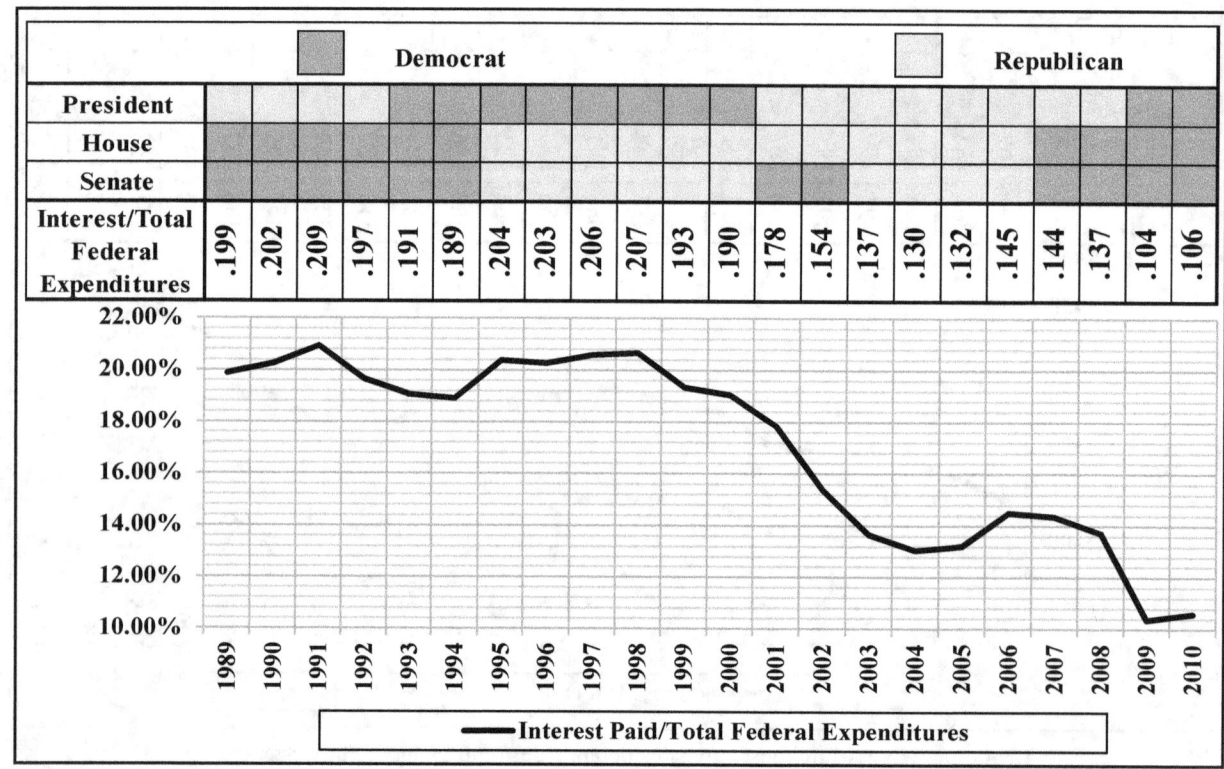

	Democrat													Republican							
President																					
House																					
Senate																					
Interest/Total Federal Expenditures	.199	.202	.209	.197	.191	.189	.204	.203	.206	.207	.193	.190	.178	.154	.137	.130	.132	.145	.144	.137	.104	.106

Source: calculated from figures 14-3 and 15-5

Finally, figure 15-9 shows the average rate of interest paid on the national debt for the period 1989 through 2011.

Figure 15-9: Average Rate of Interest Paid on US Debt, 1989-2011

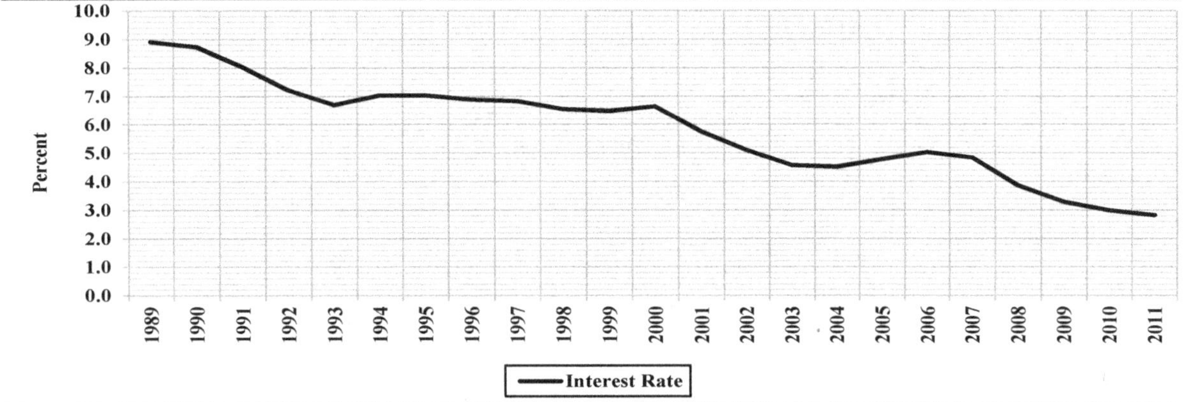

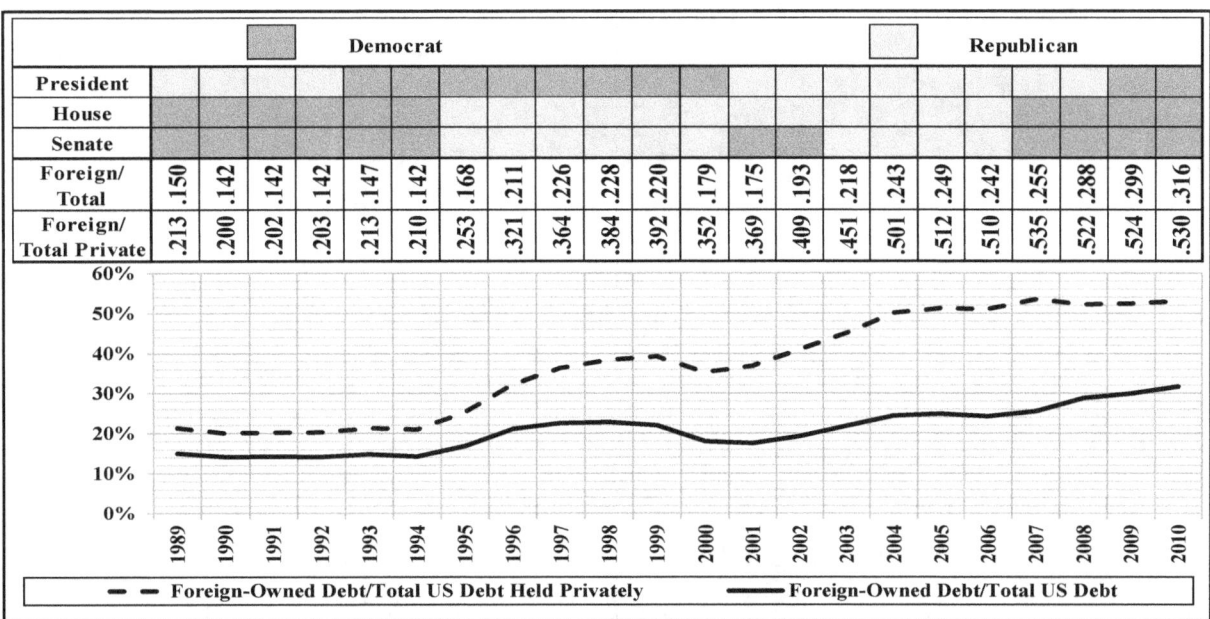

Source: http://www.treasurydirect.gov/govt/rates/pd/avg/avg.htm

15.4 FOREIGN HOLDERS OF US DEBT

One other concerning aspect of the debt is the amount held by foreign countries.

Figure 15-10 shows what percentage of the US privately-owned and total national debt is held by foreign countries over the period 1989 through 2010.

Figure 15-10: Foreign-Owned Debt as Percentage of US Debt, 1989-2010

Source: http://www.fms.treas.gov/bulletin/b2011_4.pdf

Table 15-1 shows the share of US Treasury securities (a proxy for foreign-held debt) held by major foreign debt-holding countries at the end of November 2011.

Table 15-1: Major Foreign Holders of Treasury Securities, November 2011

	Treasury Securities Held (billion $)	Percent of Total
China, Mainland	$1,132.6	23.8%
Japan	$1,038.9	21.9%
United Kingdom	$429.4	9.0%
Oil Exporters	$232.0	4.9%
Brazil	$206.4	4.3%
Caribbean Banking Centers	$185.3	3.9%
Taiwan	$149.6	3.1%
Switzerland	$113.9	2.4%
Hong Kong	$105.3	2.2%
Russia	$89.7	1.9%
Canada	$88.4	1.9%
Luxembourg	$72.9	1.5%
Singapore	$63.1	1.3%
Thailand	$62.0	1.3%
Germany	$60.7	1.3%
Other (Less than 1% each)	$720.5	15.2%
Total	$4,750.7	100.0%

Source: http://www.treasury.gov/resource-center/data-chart-center/tic/Documents/mfh.txt

US health care expenditures were $2.6 trillion for the year 2010. That represents about 18 percent of GDP in that year, nearly twice as high as in 1980. While health care costs are of concern to voters, in this election season health care primarily means two things: the rising costs of Medicare and the unknown costs of the Patient Protection and Affordable Care Act (Affordable Care Act/ACA or Obamacare). We'll look at overall health care spending in the US, then we'll look at some numbers for Medicare. At this time, there are no real numbers to see regarding the ACA.

16.1 HEALTH CARE EXPENDITURES

The Center for Medicare and Medicaid Services (CMS) publishes data on every aspect of health care administration and cost. Among the data are estimated total US health care expenditures. Figure 16-1 presents these data for the period 1989 through 2010, and figure 16-2 shows the percentage of GDP represented by health care expenditures over that same period, during which time the percentage grew by more than 50 percent. Note that this is not the growth in absolute cost but the growth of health care expenditures' share of GDP.

16.2 MEDICARE

Congress established Medicare and Medicaid in 1965. Medicare was established to address the medical care needs of the elderly, with coverage added in 1973 for certain disabled persons and certain persons with kidney disease. Medicaid was established to address the perceived inadequacy of medical care for those people on public assistance.

Congress established trust funds in the US Treasury to manage Medicare income and disbursements. Medicare taxes, premiums, and other income are credited to the funds. The Hospital Insurance (HI) Trust Fund pays for inpatient hospital and related care. The Supplementary Medical Insurance (SMI) Trust Fund comprises two separate accounts: Part B, which pays for physician and outpatient services; and Part D, which covers the prescription drug benefit.

16.2.1 Historical Performance

Figure 16-3 shows Medicare receipts and expenditures during the period 1989 through 2010. The receipts go into the trust funds, and expenditures are made from the trust funds. Figure 16-4 shows net Medicare receipts (receipts minus expenditures) during the 1989 through 2010 period, and Figure 16-5 shows the level of the Medicare trust funds over the same period.

Figures 16-4 and 16-5 warrant a little further discussion. The latter figure shows the Medicare trust funds to be valued at $381.6 billion in 2008 and declining in 2009 and 2010. These are facts, but what is misleading is the assertion that these trust funds have any value at all. All they have in them are US Treasury securities with no intrinsic value. If the trust funds were to be used to finance Medicare expenditures, the securities would have to be redeemed for cash from the Treasury, which in turn would come directly from tax dollars or newly printed money, or indirectly from the sale of additional securities.

If you look at figure 16-4, you will see that net Medicare receipts (receipts minus expenditures) were negative in 1995, 1997, and again in 2009, and really plunged in 2010.

Figure 16-1: Health Care Expenditures, 1989-2010

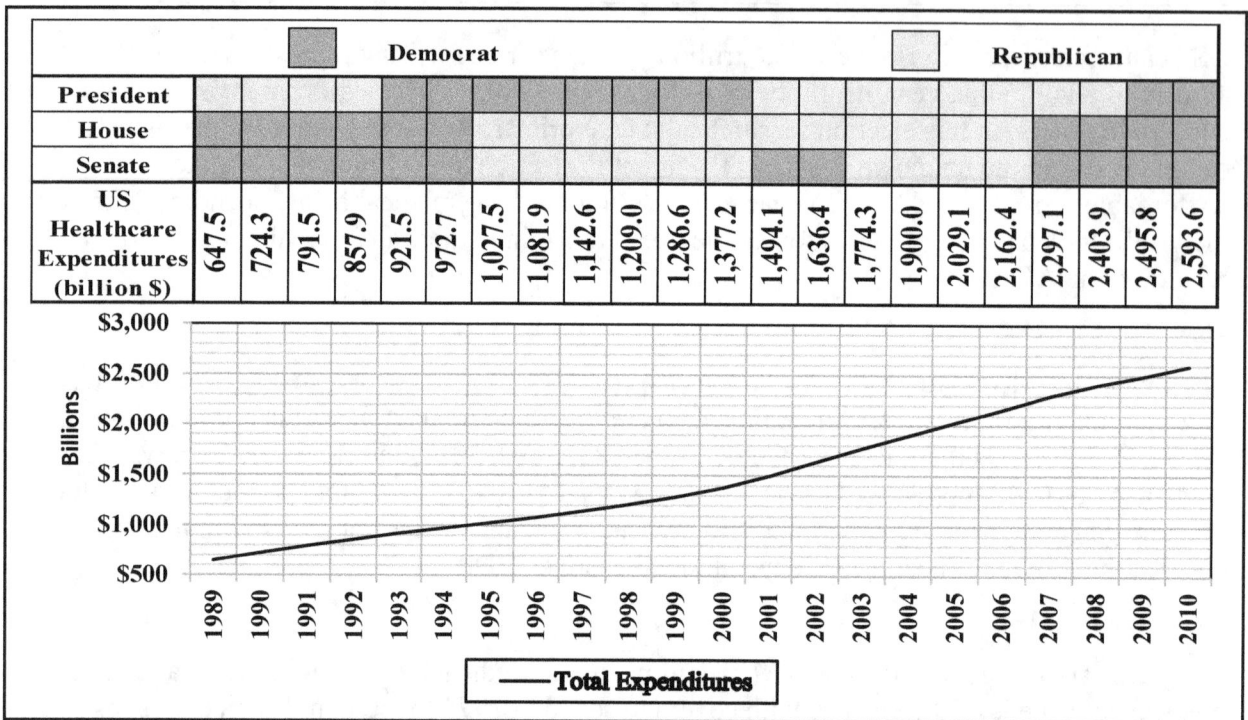

	Democrat																			Republican		
President																						
House																						
Senate																						
US Healthcare Expenditures (billion $)	647.5	724.3	791.5	857.9	921.5	972.7	1,027.5	1,081.9	1,142.6	1,209.0	1,286.6	1,377.2	1,494.1	1,636.4	1,774.3	1,900.0	2,029.1	2,162.4	2,297.1	2,403.9	2,495.8	2,593.6

Source: https://www.cms.gov/NationalHealthExpendData/02_NationalHealthAccountsHistorical.asp

Figure 16-2: Health Care Expenditures as a Percentage of GDP, 1989-2010

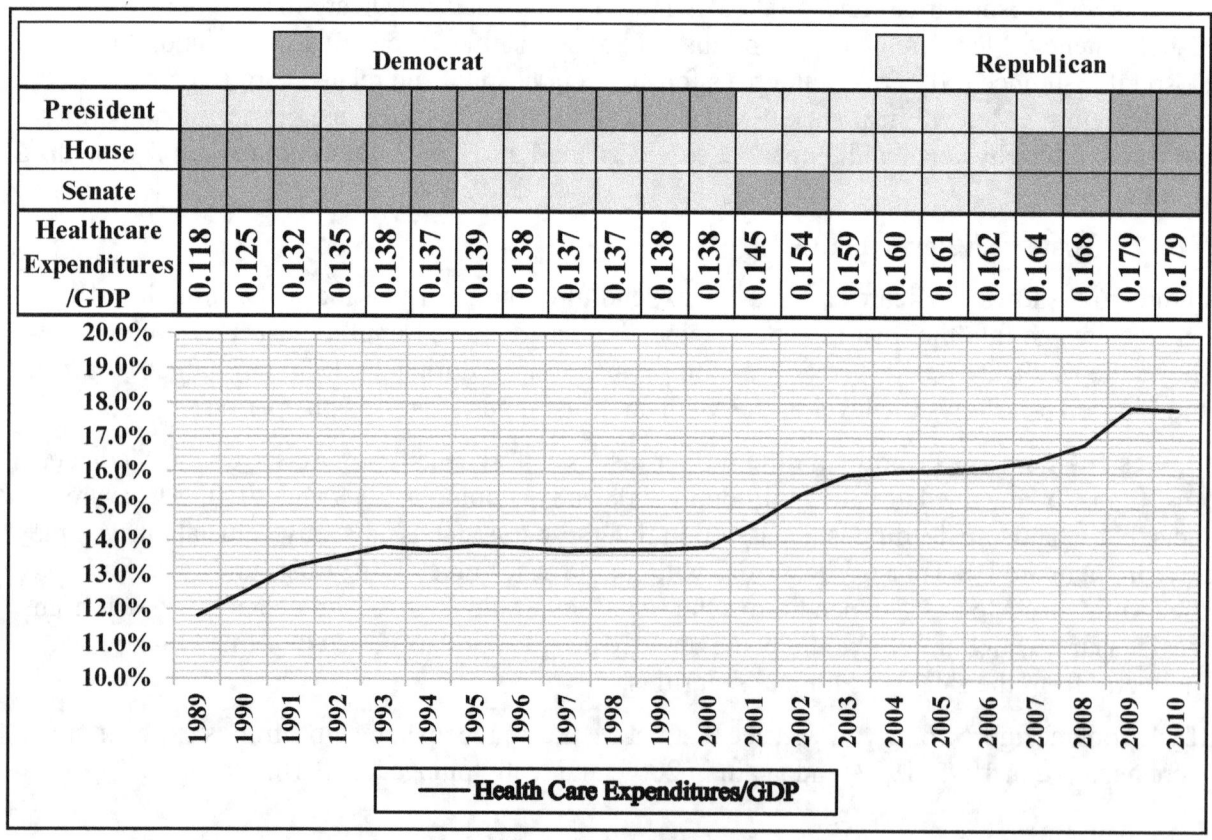

	Democrat																			Republican		
President																						
House																						
Senate																						
Healthcare Expenditures /GDP	0.118	0.125	0.132	0.135	0.138	0.137	0.139	0.138	0.137	0.137	0.138	0.138	0.145	0.154	0.159	0.160	0.161	0.162	0.164	0.168	0.179	0.179

Source: figure 7-1 and figure 16-1

16.2.2 Projected Performance

If you wish to see where Medicare might be headed, read *The 2011 Annual Social Security and Medicare Trust Fund Reports*, which present the current and projected financial status of the trust funds and can be found at the web address http://www.ssa.gov/oact/TRSUM/index.html.

Keep in mind that the projections are educated guesswork that is totally dependent on the assumptions used. The assumptions may be (in the most charitable interpretation) influenced by political factors, so the resulting projections may be as well. If you accept the possibility that these projections might be the most optimistic imaginable, they still are downright sobering. The following is the trustees' assessment of Medicare and Social Security prospects:

> The financial conditions of the Social Security and Medicare programs remain challenging. Projected long-run program costs for both Medicare and Social Security are not sustainable under currently scheduled financing, and will require legislative modifications if disruptive consequences for beneficiaries and taxpayers are to be avoided.
>
> Both Social Security and Medicare, the two largest federal programs, face substantial cost growth in the upcoming decades due to factors that include population aging as well as the growth in expenditures per beneficiary. Through the mid-2030s, due to the large baby-boom generation entering retirement and lower-birth-rate generations entering employment, population aging is the largest single factor contributing to cost growth in the two programs. Thereafter, the continued rapid growth in health care cost per beneficiary becomes the larger factor.

16.3 PATIENT PROTECTION AND AFFORDABLE CARE ACT

The Patient Protection and Affordable Care Act, as amended by the Health Care and Education Reconciliation Act of 2010 (the "Affordable Care Act" or ACA) still is too new to have a record. If you wish to learn what the Congressional Budget Office had to say about the bill, see its *Analysis of the Major Health Care Legislation Enacted in March 2010* at web address http://www.cbo.gov/ftpdocs/121xx/doc12119/03-30-HealthCareLegislation.pdf.

As with the projections on Medicare, these CBO projections are only as sound as their underlying assumptions. The underlying assumptions are strongly influenced by Congressional actions, and the assumptions are changing constantly. Any projections at this point are highly speculative.

Figure 16-3: Medicare Receipts and Expenditures, 1989-2010

	Democrat																Republican					
President																						
House																						
Senate																						
Expenditures (billion $)	100.6	111.0	121.4	135.8	152.2	164.9	184.2	200.3	213.6	213.4	213.0	221.8	244.8	265.7	280.8	308.9	336.4	408.3	431.7	468.1	509.0	522.8
Receipts (billion $)	121.1	126.3	140.1	151.1	155.9	165.2	175.3	210.2	212.1	228.3	232.5	257.1	273.3	284.8	291.6	317.7	357.5	437.0	462.1	480.8	508.2	486.0

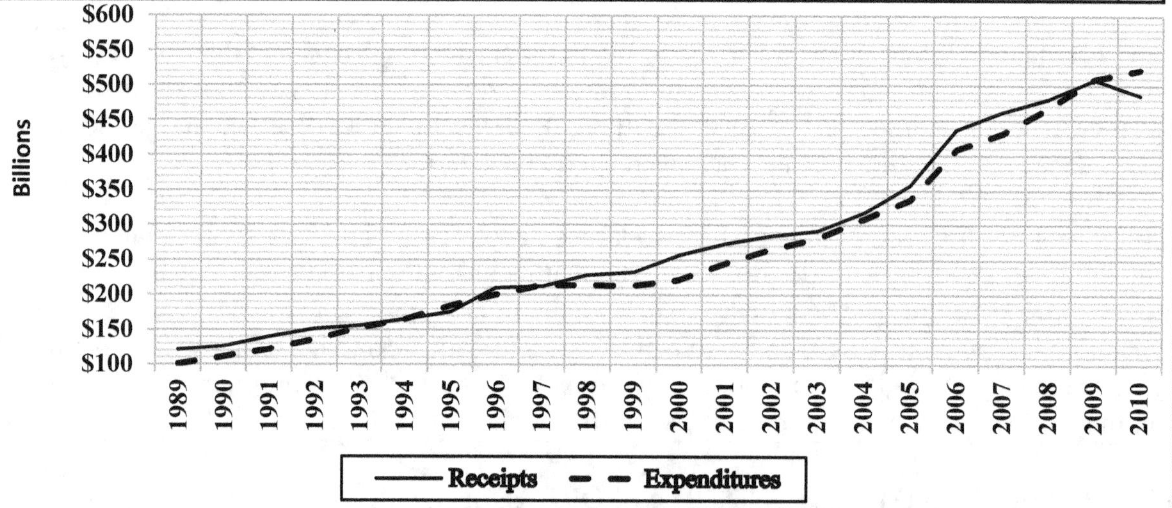

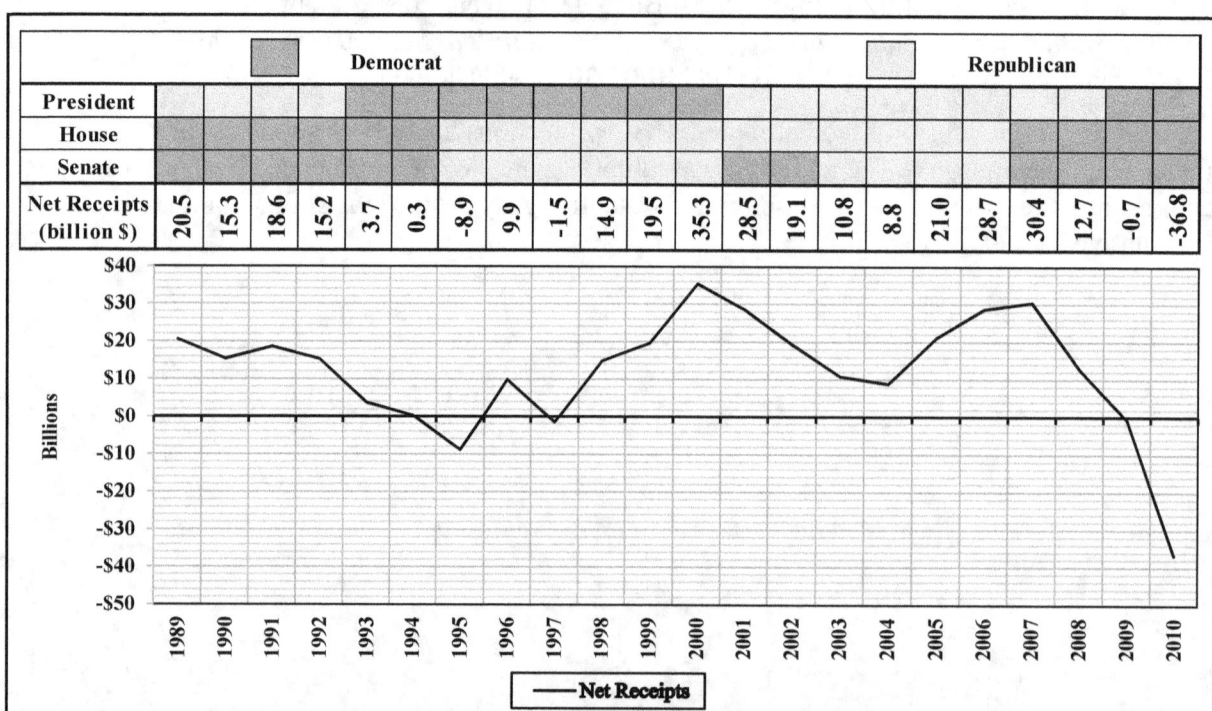

Source: http://www.ssa.gov/policy/docs/statcomps/supplement/2010/8a.pdf

Figure 16-4: Net Medicare Receipts, 1989-2010

	Democrat																Republican					
President																						
House																						
Senate																						
Net Receipts (billion $)	20.5	15.3	18.6	15.2	3.7	0.3	-8.9	9.9	-1.5	14.9	19.5	35.3	28.5	19.1	10.8	8.8	21.0	28.7	30.4	12.7	-0.7	-36.8

Source: http://www.ssa.gov/policy/docs/statcomps/supplement/2010/8a.pdf

Figure 16-5: Medicare Trust Funds, 1989-2010

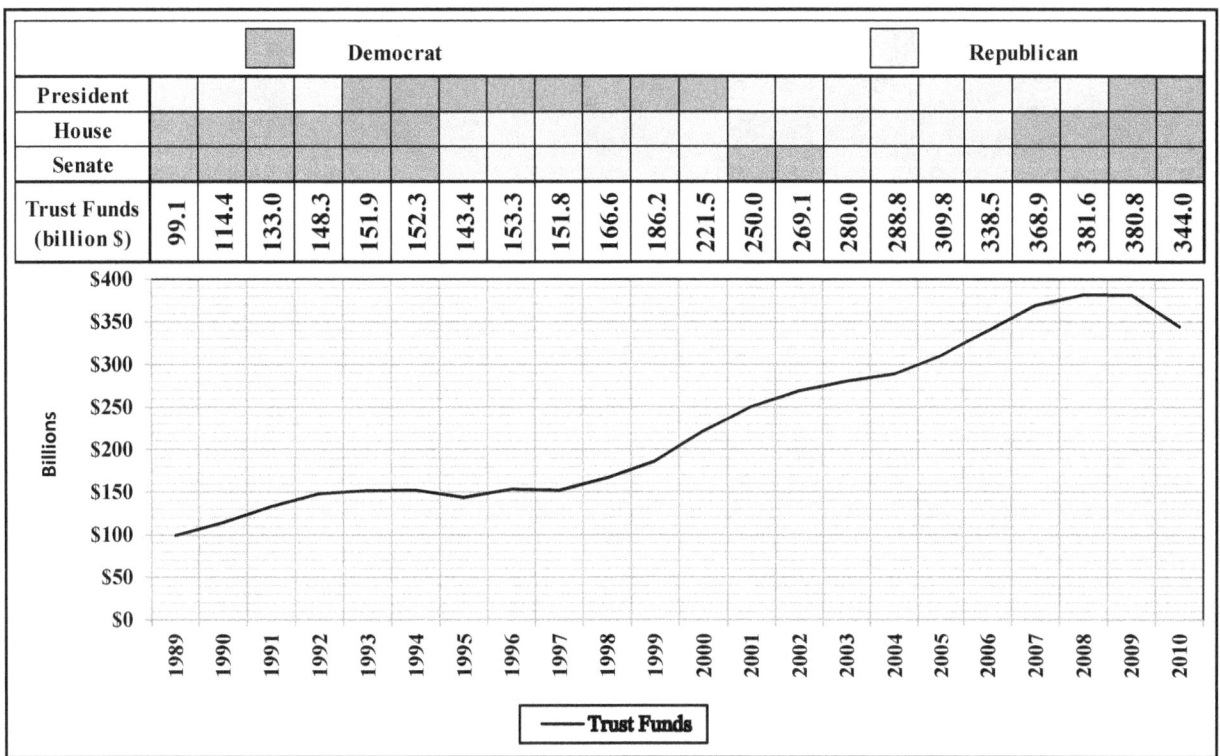

Source: http://www.ssa.gov/policy/docs/statcomps/supplement/2010/8a.pdf

17. SOCIAL SECURITY

This chapter looks at the US Social Security program, including its historical performance, a few words on its projected performance, and some thoughts on cost-of-living adjustments. It looks much like the chapter on health care because Social Security and health care are handled much the same way at the federal level.

17.1 BACKGROUND

Congress established trust funds in the US Treasury to account for Social Security income and disbursements. Social Security taxes and other income are credited to the funds. There are two trust funds for Social Security: the Old-Age and Survivors Insurance (OASI) Trust Fund pays retirement and survivors benefits; and the Disability Insurance (DI) Trust Fund pays disability benefits. The two trust funds often are considered on a combined basis designated OASDI.

17.2 HISTORICAL PERFORMANCE

Figure 17-1 shows Social Security receipts and expenditures for the period 1989 through 2010. Figure 17-2 shows net Social Security receipts (receipts minus expenditures), and figure 17-3 shows the level of the Social Security trust funds over the period 1989 through 2010.

The same critique applies to the Social Security trust funds as applied to the Medicare trust funds. Even though the Social Security trust funds were nominally valued at $2.6 trillion in 2010, they hold only US Treasury securities with no intrinsic value. If the trust funds were to be used to finance Social Security benefit payments, the securities would have to be redeemed for cash from the Treasury, which in turn would come directly from tax dollars or newly printed money, or indirectly from the sale of additional securities.

17.3 PROJECTED PERFORMANCE

If you wish to see where Social Security might be headed, read *The 2011 Annual Social Security and Medicare Trust Fund Reports*, which present the current and projected financial status of the trust funds and can be found at the web address http://www.ssa.gov/oact/TRSUM/index.html.

As with the health care projections, keep in mind that the projections are educated guesswork that is totally dependent on the assumptions used. The assumptions may be (in the most charitable interpretation) influenced by political factors, so the resulting projections may be as well. If you accept the possibility that these projections might be the most optimistic imaginable, they are even more sobering. (See the note in section 16.2.2.)

Figure 17-1: Social Security Receipts and Expenditures, 1989-2010

	1989	1990	1991	1992	1993	1994	1995	1996	1997	1998	1999	2000	2001	2002	2003	2004	2005	2006	2007	2008	2009	2010
Expenditures (billion $)	236	253	274	292	309	323	340	354	369	382	393	415	439	462	479	502	530	555	595	625	686	713
Receipts (billion $)	289	315	330	343	356	381	399	424	458	489	527	568	602	627	632	658	702	745	785	805	807	781

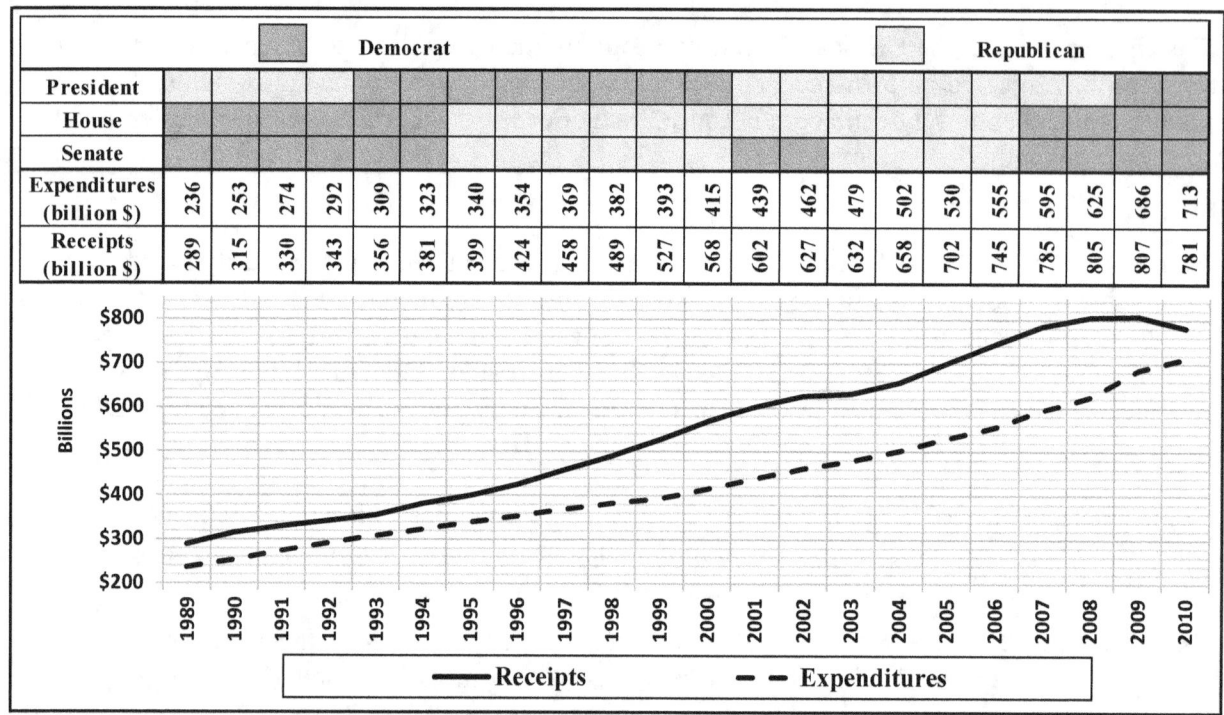

Source: http://www.ssa.gov/oact/STATS/table4a3.html

Figure 17-2: Social Security Net Receipts, 1989-2010

	1989	1990	1991	1992	1993	1994	1995	1996	1997	1998	1999	2000	2001	2002	2003	2004	2005	2006	2007	2008	2009	2010
Net Receipts (billion $)	53	62	55	51	47	58	60	71	89	107	134	153	163	165	153	156	172	189	190	180	122	69

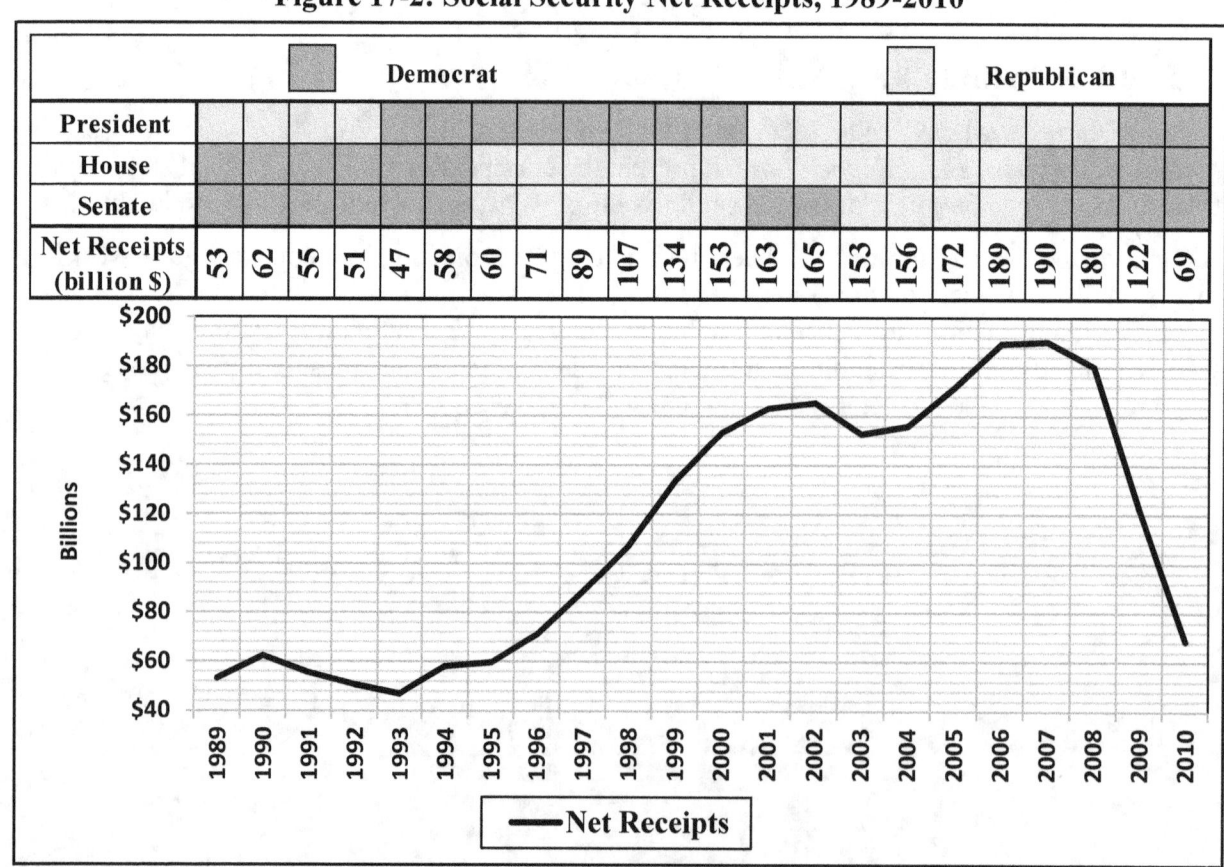

Source: http://www.ssa.gov/oact/STATS/table4a3.html

Figure 17-3: Social Security Trust Fund, 1989-2010

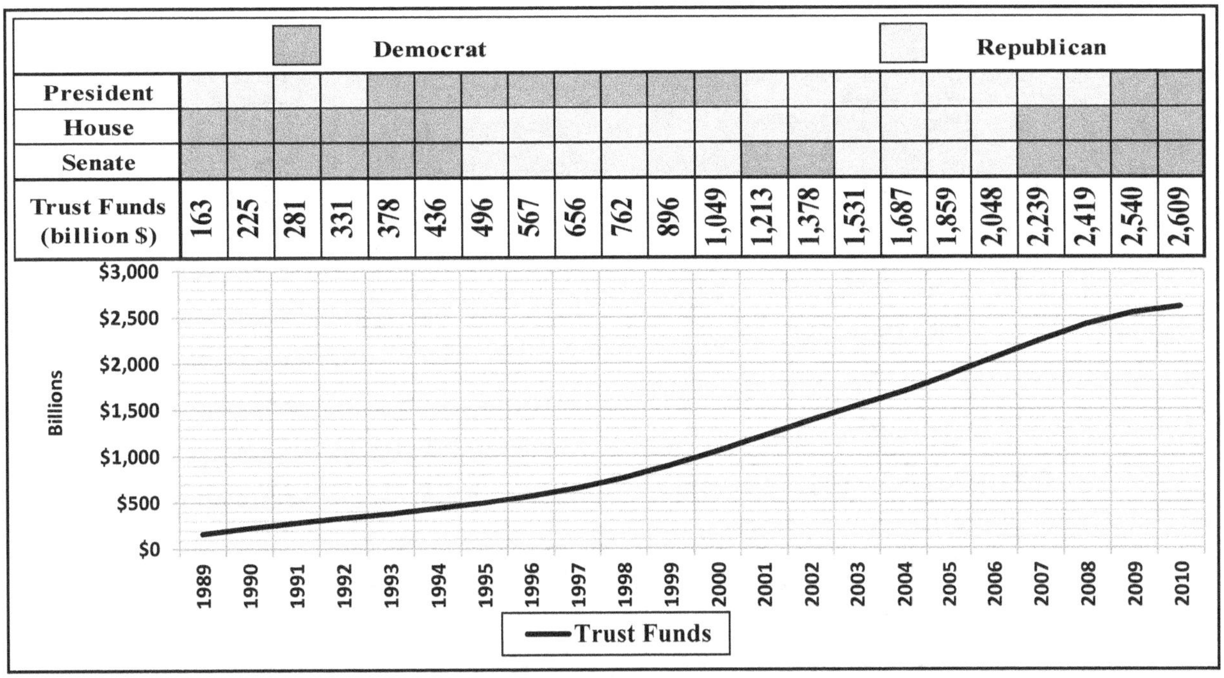

| Trust Funds (billion $) | 163 | 225 | 281 | 331 | 378 | 436 | 496 | 567 | 656 | 762 | 896 | 1,049 | 1,213 | 1,378 | 1,531 | 1,687 | 1,859 | 2,048 | 2,239 | 2,419 | 2,540 | 2,609 |

Rows shown: President, House, Senate (shaded Democrat/Republican), Trust Funds (billion $).

Years: 1989, 1990, 1991, 1992, 1993, 1994, 1995, 1996, 1997, 1998, 1999, 2000, 2001, 2002, 2003, 2004, 2005, 2006, 2007, 2008, 2009, 2010

Legend: ▢ Democrat   ▢ Republican

Chart (Billions): Trust Funds

Source: http://www.ssa.gov/oact/STATS/table4a3.html

17.4 COST OF LIVING ADJUSTMENTS (COLAS)

Cost of living adjustments (COLAs) are of keen interest to voters, particularly those who are on Social Security or some other federal pension. Those benefits are inflation adjusted. That is to say, as the cost of living goes up, benefits are adjusted accordingly. Table 17-1 shows how COLAs were determined over the period 1989 through 2011 (base periods in earlier periods may be different from those shown).

A COLA change is being discussed in Congress as a cost-cutting measure for the Social Security program. The change would see the consumer price index (CPI-W) currently used to calculate the COLA change to the BEA's chained index, which historically is lower than CPI-W. The effect would be to reduce COLAs for all Social Security recipients, federal retirees, and military retirees, among others.

Table 17-1: Cost-of-Living Adjustment (COLA) Determination, 1989-2011

Year	CPI-W Jul	CPI-W Aug	CPI-W Sep	CY Q3 AVG	CY Q3 % Chg
1989	123.2	123.2	123.6	123.3	4.7%
1990	128.7	129.9	131.1	129.9	5.3%
1991	134.3	134.6	135.2	134.7	3.7%
1992	138.4	138.8	139.1	138.8	3.0%
1993	142.1	142.4	142.6	142.4	2.6%
1994	145.8	146.5	146.9	146.4	2.8%
1995	149.9	150.2	150.6	150.2	2.6%
1996	154.3	154.5	155.1	154.6	2.9%
1997	157.5	157.8	158.3	157.9	2.1%
1998	159.8	160.0	160.2	160.0	1.4%
1999	163.3	163.8	164.7	163.9	2.5%
2000	169.4	169.3	170.4	169.7	3.5%
2001	173.8	173.8	174.8	174.1	2.6%
2002	176.1	176.6	177.0	176.6	1.4%
2003	179.6	180.3	181.0	180.3	2.1%
2004	184.9	185.0	185.4	185.1	2.7%
2005	191.0	192.1	195.0	192.7	4.1%
2006	199.2	199.6	198.4	199.1	3.3%
2007	203.7	203.2	203.9	203.6	2.3%
2008	216.3	215.2	214.9	215.5	5.8%
2009	210.5	211.2	211.3	211.0	--
2010	213.9	214.2	214.3	214.1	--
2011	222.7	223.3	223.7	223.2	3.6%

Source: http://www.ssa.gov/oact/STATS/cpiw.html

18. MILITARY SPENDING

Military spending always is an issue in presidential elections. After any period of conflict, there is talk of a "peace dividend" resulting from a reduction in military spending. The 2012 election promises to focus on how much can be cut from military spending as a result of our troops being withdrawn from Iraq and Afghanistan, with major cuts already having been proposed by the administration.

Figure 18-1 shows the annual level of US military spending from 1989 through 2011. The number for 2011 is a preliminary annual one, based on spending as of the end of the third quarter.

Figure 18-1: Military Spending, 1989-2011

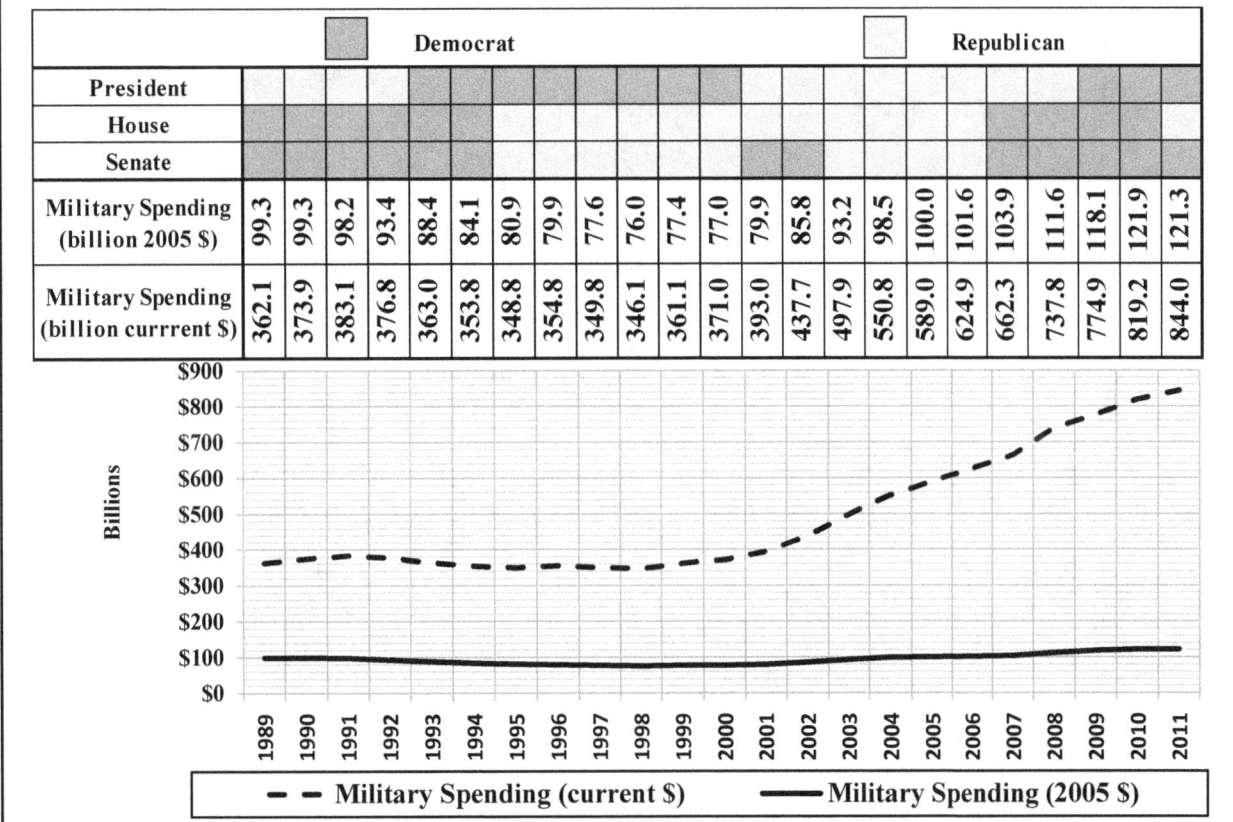

Source: Bureau of Economic Analysis, http://www.bea.gov/iTable/iTable.cfm?ReqID=9&step=1

Figure 18-2 shows US military spending as a percentage of GDP for the period 1989 through 2011.

Figure 18-3 shows US military spending as a percentage of total federal spending for the period 1989 through 2010.

Figure 18-2: Military Spending as a Percentage of GDP, 1989-2011

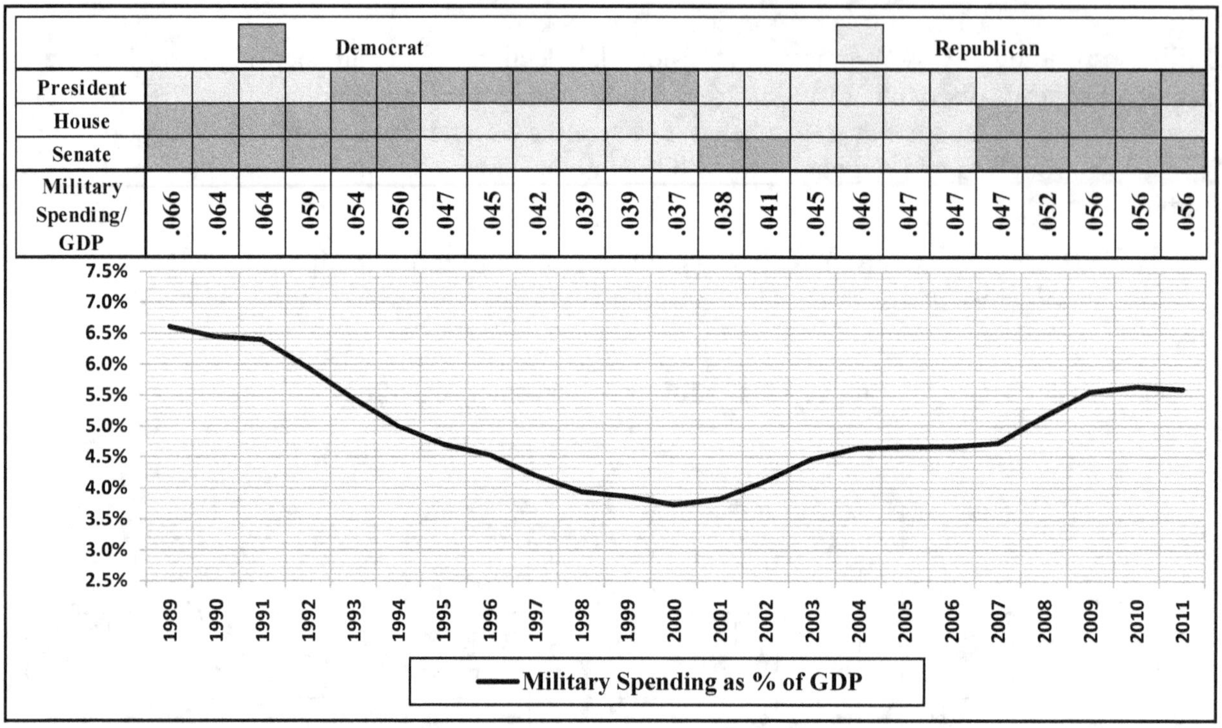

Democrat
Republican
President
House
Senate
Military Spending/ GDP
.066 .064 .064 .059 .054 .050 .047 .045 .042 .039 .039 .037 .038 .041 .045 .046 .047 .047 .047 .052 .056 .056 .056
7.5% 7.0% 6.5% 6.0% 5.5% 5.0% 4.5% 4.0% 3.5% 3.0% 2.5%
1989 1990 1991 1992 1993 1994 1995 1996 1997 1998 1999 2000 2001 2002 2003 2004 2005 2006 2007 2008 2009 2010 2011
Military Spending as % of GDP

Source: calculated from figure 18-1 and figure 7-1

Figure 18-3: Military Spending as a Percentage of Federal Spending, 1989-2010

Democrat
Republican
President
House
Senate
Military/ Federal Spending
.299 .286 .281 .253 .237 .226 .214 .209 .202 .197 .197 .195 .195 .202 .214 .223 .221 .223 .221 .224 .209 .210
35.0% 30.0% 25.0% 20.0% 15.0%
1989 1990 1991 1992 1993 1994 1995 1996 1997 1998 1999 2000 2001 2002 2003 2004 2005 2006 2007 2008 2009 2010
Military Spending as % of Total Federal Spending

Source: calculated from figure 18-1 and figure 14-3

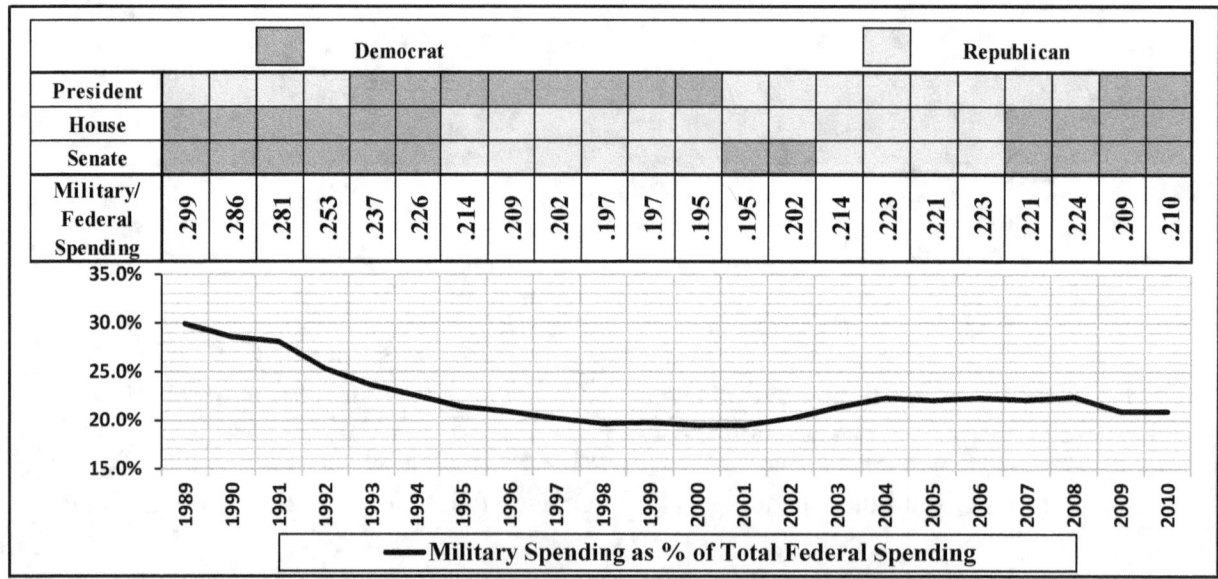

19. FEDERAL REGULATION

Federal regulation is another issue in the 2012 presidential campaign. While the intentions of the regulators may be good and the benefits substantial, there are substantial costs associated with regulation. The government spends money to write the regulations and to implement and enforce them, and the regulations impose costs on individuals and businesses. How big an impact do federal regulations have on the economy? Let's first look at how many regulations there are, then at how much they cost.

19.1 SCOPE

The *Federal Register* is the official daily publication for rules, proposed rules, and notices of federal agencies and organizations, as well as executive orders and other presidential documents. The first issue of the *Federal Register* was published on March 14, 1936. It contained sixteen pages and was a response to an urgent need for an authoritative source of federal rules and regulations. Since its establishment, it has matured technically and expanded in size as the scope of federal regulation has grown.

Below are a few statistics on the *Federal Register*:

- The largest annual edition of the *Federal Register* was published in 2008 and contained 79,435 pages.

- In 2008 the *Federal Register* published a total of 31,879 documents: rules, proposed rules, presidential documents, and notices.

- During fiscal year 2009, over 225 million *Federal Register* documents were downloaded by the public.

Figure 19-1 shows the number of pages that are devoted to federal rules and proposed rules each year from 1989 through 2010.

19.2 COST

The impact of federal regulations is difficult to quantify, and ascribing costs to them is nearly impossible. Nonetheless, Congress passed the Regulatory-Right-to-Know Act in 2001 that requires the Office of Management and Budget to report each year to Congress on the effects of federal rules and paperwork. OMB does so annually in its *Report to Congress on the Benefits and Costs of Federal Regulations*.

19.2.1 OMB Cost Estimates

The OMB report to Congress summarizes estimates by federal regulatory agencies of the quantified and monetized benefits and costs of major federal regulations. What constitutes a major rule is not defined in the 2001 act, but for purposes of its report OMB defines a major rule, among other things, to be a rule that is likely to result in:

- An annual effect on the economy of $100,000,000 or more;

- A major increase in costs or prices for consumers, individual industries, federal, state, or local government agencies, or geographic regions; or

- Significant adverse effects on competition, employment, investment, productivity, innovation, or on the ability of US-based enterprises to compete with foreign-based enterprises in domestic and export markets.

Figure 19-1: *Federal Register* Pages of Rules and Proposed Rules, 1989-2010

Year	Pages of Proposed Rules	Pages of Rules
1989	13,220	16,489
1990	12,692	14,179
1991	16,761	16,792
1992	15,156	15,921
1993	15,410	18,016
1994	18,183	20,385
1995	15,982	18,047
1996	15,369	21,622
1997	15,309	18,984
1998	18,256	20,029
1999	19,447	20,201
2000	17,943	24,482
2001	14,666	19,643
2002	18,640	19,233
2003	17,357	22,670
2004	19,332	22,546
2005	18,260	23,041
2006	19,794	22,347
2007	18,611	22,771
2008	18,648	26,320
2009	16,681	20,782
2010	21,844	24,914

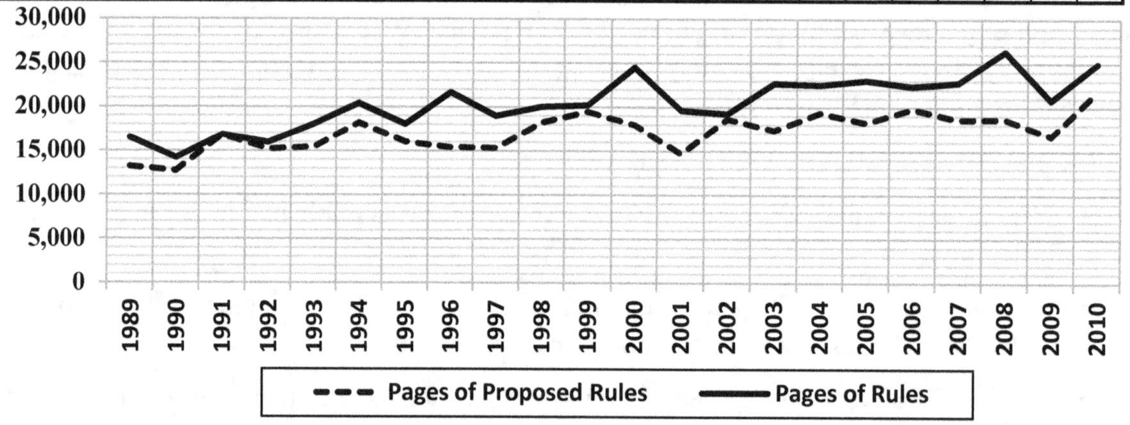

Source: www.federalregister.gov/.../07/OFR-STATISTICS-CHARTS-ALL.xls

OMB applies additional criteria from a variety of acts and executive orders, but the most significant criterion is the $100 million threshold.

Federal agencies published over 38,000 final rules in the *Federal Register* during the period 2001 through 2010. Of this number, OMB reviewed 3,325, and of this number, 540 were considered major rules.

Figure 19-2 is a compilation of costs of major rules added each year over the period 1989 through 2010. The figure also includes the cumulative cost effect of all rules over moving ten-year periods from 2001 through 2010.

OMB is very forthcoming about the shortcomings of its regulatory cost assessments. They acknowledge that the total cost of all Federal rules now in effect is likely to be significantly larger than reported (e.g., perhaps as much as ten times larger in 2005).

19.2.2 Non-OMB Cost Estimates

In spite of Congressional efforts to get a better handle on the compliance costs of federal regulations, the OMB estimates leave much to be desired. Since data from primary sources are not readily available, I refer you to *The Impact of Regulatory Costs on Small Firms* by Nicole V. Crain and W. Mark Crain of Lafayette College, Easton, PA. This study was done under contract

Figure 19-2: Annual and Cumulative Costs of Regulation, 1989-2010

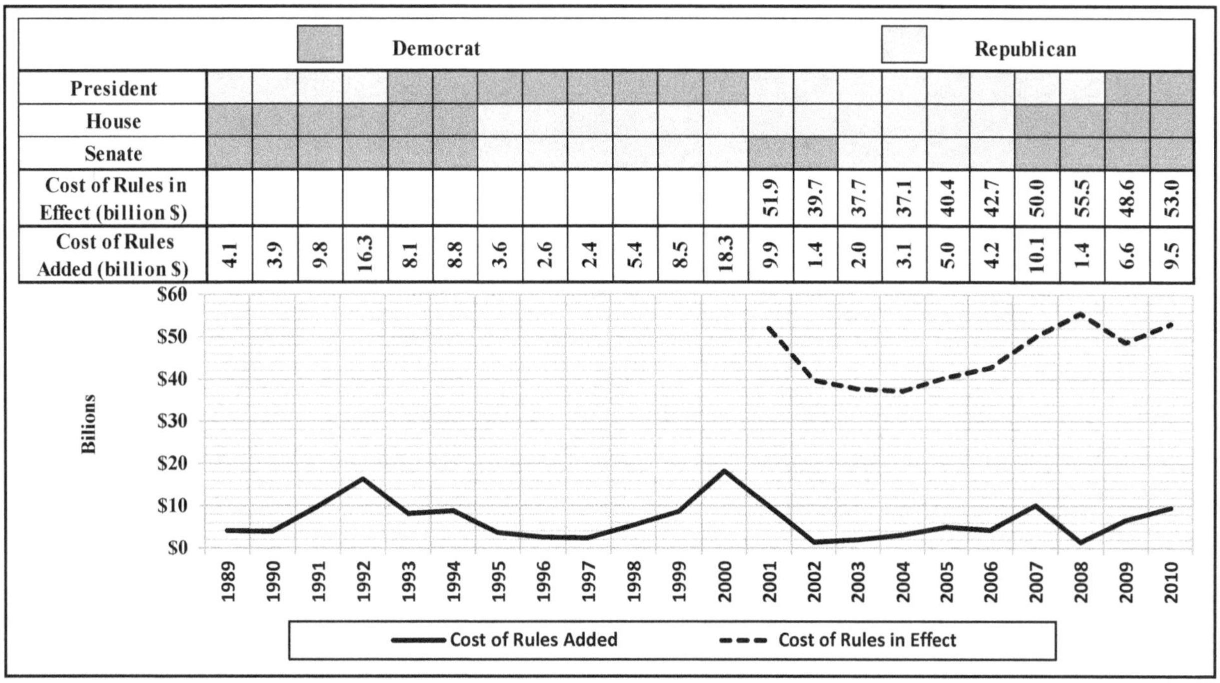

	Democrat												Republican									
President																						
House																						
Senate																						
Cost of Rules in Effect (billion $)													51.9	39.7	37.7	37.1	40.4	42.7	50.0	55.5	48.6	53.0
Cost of Rules Added (billion $)	4.1	3.9	9.8	16.3	8.1	8.8	3.6	2.6	2.4	5.4	8.5	18.3	9.9	1.4	2.0	3.1	5.0	4.2	10.1	1.4	6.6	9.5

Source: http://www.whitehouse.gov/omb/inforeg_regpol_reports_congress

to the Small Business Administration's Office of Advocacy. It was first released in September 2005, then updated and re-released in September 2010.

- OMB estimated the annual 2008 cost to businesses and individuals of major federal regulations to be in the range of $51 billion to $60 billion in 2001 dollars, or $62 billion to $73 billion in 2009 dollars. The Crain report estimates the 2008 cost of major federal regulations to be $1.75 trillion, an amount equal to 14 percent of US national income.

- The Crain report estimates that in 2004 the comparable cost of major federal regulations was $1.26 trillion based on a 2005 version of this report. If the 2005 figures were adjusted for changes in the estimating methodology, the 2005 costs would have been $1.7 trillion, suggesting a $43 billion or three percent increase between 2004 and 2008 (having adjusted for inflation).

The Crain report has a great deal of additional information on regulatory and tax compliance costs and the impact of those costs on different types of taxpayers. In deference to the Crains' extensive work, I refer you to the report for further information (http://archive.sba.gov/advo/research/rs371tot.pdf).

20. THE TRUE COST OF FEDERAL GOVERNANCE

In previous chapters of this section we looked at federal spending. In a couple of places we looked at costs of federal governance that were not reflected in the spending numbers. This is a summary chapter, in which I'm going to bring together all the numbers presented thus far that constitute costs of federal governance to US citizens and business. I've chosen 2010 as the year I will use, but recognize that some of the data were not available for 2010, so I used the most recent data available. If anything, this approach will understate the bottom line.

Here are the components of the true cost of federal governance:

- **Federal expenditures:** everything spent by the federal government in 2010, as reported by the Bureau of Economic Analysis.

- **Other factors:** the federal spending in 2010 that is reflected in changes in federal debt, but not in federal spending.

- **Regulatory costs:** the economic costs to businesses and individuals of complying with federal regulations. The government doesn't reliably collect these numbers, so I've used a privately developed number from 2008. You can be sure this number did not go down in 2010.

- **Tax compliance costs:** the value of the time spent by businesses and individuals filing income tax returns. Once again, the government doesn't reliably collect these numbers, so I've used a privately developed number for 2005. You can be sure this number did not go down in 2010.

Table 20-1 summarizes the total cost of federal governance in 2010. One can argue that if one includes regulatory cost and tax compliance costs, one should adjust GDP for their effects. I'll leave that to others. The point here is that individuals and business did not spend just 26.9 percent of GDP to support the federal government and all its programs, they spent closer to 42.1 percent of GDP as currently measured.

Table 20-1: True Cost of Federal Governance

Cost	Data Year	Reference	Trillions	% of 2010 GDP
Total Federal Expenditures	2010	Figure 14-3	$ 3.91	26.9%
Other Factors	2010	Figure 15-5	$ 0.19	1.3%
Federal Regulatory Costs	2008	Section 19.2.1	$ 1.75	12.1%
Federal Tax Compliance Costs	2005	Section 12.4.2	$ 0.27	1.8%
Total			$ 6.11	42.1%

PART 4.   INTERNATIONAL TOPICS

Immigration, and especially illegal immigration, is another hot-button issue in the upcoming presidential election.

21.1 LEGAL IMMIGRATION

The US often is described as a nation of immigrants, and statistics on legal immigration into the US are readily available. Figure 21-1 shows the level of legal immigration into the US during the period 1989 through 2010, and table 21-1 shows the countries of origin of legal immigrants in 2010.

Figure 21-1: Legal Immigration, 1989-2010

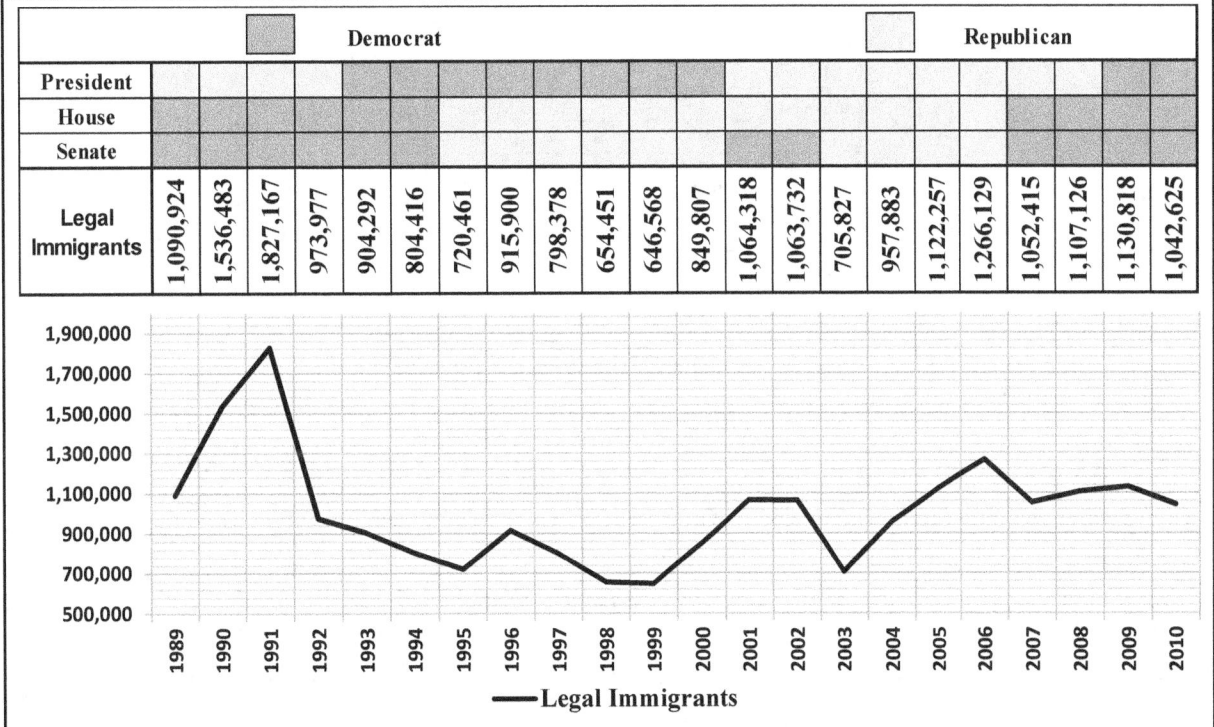

Source: http://www.dhs.gov/files/statistics/publications/yearbook.shtm

21.2 ILLEGAL IMMIGRATION

Unlike statistics on legal immigration, statistics on illegal immigration are hard to find. The Department of Homeland Security (DHS) has attempted to estimate the number of illegal immigrants in the US, but their series only goes back to 2005. Prior to that time, estimates were provided by the Immigration and Naturalization Service (INS), but only for the period 1990 through 2000. Since INS was subsumed by DHS, the methodology to produce all the estimates is similar. Basically, illegal immigrants are those left after subtracting registered legal immigrants from the total immigrant population as determined by the Census Bureau.

Note that the DHS uses the more politically correct phrase "unauthorized immigrant population" for the more accurate phrase "illegal immigrants."

Figure 21-2 shows the number of illegals in the US for selected years (those for which data are available) over the period 1990 through 2010.

Table 21-1: Legal Immigration by Country of Origin, 2010

Country	No. of Immigrants	% of Total
Mexico	3,290,000	26.0%
Philippines	560,000	4.4%
China, People's Republic	550,000	4.4%
India	500,000	4.0%
Dominican Republic	440,000	3.5%
Cuba	370,000	2.9%
Canada	330,000	2.6%
El Salvador	320,000	2.5%
Vietnam	310,000	2.5%
United Kingdom	290,000	2.3%
Korea, South	270,000	2.1%
Haiti	240,000	1.9%
Colombia	230,000	1.8%
Jamaica	230,000	1.8%
Germany	180,000	1.4%
Guatemala	180,000	1.4%
Poland	150,000	1.2%
Japan	140,000	1.1%
Peru	140,000	1.1%
Pakistan	130,000	1.0%
Other	3,790,000	30.0%
Total	12,630,000	100%

Source: http://www.dhs.gov/xlibrary/assets/statistics/publications/ois_lpr_pe_2010.pdf

Figure 21-2: Number of Illegal Immigrants in the US, Selected Years 1990-2010

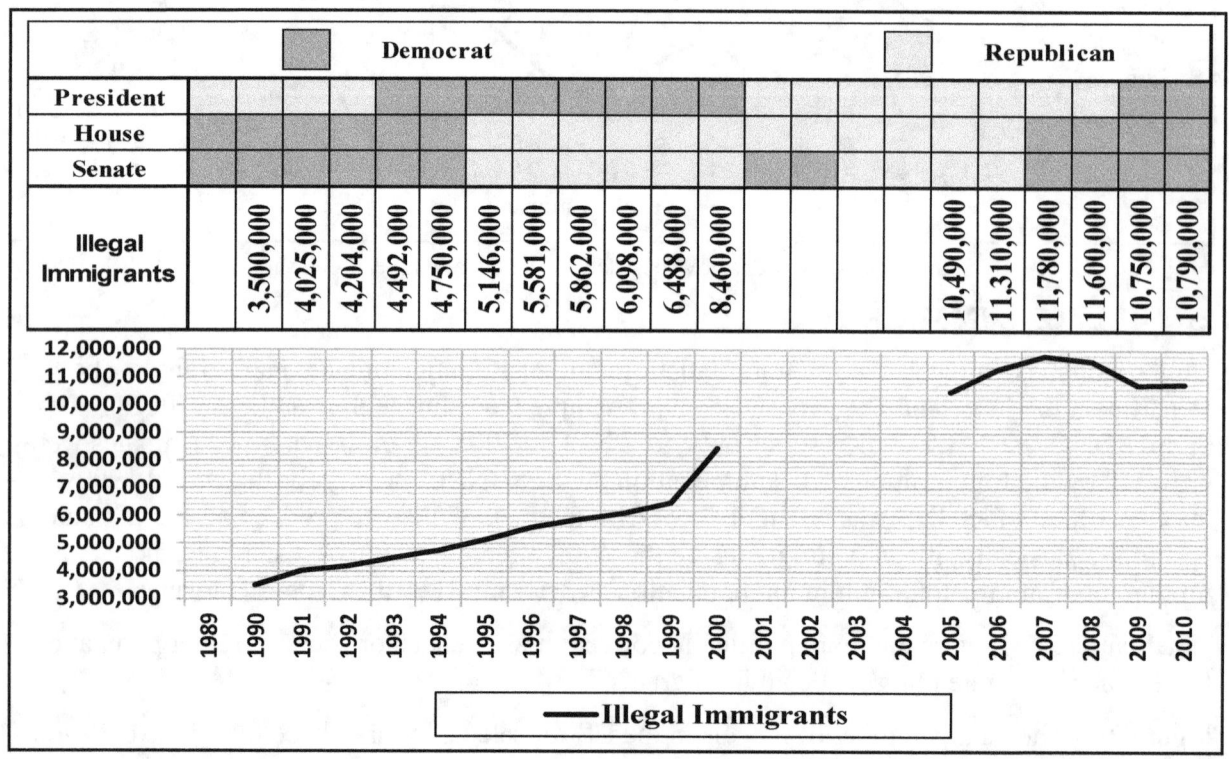

Source: http://www.dhs.gov/xlibrary/assets/statistics/publications/ois_ill_pe_2010.pdf

Table 21-2 shows for 2010 the countries from which most of the illegal immigrants in the US came, and the percentage of total illegal immigrants from each of those countries.

Table 21-2: Illegal Immigrants by Country of Origin, 2010

Country	Illegals	% of Total
Mexico	6,640,000	61.5%
El Salvador	620,000	5.7%
Guatemala	520,000	4.8%
Honduras	330,000	3.1%
Philippines	280,000	2.6%
India	200,000	1.9%
Ecuador	180,000	1.7%
Brazil	180,000	1.7%
Korea	170,000	1.6%
China	130,000	1.2%
Other countries	1,550,000	14.4%
Total	10,790,000	100.0%

Source: http://www.dhs.gov/xlibrary/assets/statistics/publications/ois_ill_pe_2010.pdf

International trade is defined as the exchange of goods and services among countries. As we've seen in previous chapters, nothing is ever that simple. In the US International Transactions Accounts Data of the Bureau of Economic Analysis, US trade is divided into three major accounts: the current account, the capital account, and the financial account. (The definitions in this chapter are excerpted from *Survey of Current Business, A Guide to the US International Transactions Accounts and the US International Investment Position Accounts*, February 2010, by Christopher L. Bach).

Please note that the accounts are constructed in such a way that the balance of international transactions for a given country in a specified period always is zero. That is to say, at the highest level, international trade must balance. One may have a surplus or deficit in the current account, or in goods and services, but overall, the accounts must balance to zero. (See section 22-4, Statistical Discrepancy for more information on this topic.)

Figure 22-1 shows the current, capital, and financial US international trade accounts over the period 1989 through 2010.

Figure 22-1: International Trade by Major Account, 1989-2010

Year	1989	1990	1991	1992	1993	1994	1995	1996	1997	1998	1999	2000	2001	2002	2003	2004	2005	2006	2007	2008	2009	2010
Financial Account (million $)	47,394	58,123	43,833	93,939	79,206	124,237	82,838	134,476	218,977	66,965	238,148	477,701	400,254	500,515	532,879	532,331	700,716	809,150	617,260	730,568	245,919	254,289
Capital Account (million $)	-207	-7,220	-5,130	1,449	-714	-1,111	-222	-7	-256	-8	-4,176	-1	13,198	-141	-1,821	3,049	13,116	-1,788	384	6,010	-140	-152
Current Account (million $)	-99,486	-78,969	2,898	-51,614	-84,806	-121,612	-113,567	-124,764	-140,726	-215,062	-301,656	-416,339	-396,603	-457,247	-519,089	-628,518	-745,774	-800,621	-710,304	-677,134	-376,551	-470,898

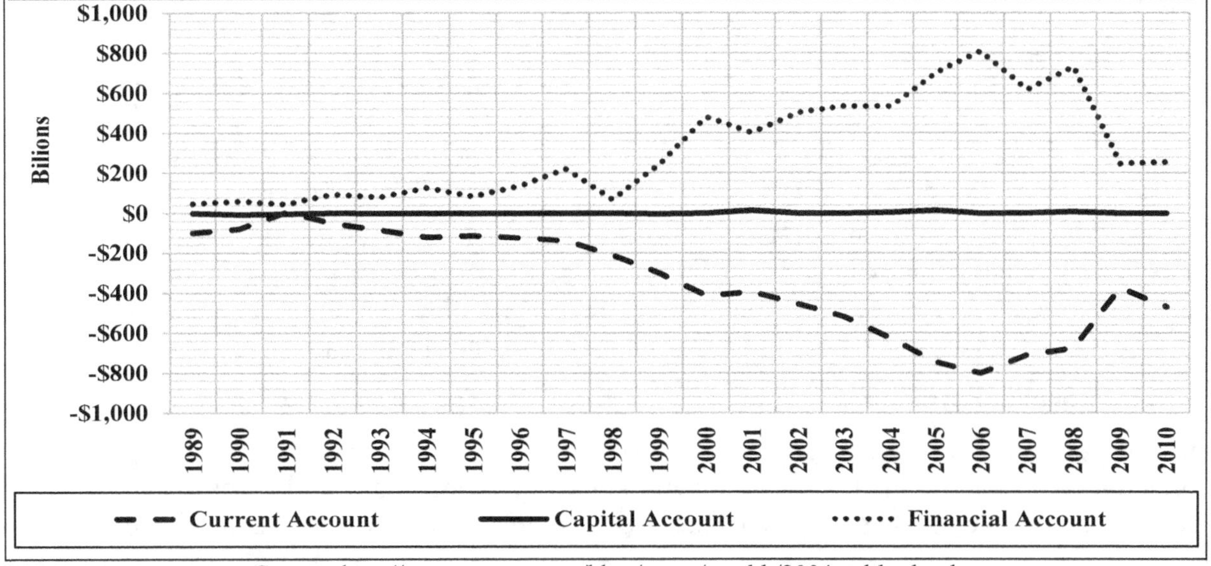

Source: http://www.census.gov/hhes/www/wealth/2004_tables.html

22.1 CURRENT ACCOUNT

The current account of the US international trade accounts records transactions in good, services, income, and net unilateral current transfers between US residents and nonresidents relating to current production.

22.1.1 Goods and Services

Goods are tangible commodities (raw materials, intermediate products, and final products). Services refer to economic output that is intangible and generally produced and consumed at the same time.

Figure 22-2 shows US imports and exports of goods and services over the period 1989 through 2010.

Figure 22-2: Imports and Exports of Goods and Services, 1989-2010

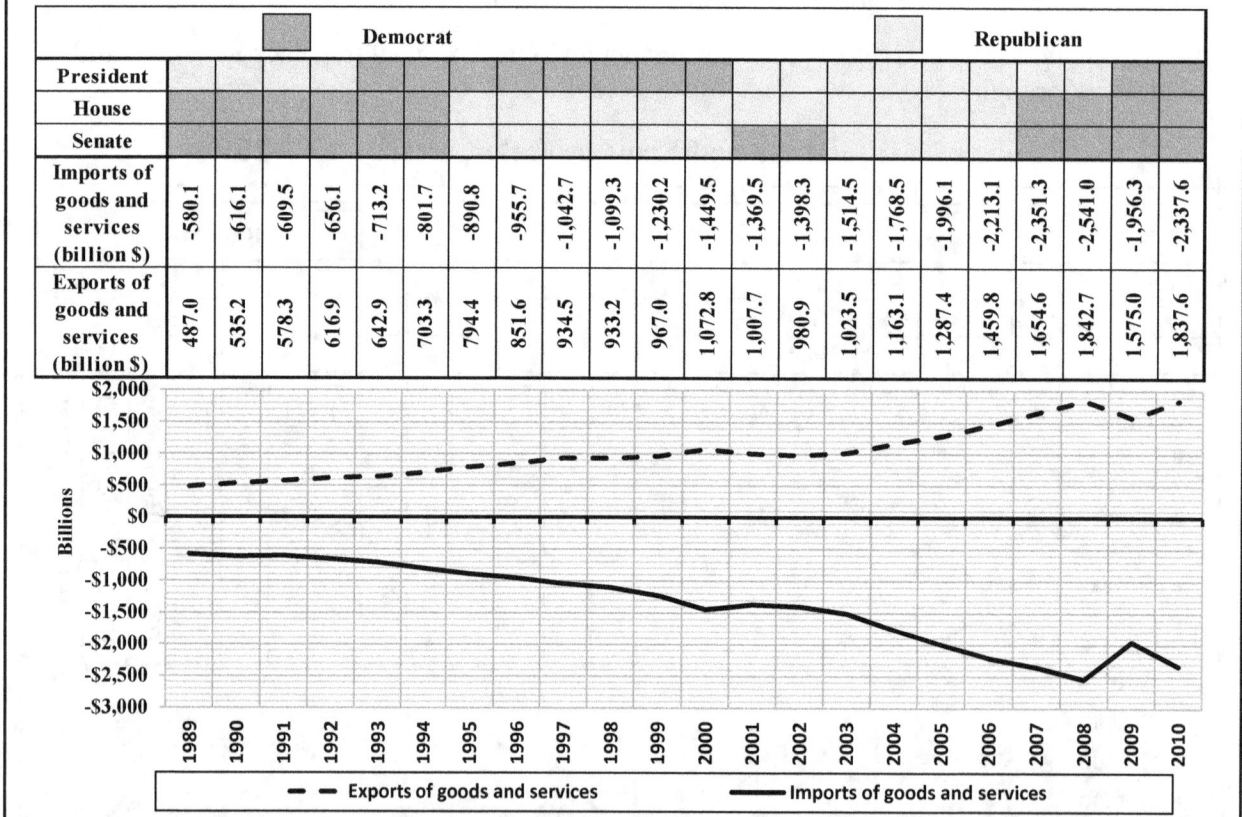

	Democrat																			Republican		
President																						
House																						
Senate																						
Imports of goods and services (billion $)	-580.1	-616.1	-609.5	-656.1	-713.2	-801.7	-890.8	-955.7	-1,042.7	-1,099.3	-1,230.2	-1,449.5	-1,369.5	-1,398.3	-1,514.5	-1,768.5	-1,996.1	-2,213.1	-2,351.3	-2,541.0	-1,956.3	-2,337.6
Exports of goods and services (billion $)	487.0	535.2	578.3	616.9	642.9	703.3	794.4	851.6	934.5	933.2	967.0	1,072.8	1,007.7	980.9	1,023.5	1,163.1	1,287.4	1,459.8	1,654.6	1,842.7	1,575.0	1,837.6

Source: http://www.census.gov/hhes/www/wealth/2004_tables.html

The difference between the imports and exports of goods and services, that is, the net exports of goods and services, is shown in figure 22-3 for the period 1989 through 2010. Note that net exports of goods and services are negative over the entire period, which means we were importing more goods and services than we are exporting the entire time.

22.1.2 Income Payments

Income payments include income receipts on US owned assets abroad, and income payments on foreign-owned assets in the US; and compensation receipts and compensation payments of temporary employees. These payments include direct investment income, other private

---

investment income, US government income, and compensation of employees. Figure 22-4 shows net income payments for the period 1989 through 2010.

Figure 22-3: Net Exports of Goods and Services, 1989-2010

	Democrat																			Republican	
Net Goods and Services (billion $)	-93.1	-80.9	-31.1	-39.2	-70.3	-98.5	-96.4	-104.1	-108.3	-166.1	-263.2	-376.7	-361.8	-417.4	-491.0	-605.4	-708.6	-753.3	-696.7	-698.3	-381.3	-500.0

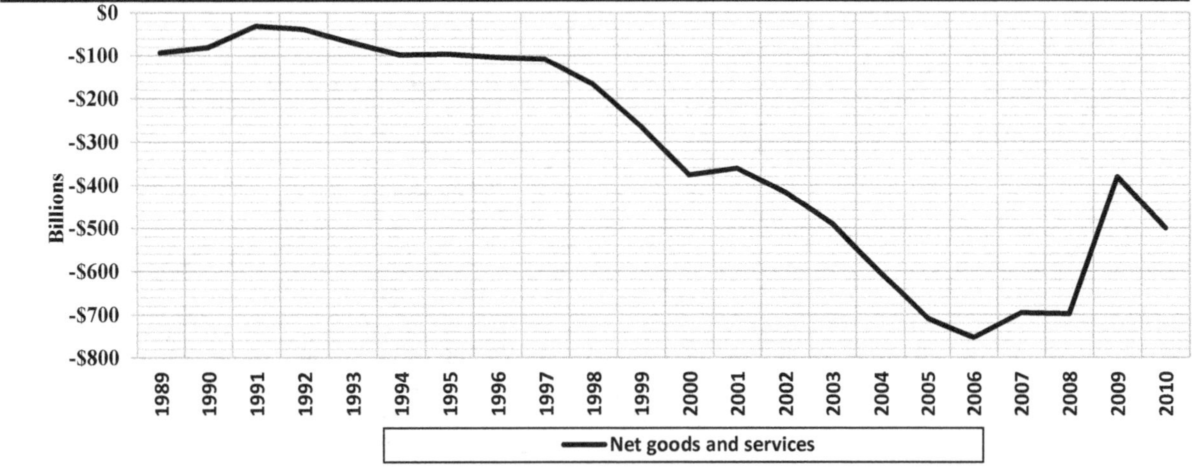

Figure 22-4: Income Payments (Net), 1989-2010

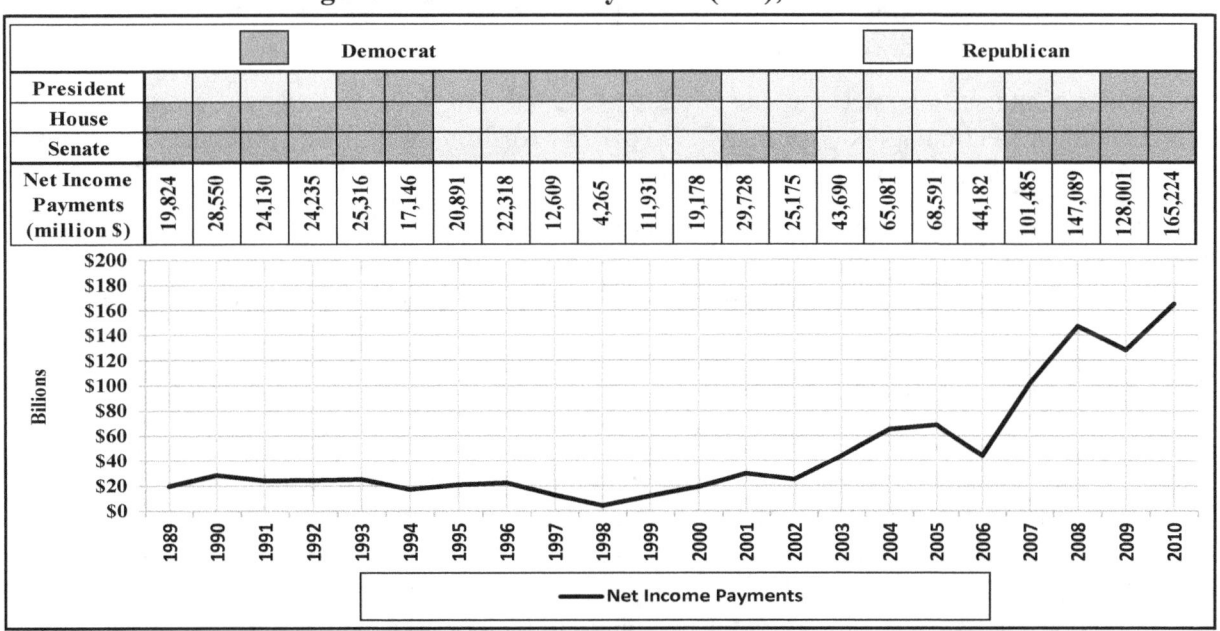

	Democrat																			Republican	
Net Income Payments (million $)	19,824	28,550	24,130	24,235	25,316	17,146	20,891	22,318	12,609	4,265	11,931	19,178	29,728	25,175	43,690	65,081	68,591	44,182	101,485	147,089	128,001	165,224

22.1.3 Unilateral Current Transfers (Net)

Unilateral current transfers are transfers by the US to another country without anything being provided in return. These include US government grants, pensions and other transfers; and private remittances and other transfers. Figure 22-5 shows net unilateral current transfers for the period 1989 through 2010.

Figure 22-5: Unilateral Current Transfers (Net), 1989-2010

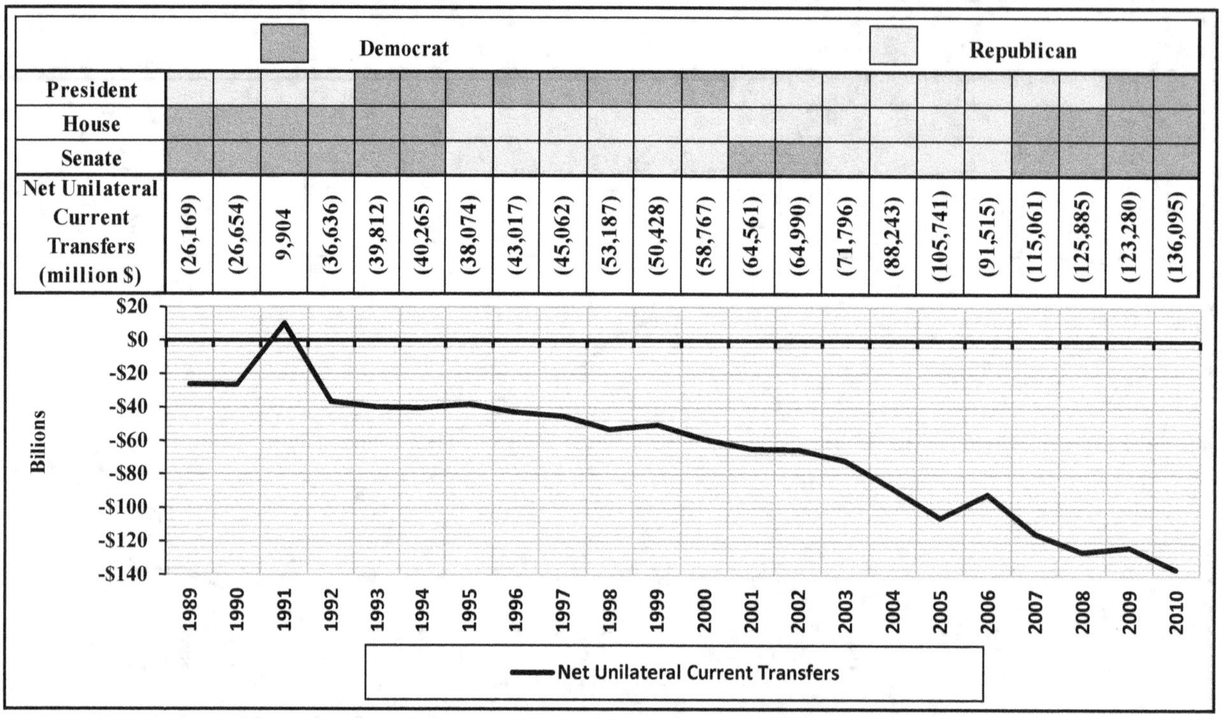
Democrat
Republican
President
House
Senate
Net Unilateral Current Transfers (million $)
(26,169)
(26,654)
9,904
(36,636)
(39,812)
(40,265)
(38,074)
(43,017)
(45,062)
(53,187)
(50,428)
(58,767)
(64,561)
(64,990)
(71,796)
(88,243)
(105,741)
(91,515)
(115,061)
(125,885)
(123,280)
(136,095)
$20
$0
-$20
-$40
-$60
-$80
-$100
-$120
-$140
Bilions
1989
1990
1991
1992
1993
1994
1995
1996
1997
1998
1999
2000
2001
2002
2003
2004
2005
2006
2007
2008
2009
2010
Net Unilateral Current Transfers

Source: http://www.census.gov/hhes/www/wealth/2004_tables.html

22.2 CAPITAL ACCOUNT

Capital account transactions result from changes in the stock of nonproduced nonfinancial assets and from changes in other capital transfers.

Nonproduced nonfincial assets include purchases and sales of rights to tangible assets (e.g. mineral rights, electromagnetic spectrum, and offshore drilling rights), and purchases and sales of intangible assets (e.g. copyrights and trademarks).

Capital transfers include transfers for insurance payments related to catastrophic losses, transfers for debt forgiveness, migrant transfers, taxes on capital transfers, and certain transactions related to the Panama Canal. Figure 22-6 shows net capital account transfers for the period 1989 through 2010.

22.3 FINANCIAL ACCOUNT

The financial accounts measure transactions in financial assets and liabilities between residents and nonresidents. Financial assets may be exchanged for goods, services, or income flows, for other financial assets, or they may be offsets to unilateral transfers. The financial account has three major components: US-owned assets abroad, foreign owned assets in the US, and financial derivatives (net). There is a fourth component, statistical discrepancy, that normally is included in financial accounts, but I will present it separately in the next section. Figure 22-7 shows net financial account transfers for the period 1989 through 2010.

Figure 22-6: Capital Account (Net), 1989-2010

	Democrat															Republican						
President																						
House																						
Senate																						
Net Capital Account (million $)	-207	-7,220	-5,130	1,449	-714	-1,111	-222	-7	-256	-8	-4,176	-1	13,198	-141	-1,821	3,049	13,116	-1,788	384	6,010	-140	-152

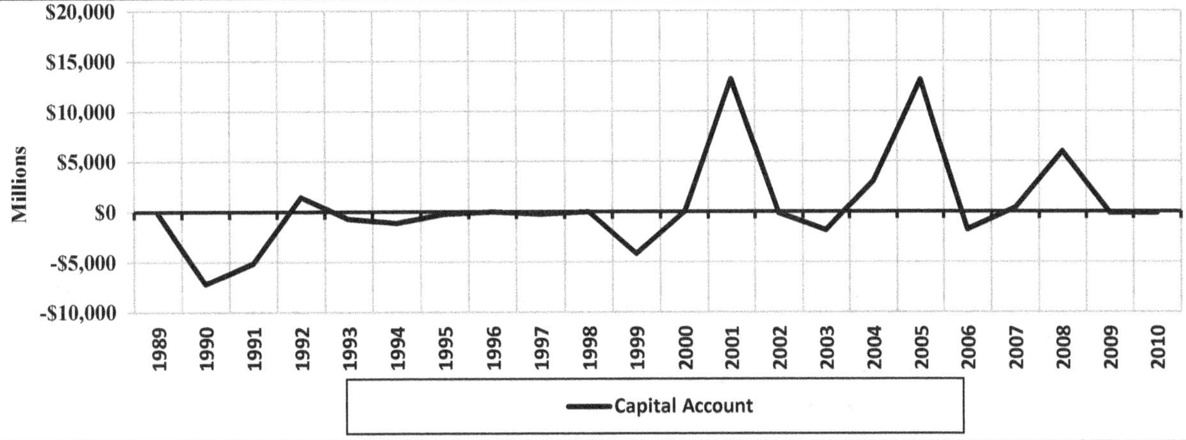

Source: http://www.census.gov/hhes/www/wealth/2004_tables.html

22.3.1 US-Owned Assets Abroad

This category includes US official asset exchanges of monetary gold, International Monetary Fund (IMF) special drawing rights (SDRs), and foreign currencies. It also includes US government credits and other long-term asset transfers arising from foreign assistance programs, repayments of US credits, and US net foreign currency holdings.

US-owned assets abroad also include flows of capital arising from US private assets abroad, but exclude financial derivatives.

22.3.2 Foreign-Owned Assets in the US

This category measures net transactions by foreign monetary authorities and other official foreigners in US government bills, certificates, bonds, and notes, and in stocks and bonds of US corporations, and bonds of state and local governments.

Also included in this category are foreign direct investment and reinvested earnings, privately held US Treasury and other government securities, plus US liabilities to unaffiliated foreigners, and net shipments of currency from US banks to foreign banks for use as a medium of exchange and a store of value.

22.3.3 Financial Derivatives (Net)

This category includes transactions in financial derivatives (forwards, futures, options, swaps, and credit derivatives) that occur in public exchange markets and private over-the-counter markets.

Figure 22-7: Financial Account, 1989-2010

	Democrat																			Republican	
President																					
House																					
Senate																					
Financial Account (billion $)	47.4	58.1	43.8	93.9	79.2	124.2	82.8	134.5	219.0	67.0	238.1	477.7	400.3	500.5	532.9	532.3	700.7	809.2	617.3	730.6	245.9	254.3

Source: http://www.census.gov/hhes/www/wealth/2004_tables.html

22.4 STATISTICAL DISCREPANCY

If all international transactions in a given period were recorded correctly and at the appropriate time, credits would equal debits and the balance of the International Transactions Accounts would be zero. In practice, this perfection is not attainable and an entry called "statistical discrepancy" is made to balance the accounts. The errors being corrected may be in any or all of the other accounts. Figure 22-8 shows statistical discrepancies in the international accounts for the period 1989 through 2010.

Figure 22-8: Statistical Discrepancy in International Accounts, 1989-2010

	Democrat																			Republican	
President																					
House																					
Senate																					
Statistical Discrepancy (billion $)	52.3	28.1	-41.6	-43.8	6.3	-1.5	31.0	-9.7	-78.0	148.1	67.7	-61.4	-16.8	-43.1	-12.0	93.1	31.9	-6.7	92.7	-59.4	130.8	216.8

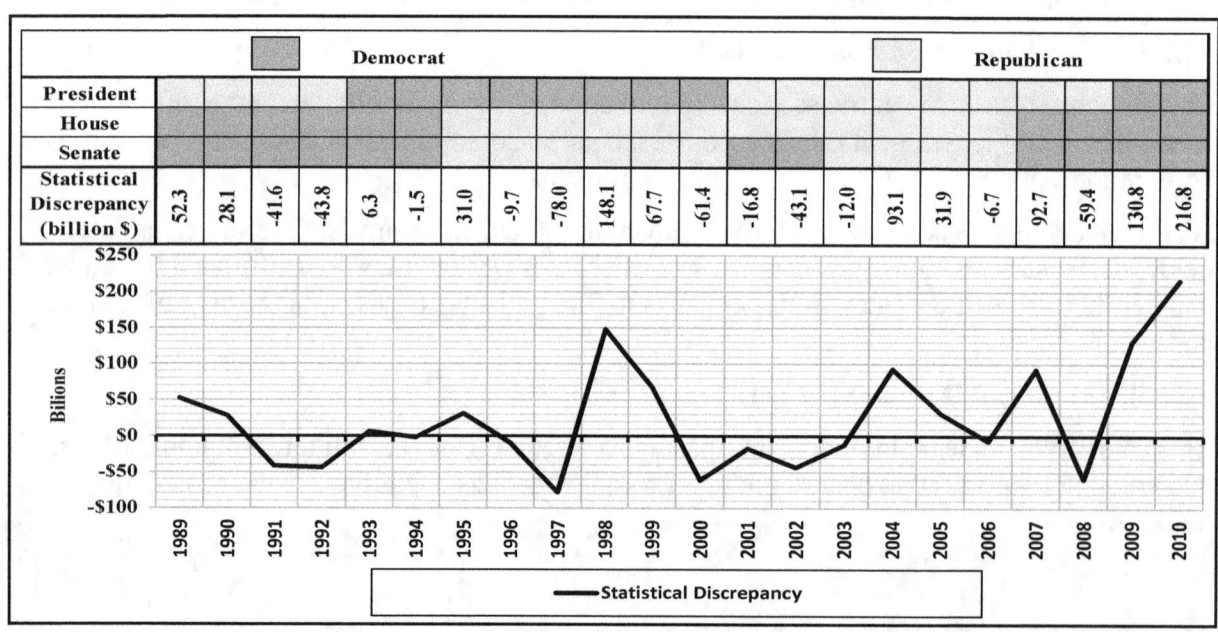

Source: http://www.census.gov/hhes/www/wealth/2004_tables.html

US foreign aid is extensive and diffuse. Many organizations participate, and funds come from numerous budgets. USAID has a central role in most, if not all, of the programs, and it is the source of most of the data in this chapter. USAID groups all foreign aid into 22 civilian and military assistance programs, presenting the data in their *Greenbook*. The *Greenbook* is updated annually, but there is a two-year lag between the present year and the most recent data reported. As a result, the most recent data available are for 2009, and the 2010 data are scheduled for release no earlier than the late fall of 2011. The collection of 2011 data will begin in February 2012 and not be available until the fall of 2012.

We will look at US foreign aid in the aggregate first, then at some of the individual programs, over the period 1989 through 2009. Note that US support to the United Nations (UN) is not considered foreign aid. For more information on the UN, see chapter 24.

23.1 TOTAL AID

Figure 23-1 shows total US foreign aid, which includes both civilian and military assistance, for the period 1989 through 2009. The total amount of US foreign aid reported by USAID for 2009 is $33.9 billion.

Figure 23-1: Foreign Aid (Including Military Assistance), 1989-2009

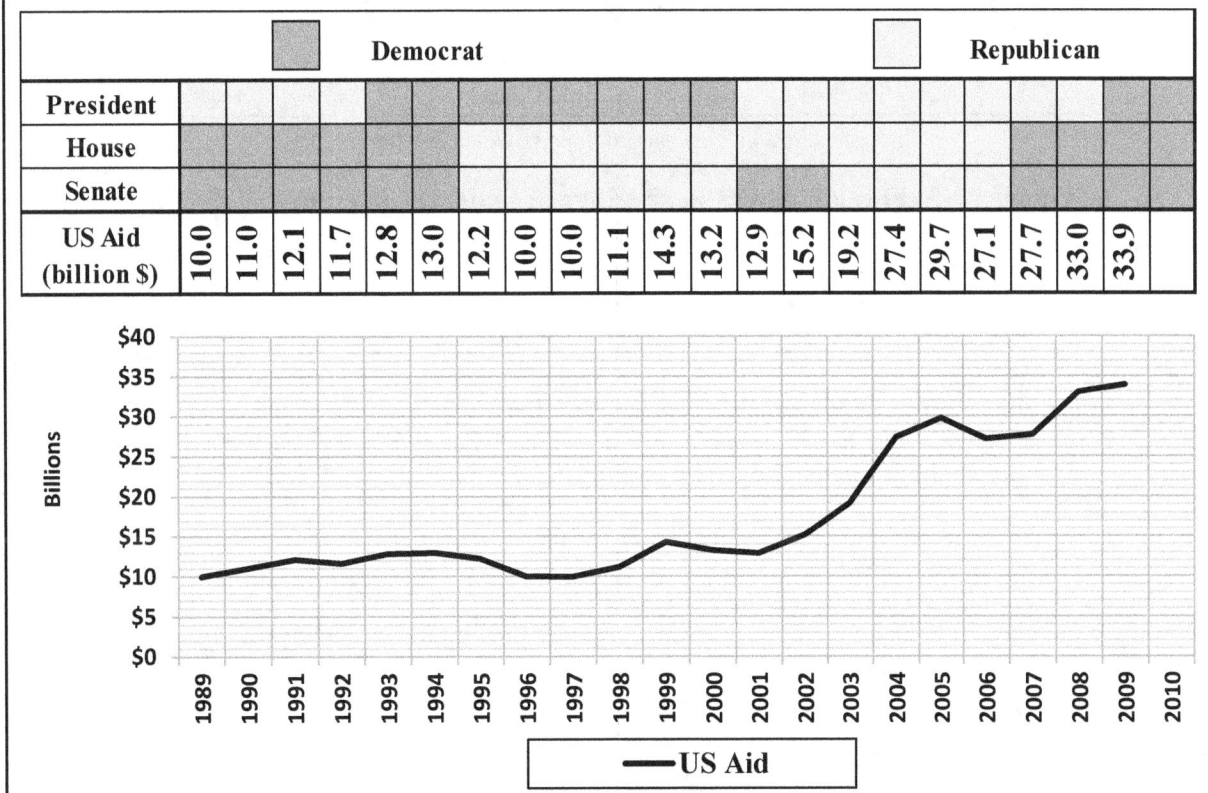

Source: http://gbk.eads.usaidallnet.gov/data/detailed.html

The number $33.9 billion isn't all that informative by itself. For example, if you look at foreign aid as a percentage of GDP, you see that it was 0.24% in 2009. That's right, about one quarter of one percent. Figure 23-2 shows total US foreign aid as a percent of GDP over the period 1989 through 2009.

Another way to look at the $33.9 billion of foreign aid in 2009 is as a percentage of federal spending. It was just under one percent. Figure 23-3 shows total US foreign aid as a percent of federal spending over the period 1989 through 2009.

Figure 23-2: Foreign Aid as Percentage of GDP, 1989-2009

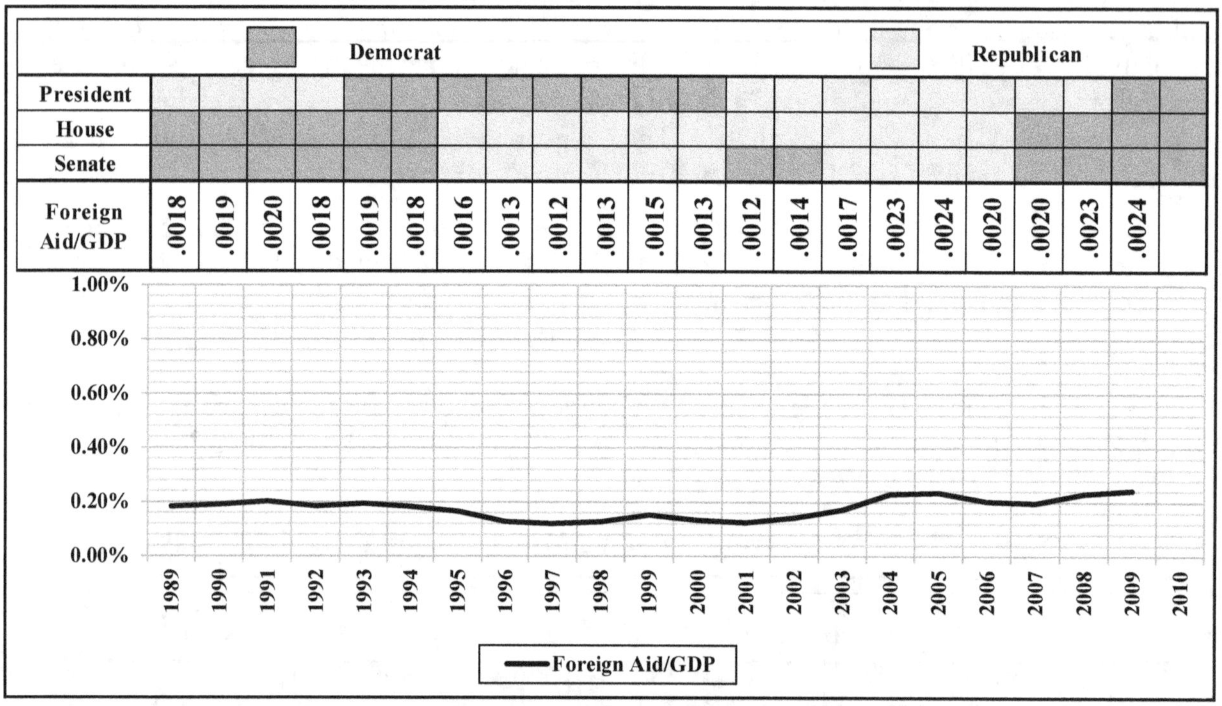

Democrat
Republican
President
House
Senate
Foreign Aid/GDP
.0018 .0019 .0020 .0018 .0019 .0018 .0016 .0013 .0012 .0013 .0015 .0013 .0012 .0014 .0017 .0023 .0024 .0020 .0020 .0023 .0024
1.00%
0.80%
0.60%
0.40%
0.20%
0.00%
1989 1990 1991 1992 1993 1994 1995 1996 1997 1998 1999 2000 2001 2002 2003 2004 2005 2006 2007 2008 2009 2010
Foreign Aid/GDP

Source: http://gbk.eads.usaidallnet.gov/data/detailed.html

Figure 23-3: Foreign Aid as Percentage of Federal Spending, 1989-2009

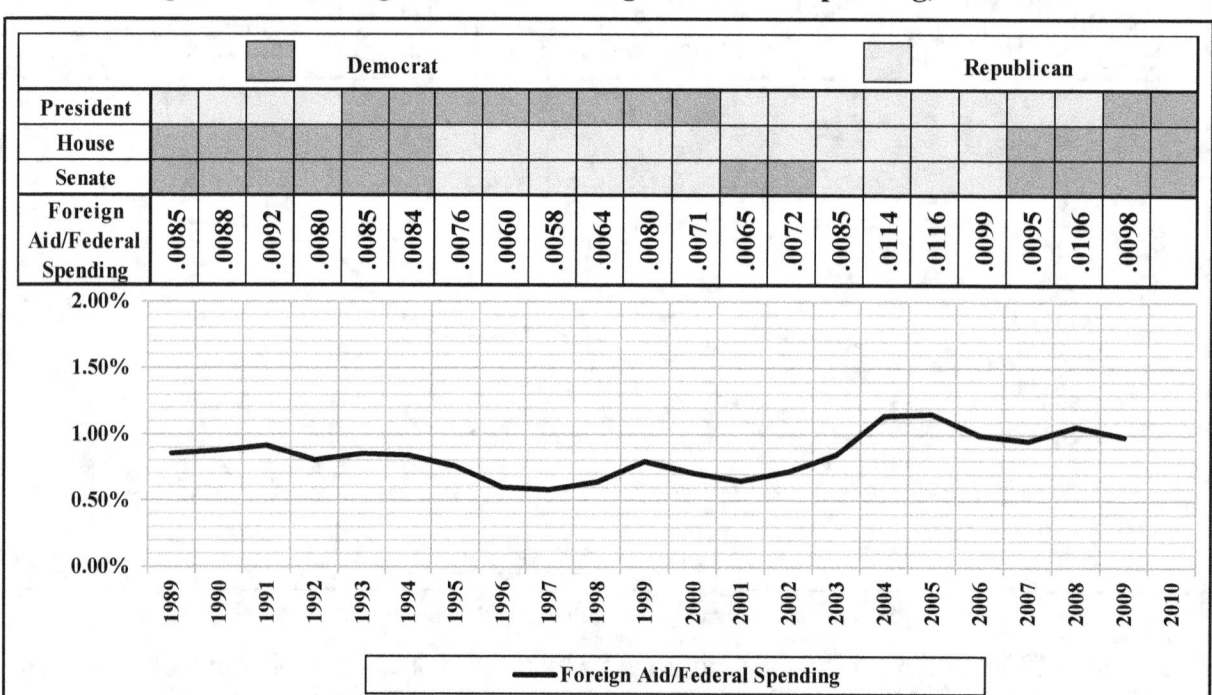

Democrat
Republican
President
House
Senate
Foreign Aid/Federal Spending
.0085 .0088 .0092 .0080 .0085 .0084 .0076 .0060 .0058 .0064 .0080 .0071 .0065 .0072 .0085 .0114 .0116 .0099 .0095 .0106 .0098
2.00%
1.50%
1.00%
0.50%
0.00%
1989 1990 1991 1992 1993 1994 1995 1996 1997 1998 1999 2000 2001 2002 2003 2004 2005 2006 2007 2008 2009 2010
Foreign Aid/Federal Spending

Source: http://gbk.eads.usaidallnet.gov/data/detailed.html

23.2 AID BY COUNTRY

Table 23-1 shows where US aid goes geographically. For the period 1980 through 2009, 26.3 percent went to "World (not specified)", and 31.7 percent went to "Rest of the World (185 entities)", but you can see the countries that benefited from the remaining 42 percent.

Table 23-1: Foreign Aid by Country/Area, Total 1980-2009

Country	1980-2009 Total	Percent of Total
World (not specified)	$ 118,169,446,364	26.3%
Iraq	$ 33,664,104,176	7.5%
Israel	$ 29,310,250,210	6.5%
Egypt	$ 24,875,288,764	5.5%
Afghanistan	$ 15,052,380,665	3.3%
Russia	$ 14,309,663,207	3.2%
Pakistan	$ 8,951,698,822	2.0%
Colombia	$ 8,064,677,922	1.8%
Sudan	$ 7,389,819,834	1.6%
Sub-Saharan Africa (not specified)	$ 6,677,300,842	1.5%
Ethiopia	$ 6,547,923,106	1.5%
Jordan	$ 5,722,446,710	1.3%
India	$ 5,439,151,565	1.2%
El Salvador	$ 5,111,790,880	1.1%
Philippines	$ 4,857,112,993	1.1%
Peru	$ 4,566,389,828	1.0%
Kenya	$ 4,539,729,394	1.0%
Indonesia	$ 4,338,833,703	1.0%
Rest of World (185 Entities)	$ 142,485,874,659	31.7%
Grand Total	$ 450,073,883,644	

Source: http://gbk.eads.usaidallnet.gov/data/detailed.html

23.3 AID BY PROGRAM

Having looked at the aggregate level of foreign aid, and at its geographic distribution, let's now look at how the aid is distributed programmatically. USAID reports on the several programs and groups of programs over time. The following sections describe selected programs, then present summary quantitative data in table 23-2 for all the programs for 1980 through 2009, the most recent reporting year. Many of the programs described below are stand-alone ones, with readily definable objectives. Others are not really programs, but catch-all categories for individual disbursing agencies. These categories are not defined below, but they appear in table 23-2.

The data presented below give only a snapshot of the overall foreign aid picture, but detailed data are available for earlier years from the cited sources.

23.3.1 Economic Support Fund/Security Support Assistance

The Economic Support Fund (ESF) program helps countries meet short- and long-term political, economic, and security needs through a range of activities, from countering terrorism and extremist ideology to increasing the role of the private sector in the economy; assisting in the development of effective, accessible, independent legal systems; supporting transparent and accountable governance; and the empowerment of citizens.

23.3.2 Emergency and Private Assistance (Title II)

Title II provides agricultural commodities to foreign countries to (a) address famine or other urgent or extraordinary relief requirements; (b) combat malnutrition, especially in children and mothers; (c) carry out activities to alleviate the causes of hunger, mortality and morbidity; (d) promote economic and community development; (e) promote sound environmental practices; and (f) carry out feeding programs.

23.3.3 Migration and Refugee Assistance

The US provides humanitarian assistance and resettlement opportunities for refugees and conflict victims around the globe. This program aims to sustain life; protect refugees, stateless persons, conflict victims, and highly vulnerable migrants; assist refugees with voluntary repatriation, local integration, or permanent resettlement in the US; and foster the humane and effective management of international migration.

23.3.4 Development Assistance

Development Assistance funds efforts in the areas of education, economic growth, and democracy and governance. Economic growth programs promote poverty reduction by opening markets, pursuing ambitious trade and investment agendas, assisting reform-minded governments to build the capacity to implement and sustain economic reforms effectively, and multiplying development efforts through private sector participation and recipient country accountability. Democracy and governance programs vary based on the challenges present in each country, but include building political parties and supporting civil society to challenge closed regimes, sustaining the work of human rights defenders, supporting independent media, promoting government that is effective and legitimate, strengthening the rule of law, and advancing anti-corruption measures.

23.3.5 Narcotics Control

The International Narcotics Control and Law Enforcement (INCLE) program supports country and global efforts to combat transnational crime and illicit threats, including efforts against terrorist networks in the illegal drug trade and illicit enterprises. These efforts seek to close the gaps between law enforcement jurisdictions and to strengthen law enforcement institutions that are weak or corrupt.

23.3.6 Trade and Development Assistance (Title I)

Title I provides for the sale of agricultural commodities to developing countries for dollars, on credit terms, or for local currencies. This program is implemented by the Secretary of Agriculture, who is granted the authority to negotiate and execute agreements with developing countries to finance the sale and export of agricultural commodities to such countries.

23.3.7 Global Health and Child Survival

This program aims at improving the health of woman and girls by increasing strategic coordination and integration; strengthening and leveraging key multilateral organizations and global health partnerships; encouraging country ownership and investing in country-led plans; building sustainability through investments in health systems; improving metrics, monitoring, and evaluation; and promoting research, development, and innovation. Resources are targeted toward countries with the highest need, demonstrable commitment to achieve sustainable health impacts, and the greatest potential to leverage US programs and platforms, as well as those of other partners and donors, and targeted to achieve ambitious outcomes on global health indicators.

23.3.8 Millennium Challenge Corporation

The Millennium Challenge Corporation (MCC) fights poverty and builds country capacity through five-year compacts with partner countries that practice good governance, control corruption, invest in health care and education, and promote competitiveness through investments in priority areas such as infrastructure and agriculture. MCC-funded programs are designed to maximize sustainable poverty reduction by fostering economic growth. MCC coordinates with other US and international donors to avoid costly duplication, and considers the role of gender and the impact on the environment as integral components of its compact programs.

By the end of 2009, MCC had signed 20 compacts and 21 threshold agreements, committing nearly $7.5 billion to poverty reduction through results-driven programs built on measureable and transparent objectives. MCC development programs have trained more than 102,000 farmers to boost productivity and food security, and have supported the ongoing construction of more than 1,200 kilometers of roads to facilitate access to markets, schools, and health clinics.

23.3.9 Global HIV/AIDS Initiative

USAID is leading an HIV/AIDS program to help bring to bear the largest and most diverse HIV/AIDS prevention, care, and treatment programs in the developing world. USAID and its partners work directly with host country governments, nongovernmental organizations (NGOs), indigenous groups, and the private sector to provide training, expert technical assistance, and essential supplies, including pharmaceuticals, to prevent and reduce the transmission of HIV, and provide care and treatment to people living with and affected by the disease.

23.3.10 Commodity Credit Corporation Food for Progress (Section 416(b))

Section 416(b) of the Agricultural Act of 1949, as amended, authorizes the Secretary of Agriculture to make overseas donations of agricultural commodities acquired through the Commodity Credit Corporation's price support program for developing and friendly countries.

23.3.11 Peace Corps

Volunteers in 76 countries help host countries and local communities improve education, encourage economic development, protect and restore the environment, increase agricultural capabilities, expand access to basic health care for families, and address HIV/AIDS prevention and care.

23.3.12 Nonproliferation, Anti-Terrorism, Demining and Related

This program provides funds to the International Atomic Energy Agency, the Global Threat Reduction Program for biosecurity, verification for the Comprehensive Nuclear Test-Ban Treaty, and UN Security Council Resolution 1540 on worldwide nonproliferation controls.

23.3.13 Food for Development (Title III)

Title III establishes a program under which agricultural commodities are donated to least developed countries. The revenue generated by the sale of such commodities in the recipient country may be used for economic development activities. The Administrator of USAID is authorized to negotiate and execute Title III agreements with least developed countries that will provide commodities to such countries on a grant basis.

23.3.14 Food for Education

This program provides US agricultural commodities and associated technical and financial assistance to carry out pre- and primary-school feeding programs in foreign countries in order to improve food security, reduce the incidence of hunger and malnutrition, and improve literacy and primary education. The program also supports maternal, infant, and child nutrition programs for pregnant women, nursing mothers, infants, and children.

Table 23-2: Foreign Aid by Program, Total 1980-2009

Program Name	Total 1980-2009	Percent of Total
Economic Support Fund/Security Support Assistance	$ 102,140,039,508	22.7%
Other USAID Assistance	$ 89,027,536,863	19.8%
Voluntary Contributions to Multilateral Organizations	$ 43,512,999,393	9.7%
Emergency and Private Assistance (Title II)	$ 32,294,935,867	7.2%
Department of Defense Security Assistance	$ 31,965,554,194	7.1%
Global Health and Child Survival	$ 24,294,787,529	5.4%
Migration and Refugee Assistance	$ 20,095,885,185	4.5%
Other Active Grant Programs	$ 19,870,363,756	4.4%
Development Assistance	$ 17,622,758,288	3.9%
Narcotics Control	$ 17,059,920,818	3.8%
Trade and Development (Title I)	$ 15,109,906,660	3.4%
Millennium Challenge Corporation	$ 7,545,165,578	1.7%
Global HIV/AIDS Initiative	$ 6,688,055,970	1.5%
Section 416(b)/ Commodity Credit Corporation Food for Progress	$ 6,443,238,853	1.4%
Peace Corps	$ 6,354,544,576	1.4%
Nonproliferation, Anti-Terrorism, Demining and Related	$ 4,119,355,251	0.9%
Other State Assistance	$ 3,479,450,593	0.8%
Food for Development (Title III)	$ 1,577,552,600	0.4%
Food For Education	$ 618,342,355	0.1%
Other USDA Assistance	$ 146,597,807	0.0%
Inactive Programs	$ 106,892,000	0.0%
Grand Total	$ 450,073,883,644	100.0%

Source: http://gbk.eads.usaidallnet.gov/data/detailed.html

24. THE UNITED NATIONS

The United Nations (UN) is of sufficient interest to warrant its own chapter and not be subsumed within the chapter on foreign aid (chapter 23). As important as the UN is, and as long as it has been in existence (since 1945), the US only started keeping and reporting comprehensive statistics on US contributions to the UN in 2006. One has to marvel at this approach to UN expenditures and wonder if this obfuscation was deliberate. After all, the European Union grew out of initially modest efforts at economic cooperation that surreptitiously expanded, largely out of the public eye, to include not only economic cooperation, but common governance as well.

We have Senator Tom Coburn (R-OK) to thank for the existence of any comprehensive data on US contributions to the UN. Prior to 2006, UN contributions were scattered among the budgets of numerous US government agencies, and it was virtually impossible to get the full picture. In 2006, Senator Coburn tasked the Office of Management and Budget (OMB) with putting together a comprehensive report on US contributions to the UN. OMB produced the first such report in 2006, covering the period 2001 through 2005.

Congress adopted legislation calling for the Administration to produce a report each year disclosing all assessed and voluntary US contributions to the UN. The President tasked the State Department with producing this report, but Congressional skepticism over the accuracy of the reports in 2006 and 2007 led Congress to designate OMB as the agency responsible for producing the report annually.

The data presented in figure 24-1 and tables 24-1 and 24-2 are based on the OMB and State Department reports for the years 2001 through 2010, the most recent year for which a report was issued.

Figure 24-1 shows total US contributions to the UN for the period 2001 through 2010. The dip during the period 2006 through 2007 could be more a reflection of the State Department's underreporting than a decrease in US contributions.

Figure 24-1: Contributions to the United Nations, 2001-2010

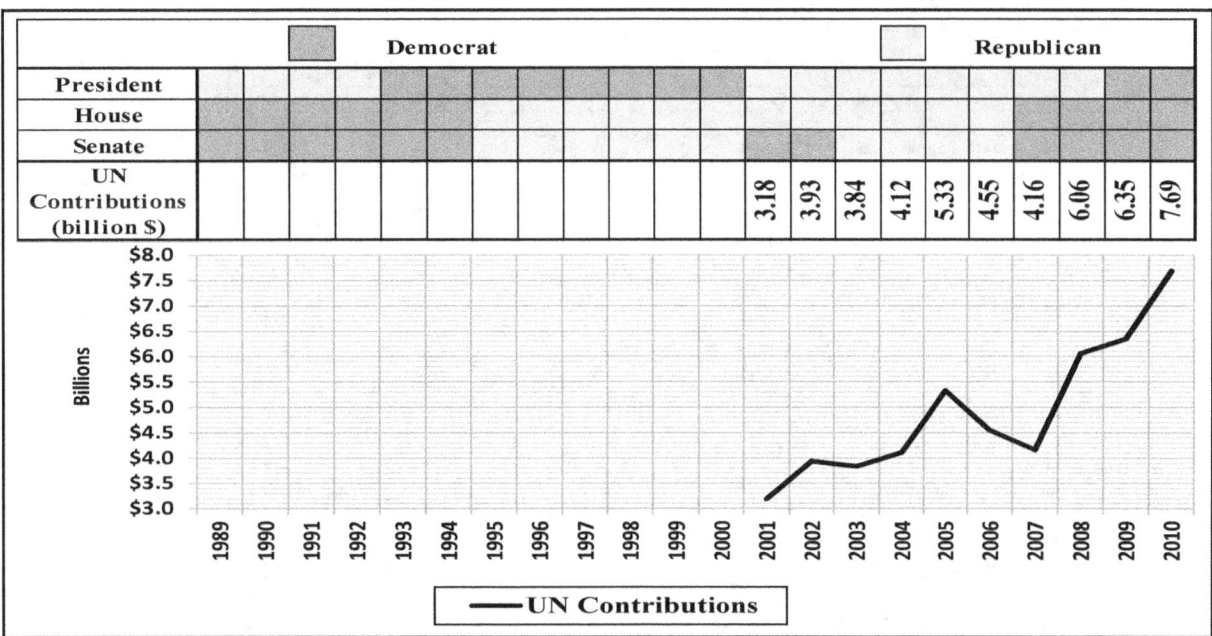

Source: OMB

Table 24-1 shows US contributions to the UN, by contributing US agency, for the year 2010. The number of sources of funds helps explain why data on UN contributions are so difficult to track.

Table 24-1: Contributions to the UN, by US Contributing Agency, 2010

Contributing Agency	FY 2010
Department of Agriculture	$ 100,309,000
Department of Commerce	$ 8,017,000
Department of Defense	$ 2,168,000
Department of Energy	$ 4,500,000
Department of Health & Human Services	$ 139,350,000
Department of Interior	$ 395,000
Department of Labor	$ 49,125,000
Department of State	$ 5,420,372,000
Department of Transportation	$ 3,348,000
Department of Treasury	$ 30,000,000
Environmental Protection Agency	$ 10,575,000
National Aeronautics and Space Administration	$ 700,000
National Science Foundation	$ 474,000
Peace Corps	$ 100,000
U.S. Agency for International Development	$ 1,921,572,000
U.S. Postal Service	$ 307,000
US Nuclear Regulatory Commission	$ 510,000
TOTAL	$ 7,691,822,000

Source: OMB

Table 24-2 shows US contributions to the UN by UN receiving agency in 2010. It also shows the percentage of the agency's total funding that the US contributed.

Table 24-2: Contributions to the UN, by UN Receiving Agency, 2010

Organization	2010 US Contribution	U.S. % of Agency Funding
Convention on International Trade in Endangered Species of Wild Fauna and Flora (CITES)	$ 5,000	22.6%
Food and Agriculture Organization (FAO)	$ 161,296,000	25.1%
International Atomic Energy Agency (IAEA)	$ 185,460,000	25.4%
International Civil Aviation Organization (ICAO)	$ 22,782,000	25.0%
International Fund for Agriculture Development (IFAD)	$ 30,000,000	7.0%
International Labor Organization (ILO)	$ 132,486,000	22.6%
International Telecommunications Union (ITU)	$ 9,361,000	8.7%
Montreal Protocol Fund	$ 25,500,000	17.0%
RAMSAR Convention on Wetlands	$ 1,292,000	22.0%
United Nations - Regular Budget	$ 650,693,000	22.0%
United Nations Children's Fund (UNICEF)	$ 255,184,000	9.0%
United Nations Department of Peacekeeping Operations (UNDPKO)	$ 2,648,234,000	27.3%
United Nations Development Programme (UNDP)	$ 22,315,000	5.5%
United Nations Educational, Scientific, and Cultural Organization (UNESCO)	$ 84,523,000	14.0%
United Nations Environment Programme (UNEP)	$ 22,957,000	9.8%
United Nations High Commissioner for Refugees (UNHCR)	$ 706,879,000	37.0%
United Nations Human Settlements Programme (UN-HABITAT)	$ 7,146,000	1.2%
United Nations International Criminal Tribunal for Rwanda (ICTR)	$ 33,607,000	18.0%
United Nations International Tribunal for the Former Yugoslavia (ICTY)	$ 42,202,000	21.0%
United Nations Office on Drugs and Crime (UNODC)	$ 35,201,000	6.5%
United Nations Relief Works Agency (UNRWA)	$ 237,831,000	26.5%
Universal Postal Union (UPU)	$ 2,373,000	6.0%
World Food Programme (WFP)	$ 1,545,666,000	36.3%
World Health Organization (WHO)	$ 386,706	23.0%
World Intellectual Property Organization (WIPO)	$ 1,097,000	10.8%
World Meteorological Organization (WMO)	$ 15,092,000	21.2%
All Other U.S. Contributions - various agencies	$ 425,934,000	-
Total U.S. Contributions to the United Nations System	$ 7,691,822,000	-

Source: OMB